AFTER IMAGE

John Grant co-founded the agency St Luke's. He has recently started a values-driven branding and innovation agency called The Generative Company. As a branding consultant John has worked on a fascinating range of projects including the relaunch of Napster, communicating IKEA's ethical and environmental initiatives, rebranding Sweden as a leading IT nation and creating a buzz campaign for Amazon. His impressive client list over the last three years includes Arthur Andersen, BT, Capco, Ericsson, Heineken, KWorld, Leisure Link, Nokia, SEB and the UK Cabinet Office, as well as numerous new technology and media start-ups. John is a frequent speaker at global conferences on marketing and has written articles for the *Financial Times* and Design Council. His previous book *The New Marketing Manifesto* was well-received internationally and won a number of awards and plaudits.

AFTER IMAGE

Mind-Altering Marketing

John Grant

P

PROFILE BOOKS

This book is dedicated to Yong Ja

This paperback edition published in Great Britain in 2003 by
PROFILE BOOKS LTD
58A Hatton Garden
London EC1N 8LX
www.profilebooks.co.uk

First published in Great Britain in 2002 by
HarperCollins Business

1 3 5 7 9 10 8 6 4 2

Printed and bound in Great Britain by
Bookmarque Ltd, Croydon, Surrey

A CIP catalogue record for this book is available from the British Library.

ISBN 1 86197 640 2

CONTENTS

SECTION 2: APOLLO RISING 49

SECTION 3: RETHINKING BRANDING 79

PREFACE TO THE
PAPERBACK EDITION

When I give talks based on my books, people often ask how I have been applying the theory in my own work. Since my books are based upon my work, it's also the best way to answer that journalist's question; 'so what will your next book be about?' And it certainly fills in the time that has passed between hardback and paperback. So what follows is work in progress.

This book is about brand value shifting from image to learning. It places this trend within recent developments in consumer culture and media. And it recognizes that this approach is probably not for everyone, and most applicable to new markets and tackling customer mental models; the fundamentals of beliefs, habits, unwritten rules and so on.

There is another, implicit, agenda in this book, which has come to the fore in my recent work with client companies. In fact, this agenda has become so important to me that I and a colleague (Russell Lack) have launched a new company – The Generative Company.

This new agenda is a marriage of ethics and innovation – both key themes throughout this book – to create a hybrid which we call Generativity. The concept is one many readers will recognize from their own lives. Erik Eriksson, the psychoanalyst, introduced the term 'Generativity' to describe a phase in adult mid-life when we normally move on from competitive and social concerns to a broader 'concern for the species'.

This is, we believe, an apt analogy for where business leaders have got to, corporate social responsibility and long-term legacy being hot topics in the boardrooms of today. It is also a pointer to what they can do about it, as Generative activities tend to take one of only a few forms:

- Sharing fresh ideas and thinking
- Passing on knowledge, skills & resources
- Caring for, enabling & assisting
- Establishing relationships and building trust
- Developing new talent

These headings are a very good fit with strategies for knowledge branding, as set out in the second half of this book. They also point to a number of new opportunities and avenues. One half of our business aims to help clients build Generative media platforms; to develop their brand and market as well as building trust, authenticity and salience. And hopefully doing a little good in the process.

The other application of the Generativity concept is to innovation. This connects with parts of this book explaining how insights into the cognitive structures shaping everyday life can be used in creating meaningful branded concepts (such as 'organic', 'SMS', 'dating rules' and 'life management' not to mention 'lifelong learning').

In the twenty-first century we need a new type of new idea.

It's no longer about incremental improvements and the little luxuries that characterized marketing innovation in the twentieth century. It's about solving life's REAL problems. This means products that genuinely improve daily life of individuals and society and also provide economic growth, profit and value. As one person put it at a corporate ethics event I attended recently; 'we need to start developing sustainable business models'.

This kind of idea has often come from the entrepreneur, science park and inventor rather than from corporate marketing department or leadership team. But we believe that is fundamentally a 'how?' issue rather than a 'where?' issue. And innovation is too important to leave to the niche players. In the past corporate structures have straitjacketed people's thinking. These days that is changing.

Our approach – which we call Innovology – turns our creative, branding and media content skills to the innovation process as inputs. We help innovators get inspired about human needs, insights, problems, ways of seeing, the adjacent possible.

Many companies pay attention to their innovation process (such as brainstorming) and outputs (such as route to market). But few look hard at the innovation inputs – the building blocks of information, knowledge, insights, experience, problem definition, expectation – that new ideas are made of. And as the saying goes 'garbage in, garbage out'.

In this work we have been drawing on the findings of cognitive creativity (a few of which are quoted in this present book). This is a very exciting field of current research, which has brought many new insights into the thought processes underlying creativity and how these can be enhanced.

Hopefully, all being well, that will be the next topic of my (our) next book. Meanwhile we have a lot to learn, build and play with! I hope you enjoy this book and that it adds helps you in forming your own future plans.

ACKNOWLEDGEMENTS

This book intertwines with my work as a roving consultant, and in the course of that work as well as the writing, so many people have inspired, helped and encouraged me that I'm sure to have missed a few in this list, for which my humblest apologies.

For direct help with the book I must first thank Lucinda McNeile who challenged me to write something new and Tamsin Miller who forced me to keep in touch with reality (as well as current English usage). Thanks to James Parr for the drawings, which are just a fraction of what he's really put into the book. And to Jon and Dan, their team at Karmarama and beyond, whose cover so captures the idea of the book.

Thanks are also due to Lena Simonsen-Berge, Maria Borelius, Terry Finerty, Herman Hauser, David Magliano, David Patton, Jonathon Porritt, Sue Unerman, and Gerry Zaltman who took the time to read the drafts at various stages and give me feedback.

Special thanks are due to those people who not only helped with the book, but took a similar interest in the direction of my life and in very different ways have acted as my mentors over recent years; Alex Wipperfurth, Annie Wegelius, Bill Lucas, Christie Franchi, Matti Naar, Nick Hahn, and Stephen Hailey.

Then there's the much longer list of people whose conversation, support and inspiration are the very fabric of this book; Anders Dahlvig, Andrew Hill, Anne-Marie Nilsson, Anne Gro Gulla, Anthony Bouchier, Bede Njoku, Brian Akers, Charles Handy, Charlie Crowe, Chris Smithers, Colin Mattey, David Pharo, Eric Bartells, Gary Swindell, Goran Eriksson, Graham Bednash, Stephen Heal, Herman Hauser, Ivan Pollard, Jason

Gormley, Javier Bajer, Jean Gomez, Joyce Taylor, Joel and Laura Hagan, John Griffiths, John Parkin, Jose Evers, Keith Hare, Ken Sacharin, Klas Dahlhof, Kola Ogundipe, Mike Liebling, Magnus Andersson, Magnus Westerberg, Mark Boston, Mari Cortizo, Martin Liu, Martin Payne, Mats Engelmark, Michael Ellis, Mitain Patel, Montse Maresh, Naresh Ramchandani, Neil Cohen, Nigel Jones, Noel Wilsmans, Peter Csoregh, Petteri Kilpenen, Pieter Vereertbrugghen, Phil Teer, Ramona Liberoff, Richard Boulton, Ricki Seidman, Robert Colwell, Russell Lack, Robin Drinkall, Russell Hart, Ryusei Kogure, Simon Nowroz, Sanjay Nazerelli, Scott Barnum, Simon Chung, Simon Warner-Bore, Stephen Carter, Steve Hewlett, Ted Polhemus, Tessa McLoughlin, Thomas Gad, Tim Hoad, Tim Parker, Tom Taniguchi, Verity Johnston, Will Gosling, Yukiteru Nanase.

I'd also like to thank my family and also my onetime surrogate family at St Luke's, whose values are the driving force in what I've written.

And most of all I'd like to thank my wife Yong Ja who is my guiding light.

INTRODUCTION

Something wonderful is about to happen.

DAVE BOWMAN, *2010*

A great phase in human society appears to be drawing to a close – the Age of Image.

Some called it the society of the spectacle:[1] a time saturated by images from the new media of cinema, magazines and television. These fused with the growth of leisure, lifestyle and mass-produced goods to create a Consumer Society. It's now being challenged by everyone from anti-globalization protestors to non-conformist geeks.

As one phase closes, another opens – the Age of Intellect.

Why 'Intellect'?

For one thing people are getting smarter. Not only in the limited sense of being media literate and seeing through the false images projected by brands (although this is a factor in the demise of image marketing), but *more intelligent* and *better-educated*, in general.

We easily accept that people are getting taller, faster at running the 100 metres, and so on. It's a less well-known but no less established fact that people are getting smarter. One landmark survey across fourteen countries found 'massive IQ gains'. This study found differences in average IQ test scores between generations of two to twenty-five points.[2] This means that we are (on average) 2 to 25 per cent smarter than our parents' generation. The phenomenon even has a name (after the psychologist who discovered it) – the Flynn Effect.

To explain the increase, Flynn applied a distinction which psychologists have accepted for over thirty years: crystallized intelligence versus fluid intelligence.[3] Fluid intelligence is measured 'by tasks that require adaptation to new situations for which past learning provides relatively little advantage'. Whereas crystallized intelligence is measured 'by tasks in which the problem solving has been learned as a result of education and enculturation, or both'. When Flynn applied this distinction to his findings he found that the main gains were in fluid intelligence.

So people are getting smarter in a specific way – they are better at *dealing with new situations*.

Doesn't that strike a chord? Everyone reading this book will have their own experiences of a society which constantly confronts us with new situations: which forces us to live on our wits (even if this sometimes drives us to our wits' ends). It's why our times are so stressful and thrilling at the same time. Everything keeps changing. We are constantly having to solve new problems, ranging from 'how to be a man these days' to 'what to do when my new operating system doesn't work with my old software'.

Then there is the whole shift from manual work to knowledge work, which has fuelled the greatest education boom in human history. Before the modern age, 98 per cent of humankind were engaged in manual (mostly farm) work. Now nearly 70 per cent are in skilled work – and university admissions are fast approaching 50 per cent of all young people.

Not only does this mean changes in the spread of education (many more people get to hone their intelligence to a critical sharp point) and in its scope (people are engaged in learning throughout their lives), but all this extra learning also has a huge effect on people's values, their individual self-confidence and in the amount of trust and credence they place in the authorities.

In a short space of time we've gone from a 'couch potato' audience which was receptive to 'dumbed down' marketing daydreams, to an audience which is sharply critical, in every sense. Some commentators look at all this and see 'the death of marketing'. But I think that this is naïve. Companies still have the budget and will continue to use marketing to promote their business. It's just that the main means of doing this – used for the last fifty years – have stopped working. And new ways have started to emerge.

For the last seven years, I've been working out a new marketing system. I started on this trail because the concepts we've inherited – like brand image and positioning – were all too often an uneasy fit with briefs I was getting from clients. A typical marketing project now – for financial services, a retailer, new media or technology – is simply *different* from the projects which established modern brand marketing in the 1950s.

The differences include:

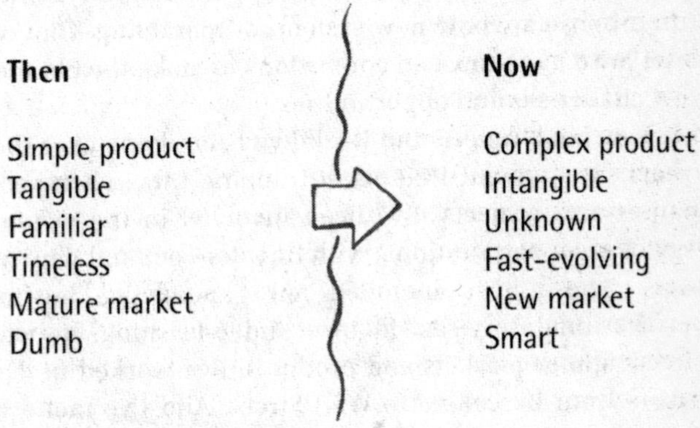

Then		Now
Simple product		Complex product
Tangible		Intangible
Familiar		Unknown
Timeless		Fast-evolving
Mature market		New market
Dumb		Smart

Fig. 1   *Marketing differences*

And that's just the business.

Society has changed too. Ours is one of the only times in human history when most of the learning happens *within* a generation, rather than being passed *between* generations.

Nowadays, we make up our own life stories, instead of following traditional patterns. Every month could bring a new twist in our personal situation, our work, our community and society. So we have learned to be more flexible, active and dynamic in forming our concepts and outlook. We have discovered how to *learn as we go*.

In my last book, *The New Marketing Manifesto*, I presented a toolkit of twelve rules for building brands, based on successful new approaches to marketing which had emerged in the late 1990s. These rules were all, in some sense, about 'getting real': for instance, being more intimate, true to people's real lives and attentive to their fundamental needs and the changes in their lives. The feedback I'm still getting is that it was quite a good summary of where we'd got to.

A typical example, which I'll return to in this book, is the shift from selling branded drinks to teaching people to appreciate whole categories like wine. This was already a challenge to building a 'false image'.

Now I want to take marketing thinking to the next level. Rather than try to stretch the existing paradigm any further, I want to propose a whole new system for marketing. One where we don't have to go through contortions to make the old tools fit the new challenges and opportunities.

This new book reflects the work I've been doing over the last few years, as a global free agent, dipping into other people's companies and projects. I've been involved in the vision and strategy of great corporations, with tiny dot-com and new media start-ups. These have included pure knowledge businesses like professional services, finance and e-learning, as well as classic consumer markets and products. I've worked in diverse cultures – from Barcelona to Wall Street. And I've met a lot of interesting people with new visions of marketing along the way.

I have had to constantly alter and challenge my assumptions and my overall map of marketing. Common themes have emerged in my work, which I believe are signposts to a new way of thinking about, and doing, marketing. And slowly these themes have united into a whole new theory and system.

Marketing on the next level will be about expanding people's minds with new concepts – rather than hypnotizing them with brand images.

We need to know *why* marketing is moving in this direction (based on business and social trends), *what* the core strategies of marketing will be (to replace or update branding) and *how* these can be executed (in the new media landscape).

To start, let's divide marketing, from 1900 to 2000 and beyond, into three phases, each of fifty years. Each of these phases has a different marketing paradigm. Each new paradigm has not replaced the preceding one. But rather it has relegated it to a lower place in the marketing plan.

This is how I see things moving forward too. With mind-altering marketing *eclipsing* image marketing, rather than replacing it.

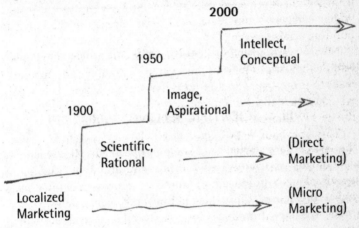

Fig. 2   *Step changes in marketing*

To put this in a contentious way, brand-image advertising is the new junk mail.

Why the step changes? Marketing is, of course, a consequence of the types of businesses that pay for it and their priorities, the social context and the media used. When these three components change, marketing must change too.

Figure 3 makes a simple point – marketing is not an island. When everything around marketing stays fairly constant then it is right for marketing tools like advertising to stick to roughly the same formula. But when all three of the other areas go through big changes, then marketing has to change not only its content, but also its formulae.

Ours is not the first time in which business, society and media have all gone through step-changes. Let's start with the first big

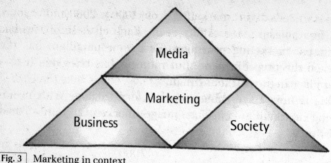

Fig. 3 | Marketing in context

step within living memory, which came with mass media and mass consumer products . . .

LEVEL 1: SCIENTIFIC SELLING, 1900–1950

The last century started on a wave of optimism. New sciences, technologies and industries had brought, and kept bringing, a stream of mass-produced products to improve people's lives such as medicines, affordable clothing and electric lights.

The business frontier – and nearly all of marketing – was about launching new packaged goods, across national markets. A typical advertisement would extol the virtues of the new product and contain a coupon, to be redeemed with a trial pack, at the local grocery store. This was the start of 'scientific advertising'.[4] Campaigns were for the first time based on research into what pulled the greatest response. The advertisements tended to emphasize rational propositions; like the fact that shaving cream produced 'a hundred times more lather' than normal soap. There were also the first signs of modern brand personality, like the use of an invented character (in a series of ads for dress-making kits), or the use of exotic sounding ingredients (like palm oil). But it was all about selling.

There were some innovative marketing campaigns in this period. Kellogg's Corn Flakes launched themselves into the national diet using my favourite sales promotion of all time, 'Wink at your grocer and see what happens'. (When a housewife complied she was handed a trial pack of Corn Flakes.) But these were not devised as 'brand building', so much as impactful and ingenious ways of generating trials of new products.

The marketing behind national product launches was greatly helped by the growing mass media of magazines (like the *Ladies' Home Journal* and *Good Housekeeping*). Other media like commercial radio and posters emerged at this time. But they all took their lead from the printed advertisement.

A key social trend was the war on dirt. New discoveries in science had shown that many diseases were due to tiny micro-organisms. These tiny bugs gripped the popular imagination – a dirty home was a diseased home.[5] Cities and homes were sanitized. The concept of the housewife was already well established – it dated back to the early Victorian age. A woman's place was in the home, at least for the middle classes, and many working class women worked as domestic servants.

If I had to isolate one value that stood for the whole culture of that time it would be *duty*. People knew their place and accepted the strict responsibilities that went with it. They did 'a hard day's work for an honest day's pay', and they didn't get 'ideas above their station'.

Overall the marketing paradigm for 'Level 1' looks something like this:

Fig. 4 | *The 'Level 1' marketing paradigm*

LEVEL 2: FANTASY IMAGE, 1950–2000

The mid-1950s was another time of great hope and improvement in the quality of life.

The war was over. Rationing had ended. New 'miracle products' like washing machines and vacuum cleaners released women from domestic chores. Luxuries like a motor car and blended whiskies became affordable by the mass middle class. Leisure time became a part of everyday life, alongside work. Surveys show that, of all recent decades, this was the time when people were most happy.[6] They'd 'never had it so good'.

The business priorities that drove marketing campaigns changed. Many markets for consumer goods had matured. This meant that a number of similar products at the same price point were competing for customers. The battle was on for loyalty and share. Which forced marketers to consider how consumer habits were formed and maintained. Generic product benefits were no longer enough. They needed a little 'extra edge'.

Advertising agencies hired psychoanalysts, to help them figure out how to get deeper into the psyche of the consumer. These psychoanalysts introduced the focus group interviews and projective techniques, which are still with us today. They came to the field with a (Freudian) assumption that people did most things for unconscious and irrational reasons. And they soon found plenty of examples in the world of consumer goods to support this assumption.

Ernest Dichter was a Vienna trained psychoanalyst turned marketing shrink. His *Handbook of Consumer Motivations* catalogues the psychological factors involved in people's choice of car, beer or lipstick.[7] He and other analysts came to an overall conclusion, which changed the way that marketing conceived its whole approach:

> Most cars in a similar price category are more or less alike technically. They may differ as far as design is concerned, but the major distinction people are interested in is this vague, subtle, overall feeling of personality. A Ford is different from a Chevrolet; a Citroen

is different from a Simca. It is this image, this personality that we usually buy and on which advertising must concentrate.

And concentrate on image it did. The advertising of the time (and ever since) shifted: from words to pictures, and from print media to the more emotion- and personality-driven medium of commercial television. Ads were no longer selling a product. They were selling an image, a fantasy escape, a lifestyle. Consumers found themselves in an Aladdin's cave of luxury, status, glamour and aspiration. The consumer society was born.

Brand image became the central concept of marketing. It was seized by the ad agencies as all the justification they needed to make creative, entertaining commercials (which is all most advertising people I've ever known have ever wanted to do); and by design and other marketing services to justify their more creative, artistic proposals.

A new line was drawn in marketing. 'Above the line' was brand image-building in expensive, flamboyant ways. It was creative rather than scientific. 'Below the line' the old rule-based scientific selling continued – now known as direct marketing. The dominant marketing paradigm for 'Level 2' looks like this:

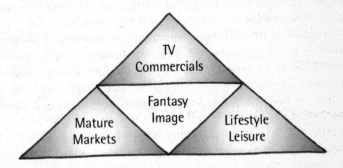

Fig. 5 | *The 'Level 2' marketing paradigm*

LEVEL 3: MIND-ALTERING MARKETING, 2000–?

The main social change happening now – and it towers above all other trends – is the addition of a third realm of everyday life, alongside work and leisure, which is learning.

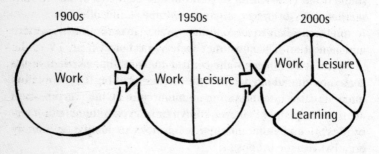

| Fig. 6 | *The work, leisure and learning mix*

This has cut into work time. For instance, nearly half of UK adults have had training recently to update their computer skills. Learning has also cut into leisure time. With over two-thirds of people taking on some form of learning, either on their own, at a local class, at a formal college, or increasingly online.

Vocational learning is an essential survival tool in modern working life. People need to constantly improve their skills and ways of working in order to be employable. The average individual leaving school in the mid 1990s will go through five different careers in their working lifetime, with major retraining for each stage.[8]

There is a broader learning trend as well: updating our fundamental ideas about who we are and how we live. We are the first generation not to rely on instruction from previous generations. How to be a mother, a man, what to wear, what to eat . . . everything is up for question, and subject to constant revision with new information.

The same changes in technology and society that are driving people into lifelong learning are also driving companies into rapid development. Business strategy now aims at creating whole new markets and industries, not just new products and services.

The first level for business was about new products, the second level was about brands, the third level is about new concepts. This trend is typified by the information and communication industries. But it is also true of older markets, transformed by new technologies and channels. It's even true for some basic commodities. Starbucks has created a whole new market concept for that ancient product called 'coffee'.

The media shift is from passive, single media to interactive mixes of media. That doesn't just mean a shift from TV to the Internet. It's a shift to anything *with* anything. Sony describe it as moving from 'broadcast to anycast'.[9] A big TV show now often has an interactive component and at the very least a website. Technically, interactivity is still in its infancy. But interactivity, the way the audience relates to the content, is already established.

The new learning culture means that individuals are interacting with the media to work things out. It's about using the media in an active way, to form and revise our mental models. We used to doze or chat through the stock market news on TV. Now we sit forward a bit and wonder what it means for our mortgage, job security and pension.

The marketing concept which fits these changes – to learning for individuals, new markets for companies and the new interactivity and other options in media – is *Mind-Altering* Marketing – creating new mental models.

This doesn't, in most cases, mean instruction. That is a form of learning from the non-interactive, non-empowered age. Knowledge now is 'just in time'. We learn fast, but only when we need to learn. Parents-to-be learn the latest dos and don'ts in ante-natal classes. Patients learn about new treatments from support groups. People buying a new computer buy the latest computer magazine.

There is no point in learning in advance, because human knowledge keeps evolving at a rapid pace. And there is just too much of it, to take all of it in. This year's health fad can be next year's health scare. When this happens, the media will let us know.

The paradigm for marketing, at Level 3, looks like this:

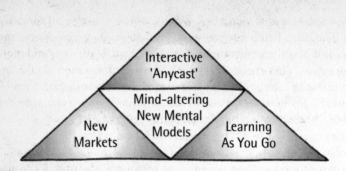

The 'Level 3' marketing paradigm

An example of all this is alternative remedies and regimes:

- **LEARNING:** whether you are into yoga, ayurveda, acupuncture or homeopathy, one of the key attractions to alternative remedies and treatments is that there is a whole philosophy and vocabulary to absorb.
- **NEW MARKETS:** These treatments do not fit simply into healthy eating or exercise. They tend to be holistic in their approach, and they deal with healthy people (who are at most stressed out) unlike Western medicine which deals with the 'sick' – a new market by definition. If alternative therapies replace sales of something it's most likely to be cigarettes or alcohol.
- **MIND-ALTERING:** People who adopt alternative therapies tend to make sweeping changes across their lifestyle, because they take on new mental models of 'how to live'.
- **INTERACTIVE:** Compared with Western medicine, holistic therapies are intensely interactive and participative. A good deal of a consultation is taken up with communication in both directions, let alone with classes etc. One popular claim from converts to alternative medicine is that 'it treats me like a person' which is a good yardstick for any modern marketing and service.

'The body and soul' market has become a huge industry. Reports from the US where New Age is most advanced suggest that there are more visits to alternative medicine practitioners than conventional GPs. Nearly every lifestyle magazine gives over some space to the topic and major retailing chains like the Body Shop have got in on the act.

A NEW MENTAL MODEL OF MARKETING

When people from the two previous paradigms (brand image versus direct marketing) meet, the result is usually confusion, because they have their own – very different – mental models. I remember working on a recruitment press campaign for First Direct. I simply could not get my head around it. Why adjust the ad a little and measure the response, rather than coming up with bold new ideas? I did not have a scientific sales mentality.

I've met the same incomprehension, in reverse, from direct-marketing agencies. 'What are the main selling messages?' they'd ask. 'Whatever you like,' we'd reply: 'People don't really buy it for those product points, they buy it because they love the brand.'

The same goes for crossing from brand-building to mind-altering. You need a new set of concepts to work in this space – different assumptions about the role for marketing communications, different kinds of ideas, for different mixes of media.

This book is an attempt to articulate the new approaches needed to work at the next level of marketing, and in its four main sections, I will explore the four segments of the new paradigm:

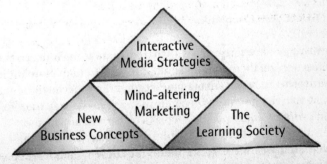

Fig. 8 *The new marketing paradigm*

Each reader will have their own area of expertise and interest. A market researcher might be glued to section two, while a media planner would feel more at home in section four. But it's important to grasp the whole picture. That's what's often missing in the debate in each 'corner'.

I sat opposite a manager from a big interactive advertising agency at an e-learning event recently. They must be deep into this area by now? (I enquired). After all, learning is one of the key possibilities in interactive media? No, they weren't at all, he replied. They were still trying to shift their clients from direct sales into brand building.

To change the way you do marketing, you have to change your whole mental model.

Having pulled marketing apart, section five will put it back together again. Using the mobile-phone market as an example, I'll show how the model can be used to drive the marketing process, from start to finish, by answering four basic questions:

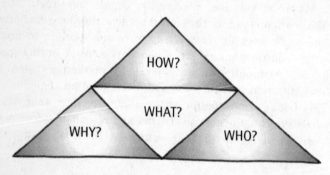

Fig. 9   *Basic marketing questions*

Now that we are heading into what appears to be a deep recessionary freeze, there will be another incentive to explore radical alternatives to brand-image marketing. Like a decadent monarchy it may have simply become too expensive and too out of touch with ordinary people's lives to be carried any further.

In the 1950s, Lord Leaverhume said that he knew half his advertising was wasted, but he didn't know which half. Nowadays the situation is much worse. Media inflation alone means that, if in 1955, 50 per cent of your advertising budget was wasted, then by 1995, 90 per cent would be wasted, all other things being equal. And if 90 per cent of your advertising budget is wasted, does it really matter 'which 90 per cent'?

It's the lack of established alternatives that have held many companies, but not all, back from radical change. While I'm as gloomy as the next marketer about the prospect of a recession, I'd definitely take the winter in the hope of the spring.

Personally I hope that marketing is indeed moving up to this next level, as learning, in the liberated, self-directed and passionate mode that I describe in this book, is one of the only forces for lasting good I can see in our universe. If marketing is to drive this trend – as strongly as it drove the consumer society in the 1950s and 1960s – then it might just be worth hanging around for.

As marketing people, it would be great for us to be on the side of the angels, for once.

Don't you think?

META-BUSINESS STRATEGY

Business strategy has shifted, from developing new products and services, to developing whole new business models and markets. This is a natural consequence of the Information Age, which affects the whole economy from the capital markets to individual workers. The implication for marketing is that 'the brief' has changed. It's no longer about promoting an enduring brand. This is too narrow and inflexible. It's about establishing a whole new concept in people's minds. It's the next level up.

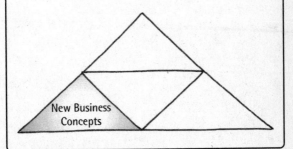

New Business
Concepts

understanding and overcoming our
so that we can save the planet, stop
logies, adopt a humane set of rul
This may well be true. And
more pragmatic level, evol
the limited human repe
link between chang
doing so in a fairl

Evolution is

> We are entering a period in which evolutionary thinking is being
> applied to every conceivable domain of inquiry. Witness the
> development of fields such as evolutionary ecology, evolution-
> ary economics, evolutionary psychology, evolutionary linguistics,
> evolutionary epistemology, evolutionary computational science,
> evolutionary medicine and psychiatry – even evolutionary chem-
> istry and physics. The new millennium can therefore be called the
> Age of Universal Darwinism.[10]

It is also enjoying quite a surge in popularity in business theory.
Evolution appears to be taking over as the key metaphor used
in business (the previous one being warfare). My search of the
McKinsey Quarterly database, using keywords, revealed that
among 300 articles on 'business', 175 also refer to 'evolution'.
If I were a management consultant, I'd conclude that evolution
accounts for 58.33 per cent of business thinking now!

Evolution is not a new idea. So why is it suddenly all the
rage?

In a recent book, Mihaly Csikszentmihalyi describes evolution
as 'a psychology for the third millennium'[11] as well as our 'creation myth'. He sees the main challenge facing humanity as:

evolutionary inheritance,
killing each other over ideo-
es for social life and so on.
it's certainly fascinating. But on a
tion is uniquely helpful as an idea (in
rtoire of 'standard ideas') in describing a
and *information* in *complex systems*. And
intuitive way.

THE CAMBRIAN EXPLOSION

ness change is about more than globalization, competition
nd innovation. It is about a step change to another level of
organization and complexity. The key business evolution right
now is the development of whole new business models and
industries, rather than just the development of new products and
services. A similar step change happened, 540 million years ago,
in the evolution of life on earth. Because of a very special set of
conditions, which are a good analogy for what is driving business
innovation now.

This step change can be seen in the Burgess Shale, an amaz-
ingly rich fossil deposit. It was found, high in the Canadian
Rockies, by a Victorian geologist called Charles Doolittle Walcott.
It's a fossilized mud-slide. The animals had been buried so fast
that their soft tissue was preserved. In rocks dating from any time
before this deposit no higher organisms – i.e. animals with more
than one cell – had ever been found. It appeared that living creatures leapt from single cells to the rich diversity of life today, in a
very short period of time.

Putting the Burgess Shale together with several other contemporary fossils finds across the world, it appeared – according to
my geology lectures a few decades ago, anyway – that 540 million
years ago, over a period of 40 million years (or 1 per cent of life's
history on earth), every single design subsequently used by any
higher animal (about 35 distinct architectures or phyla) was
invented.

A number of factors, with direct parallels to business now,

conspired in the rapid development of such a diverse range of complex creatures:

- **OXYGENATION:** At that time the amount of oxygen in the sea, produced by algae through photosynthesis, shot up. Oxygen is the basis of animal life. Abundant oxygen is important for larger creatures, with higher metabolic rates.

The oxygen of business is capital. This has always been in short supply. So that the metabolism and growth of companies has been limited. And the power has been with the lenders (banks) and owners (shareholders). Until recently, when we switched to a global capital surplus, caused by the capital markets revolution and the individual investment boom (our 'algae'). So that capital was suddenly freely available to anybody with an ambitious growth plan. So big was the glut, that capital migrated to riskier sources of growth, like the hedge funds, and most recently venture capital. Between 1990 and 1999, the amount invested in venture-capital funds increased from $1 billion to $90 billion. That's a lot of extra 'oxygen'.

- **THE SPREADING SEA:** In the Cambrian era, the sea level rose over the continents, providing rich nutrients and, with those new long ocean shelves, also a lot of new ecological niches to adapt to.

The spread of capitalism and markets – through globalization, rapid industrial development and the end of the Cold War – and the new (and still developing) Internet phenomenon have created huge new 'ocean shelf' markets. There are new geographical territories open for business; for example, it's a great time to expand your business into China. And also new virtual geographies within the Internet, joining up niches into big opportunities – the difference between a local auction house and e-Bay.

- **PREDATION:** This phase of evolution was rapid because it was an 'arms race'. Once you have multi-cellular creatures, the

life or death question is 'eat or be eaten?' Geologists think this
favoured both the new armoured creatures (with shells) and
also increasing size, complexity, locomotion and attack/
defence possibilities.

The pace of business innovation now is also based on competition. Global competition threatens every formerly protected
locale. No business is safe. One defence is to be constantly inno-
vating. If you take a business plan to a venture capitalist, their
two main concerns are is it *scaleable?* (bigger organisms) and, if
so, is it *defensible*? (hard shells).

The main body armours used by business are intellectual
property and partial monopoly protection, eg 'owning' the distribution channels.

But all of this – for the Cambrian Explosion and for our times –
is insufficient to explain the sudden arrival of an astonishing
variety of whole new forms.

■ In the pre-Cambrian Explosion we see the emergence of
   whole new designs for creatures. Not just extensions of
   existing creatures, but totally new phyla (forms).

Whole new phyla have arrived in business. There are new
internal structures, like flattened hierarchies, self-managed
teams and distributed innovation. There are new arrangements
between companies, like the value network, where many separate companies co-ordinate seamlessly to replace the corporate
monoliths, for instance in the car and finance industries. And
radical forms that challenge the very notion of 'company' itself,
like Linux. And most importantly for this book, there are many
examples of new ways of bundling or dividing a market – like
Starbucks, Intel and ready-to-eat salad.

THE INFORMATION STEP CHANGE

What happened in both the Cambrian Explosion and the
Network Economy was a step change in information capabil-

ities. Which allowed the creation of vastly more complex and competitive designs.

The design of an organism is held as information, in the genes. At the start of the Cambrian Explosion a new kind of super-gene emerged. It's called the homeotic gene. The homeotic gene governs the arrangement of cells in three-dimensional space. Without this, different cells cannot specialize and will not grow into different parts of a body.

The homeotic genes of any multi-cellular animal have been found to be very similar. Which probably means every higher animal is descended from one little creature that first cracked this code. Hence the sudden 'explosion' of forms.

The equivalent of the homeotic gene in modern business is information and communication technology. This allows complex new forms of organization, which are more efficient.

One example is retail banking transactions.[12]

Cost per retail banking transaction

Branch	$1.07
Telephone	$0.68
ATM	$0.27
Internet	$0.10

Not only do these technologies bring more efficiency within companies, they also permit more efficient transactions between companies. This is the new frontier for business development. My Andersen clients call it the Network Economy.

One implication is that a big company, covering a whole value chain, can now be replaced by a hyper-efficient network of smaller specialist companies. Each can focus on what it does best and outsource all non-core functions. And these companies can co-ordinate efficiently, for instance in 'business-to-business exchanges'. These developments are extending to consumers; for instance in purchasing power aggregation (Priceline.com) and customer agents. We're all part of the same matrix now.

Sociologist, Manuel Castells, studies *The Network Society*.[13] His three-volume book on the subject charts a global shift, taking in the rise of the Internet and the fall of Communism. Castells describes the overall trend as 'Informationalism'. Which means a technology-driven change in the organization of society.

He points out that it's not enough to say we live in a 'knowledge age'.[14] Knowledge has been the key driver of progress in many past societies. The Romans had roads, laws, engineering and drainage. The Protestants had printed books and accountancy.

What other 'knowledge ages' didn't have, according to Castells, was a new technology paradigm with three special features:

- a self-expanding processing capacity (eg, integrated circuits)
- a recombining ability (eg, the World Wide Web)
- a distributional flexibility (eg, networks and mobile phones).

These aren't just Internet or IT properties. Castells shows that they also apply to genetic engineering, which has the same potentially explosive impact on society and economics. His point is that we have invented technologies for self-reinforcing, accelerated learning.

Castells sees the key impact of these technologies as changing society: 'the network society emerges and expands as the dominant form of social organization in our time'.

Informationalism changes society at all levels at once: it has revolutionized the capital markets and nation state politics. It also changes people's minds. This is because '*the global hypertext provides most of the sounds, images, words, shapes and connotations that we use in the construction of meaning in all our domains of experiences*'.

The latest findings from geology suggest that the Cambrian Explosion may have had a long fuse. The current view is that there were earlier complex life-forms, which were less likely to be fossilized, because they had no shells. And which were much smaller and harder to find. An example has been found in China. So the explosion may have built up over a longer time, but only 'appeared' when creatures became big enough to see.

This is quite a good corrective to the 'New Economy' boom-and-bust viewpoint. The roots of the business explosion are in the preceding decades: in more efficient capital markets; in more open-minded (less traditional) values; in rising education levels and individual investment. The dot-coms were not the first or last new forms to emerge.

The balanced view, coming out of that frenzied period, seems to be:

- it's still all about new business models and new markets
- with a proviso that companies *do* have to make money
- the 'New Economy' is better described as the Network Economy
- with new ways of organizing and combining companies
- which is the true equivalent of multi-cellular organisms.

That's the line taken by my mentor at Andersen, Stephen Hailey, head of consulting in Europe. He sees the 'correction' as a weeding out, but not a return to the 'old economy'. The network is here to stay and with it dramatic new forms of business.

Weeding out was also a feature of the Cambrian period. First came a great fan of diverse forms. But then some won out, and others died out. And these developments came in waves. The trilobites nearly all disappeared. But the vertebrates (our ancestors) made it.

Informationalism has many more new technologies up its sleeves. The next thirty years, at least, look likely to be heated up again and again, by scientific breakthroughs, underway or anticipated. With developments in areas such as:

- cognitive neuroscience and artificial intelligence
- pharmacogenomics
- new forms of super-networked computing
- nano-technology
- fuel cell and other energy technologies
- quantum computing
- genetically modified foods.

As the last example shows, culture has a big role to play in the shape of the future too.

2

INFORMATIONALISM
CHANGES EVERYTHING

'Informationalism' is Manuel Castells' word for the whole system
of change, catalysed by the Internet and other technologies, but
acting on human culture and society. It's not enough to say that
'the Internet changes everything'. So did the credit card. And
the Internet would be very little without the shift to mobile
technologies etc. The difference between Informationalism and
other lesser shifts is that it is a new homeotic gene. It allows the
creation of whole new phyla in business and society.

INFORMATIONALISM AND ECONOMICS

There are two kinds of economic thinker, the optimist and the
pessimist. The optimistic school held court in the 1990s under
the banner of the 'New Economy'. With the American downturn,
re-engineering, mergers and redundancies are staging a comeback. Monetarism and pessimism are back (for a while); from
Clinton to Bush, who is the only recent political leader anyone
can remember talking *down* their economy.

In the 1980s, monetarists ruled, in the UK and the US (and
later worldwide, through the IMF). Then New Growth theory
came along to challenge these pessimists. 'New Growth' is to the
Information Age what Adam Smith's theories were to the Industrial Age: it explains how a change in the means of production
might create a new 'universal opulence'.

The crux of New Growth theory is the notion that *ideas*, of themselves, have the capability of producing economic growth.

Paul Romer, the leading proponent of New Growth, argued that ideas are different from moving parts (production technology or human capital) because they are 'non-rival'. If one person uses an idea, another person can use it too. Whereas human capital (a person), or production technology (a machine) can only (conventionally) be used for one task in one place at a time.

It's a theory that seemed to fit the facts.

In the US, natural resources and fixed assets – the 'weight' of the economy – have barely increased in the last fifty years. But productivity and the resulting value of the economy (GDP) have increased five-fold, in real terms. This weightless new growth is the result of 'concepts and ideas' according to Alan Greenspan, president of the Federal Reserve.[15]

The rate of innovation has increased, with advances accelerating the rate of further advances, not only in computing power, but in disparate fields enabled by these advances in IT, like software, genomics and financial services. Applications, per year, to the US patent office roughly doubled across the 1990s.

New Growth theory explains why an advanced nation could go on investing, without deminishing returns. It is the tendency of ideas to slip out of their inventors' hands, into the public domain, that leads these economies to show increasing returns on investment. The theory is borne out by data tracking US investment. And it's no fault of New Growth theory, which says that 1 + 1 = 3, if American investors started to believe that 1 + 1 = 50 (the stock price multiples).

This leaking of ideas between companies was key to the Silicon Valley phenomenon. So was the sheer scale of inbound investment. Heavy investment gives a business the resources to constantly innovate. If these investments are 'good bets' then the corresponding return on investment is higher. High investment creates a 'can-do' energy in a company. Ideas are doubly productive when people are excited about working with them.

Another new growth theory is the 'law of increasing returns' which says that for knowledge products, such as software, there is very little cost of an extra sale. The problem occurs if, when something hardly costs anything, ownership is intangible too.

Microsoft sells knowledge. Their mainstay is the operating system. Before Microsoft came along, no-one had thought of selling this. It was just a stack of generic code, shared among developers. Selling the operating system is a bit like selling the washing instructions separately from the clothes. Linux have challenged the idea of 'owning' it, as have software pirates. It's estimated that one third of all Windows software in use was illegally copied.

This says that not paying for your software is very popular. 'Pirate' makes it sounds like illegal companies producing counterfeit copies for sale. But my guess is that most copies are 'cracked' and circulated for free. There are huge file-sharing sites on the Web where you can find most 'big brand' software available free in a cracked form. And there is a running battle between the crackers and the 'software police' who scour the Net for such sites and threaten to close them down.

A tricky issue is how to own something that is *just an idea*. Say I discovered the deep structure of carbonic crystals. Could I claim that I owned all the diamonds in the world? I didn't make them. But Celeron did not make the human genome either.

Assuming we agree through legal contracts that I do own this idea, how can something that can be copied be protected? This will almost certainly be the century of the lawyer – if we're not careful.

All of this suggests a more important role for brands than jockeying for position with emotional images. Brands link ideas with companies, in people's minds. A brand can make you the *author* of an idea. It's difficult to stop you from photocopying parts of this book and passing them to colleagues. But it's much harder for you to claim ownership of the book as your own work. And there's a danger your colleagues will have read it too.

Sony invented the Walkman. Now, all electronic companies have their version. And the technology has moved on, through CD, Minidisc and MP3. But Sony still owns the idea. A Sony Walkman is the prototype, the standard against which others are measured. There's still something special about owning a Sony Walkman. It's the original.

That's why, while brand image (the creation of an appealing personality) is too narrow and inflexible an idea for many fast-moving markets, the notion of branding will continue, but on a higher level. It's about the author, not the book cover.

INFORMATIONALISM AND MARKETS

Markets grow through learning.

Until 200 years ago, most value was in agriculture, land, metals etc. – in the ownership of natural resources. Even then, learning added value. The knowledge that a herb had medicinal properties increased its value, and also created value in books of remedies, herbalists etc. But most value was in raw materials.

Since then, human inventions have increased the value of this stuff, off the scale. The motor car, computers . . . are all worth many times more than the raw materials.

Learning-value progresses in a sawtooth way. New market-creating inventions bring a step change in value. But they often have associated costs that limit their affordability. Creeping improvement then reduces the costs, so that many more can afford them, decreasing the value per unit, but increasing the overall value further in the process.

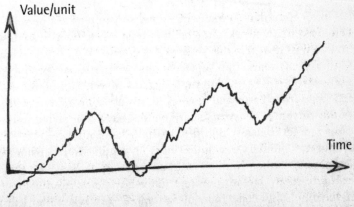

Fig. 10   *Value/time product graph*

Consider air travel. Invented less than a hundred years ago, this offered the opportunity for the rich to travel to far-flung places faster. It was a whole new market.

Innovations in production and design, largely for military aircraft, made air travel by jets affordable for the masses by the 1970s. What started with the Wright brothers ended up with bucket and spade holidays in Majorca. Within this progression, there have been smaller step changes, such as the invention of the package holiday (the bundling of a flight plus a network of 'foreign hotels' and rep services into a 'predictable' experience).

The current thinking in business strategy is that discontinuous change, or 'Revolution' as Gary Hamel calls it, through reinventing markets, is the key to creating company value.[16] Hamel points out that existing market boundaries are not fixed. And that there is enough new technology (and good old-fashioned inventiveness) in the system, for companies to make great leaps forward. Some of his examples include:

- Starbucks – whose average customer visits eighteen times a month
- e-Bay – who grew from Pez dispenser specialists to having 2.5 million items on sale
- IKEA, Home Depot and Sephora (a French cosmetics retailer that is now expanding in the US).

It's interesting that so many of Hamel's examples are retailers. Retailers already work at the heart of business networks, so they may be well placed in the Network Economy.

In recent years the supermarkets in particular produced aggressive market discontinuities; like supermarket petrol, the £25 Levis from Tesco and moves into twenty-four-hour opening. In the current downswing shareholders have stampeded to the same retailers because they deal with life's essentials.

Market boundary revolution puts an emphasis on customer learning. Whether you rebundle an existing market, like Starbucks, or create a totally new one, like e-Bay, the value only exists in the minds and behaviours of customers. Only when they learn to grasp, use and appreciate your new business, will it take off.

You need to develop a new concept with a new value proposition – like the packaged holiday. But it won't succeed until it becomes tried, popularized and adopted as an idea. The bulk of business success with new concepts is about a change in the customers' mindset.

The holy grail of lasting value is created in two ways:

- companies learning – to invent or improve business concepts
- customers learning – to appreciate and adopt these concepts.

Brands are usually the most public and visible part of a business, by definition. So whenever a business is successful it is tempting to think that it is due to strong branding. But if you look a little deeper you usually find that, recently, when companies have been successful it is because they worked in these two broader and deeper ways.

I imagine that you might be drinking a cup of coffee right now. Let's assume you got it from Starbucks. What factors make this bundle of coffee, water, milk and styrofoam worth about £2 (the ingredients cost one tenth of that I'd guess)? Is it the 'brand'? Starbucks certainly has a strong brand. So it's easy to assume that the brand caused or at least played a big role in the final price.

But I can't help thinking that my cup of cappuccino from Costa, Pret a Manger, or Aroma is worth pretty much the same to me. Or the cup I'm drinking now, from my own Pavoni espresso- and milk-frothing machine. Isn't it possible that most of the value in the gourmet coffee sector comes from customers learning.

- to appreciate 'gourmet' coffee
- to value 'authentic' foodstuffs: eg organic and freshly squeezed . . .
- to value little luxuries and breaks in a faster paced life
- to value American 'energy'.

What Starbucks did was drive this learning (with their mission to convert the American coffee drinker to better coffee made from better types of beans). Starbucks' success is exemplified by the little leaflets it produces about coffee roasting, not by its more obvious and extrovert branding. Think about the difference between Starbucks and McDonald's. Is it the way they brand themselves? Or a change in the food and drink culture.

Information-age markets thrive by nurturing new customer concepts. This is where the branding action is. The information age also brings new possibilities to how companies are organized to serve these markets. And these new forms mean that what is being branded changes. To illustrate the shape of things to come, here's one new form (among many alternative 'phyla'): *Customerization*.

Customerization (not to be confused with Customization) is the centring of an industry on the individual end-consumer. One area where it's likely to happen sooner rather than later is finance. Because finance is pure knowledge – money, advice, transactions, credit ratings, risk – it's all information.

The old paradigm is the 'value chain'.

This was often owned by a single company which also 'owned' the customer. Banks controlled the 'birds nests' of information about my routine transactions, standing orders, pay-roll and so on, which used to mean that people changed bank accounts, on average, less often than they changed marriages. It was just too much hassle.

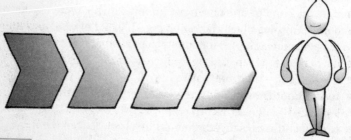

Fig. 11   *The value chain*

The new paradigm is a network of suppliers clustered around the individual, meeting different needs in an optimal way, and also able to co-ordinate seamlessly.

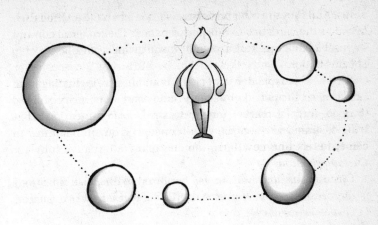

Fig. 12 | *Value chain orbits*

Understanding that the world is centred on customers, not companies, highlights quite a number of directions in which things are headed:

- the customer is self-directed, educated, informed and in control
- there is potential to do business better through efficient networks
- the best firms do one thing very well
- companies work best when they are in rich dialogue with the end consumer
- it's hard to develop your company without changing the market
- value should now be measured in terms of the customer, as an individual not in terms of a company or economy – that's where it all comes together.

This new arrangement means that branding has to deal with being part of a bigger whole. A great example is Intel. On the old model of branding they would have created an image for their microprocessors, which was slightly different from others'. But they have seen the bigger picture. People buy computers, not chips. And they are after performance. So Intel have pitched their brand as the yardstick of this performance. Their overall concept is 'Intel Inside', part of a mental model which says faster chip speed = better.

This new perspective is not just about finance, technology and other complicated 'knowledge industries'. As Gary Hamel pointed out, the market for pre-washed, 'ready-to-eat' salad (a truly customer-life-centred value concept) grew from nothing in 1980 to $1.4 billion by 1999:

> *Send an e-mail to everyone you know in your company: table-ready lettuce, $1.4 billion. If someone can do this with a vegetable, what the hell is our excuse?*[17]

Moving to complete customer solutions, rather than just selling 'stuff', is a general trend. The utility of what is being sold is much greater, while the cost of the elements is roughly the same. The missing step between an ingredient and a complete solution is information or some form of 'software' in the broadest – New Growth theory – sense.

A client of mine from an e-learning company sat on a flight next to a manager from SKF, the world's leading ball-bearing manufacturer. He told her that they are in the knowledge business too. His product's main added value is the software for operation, maintenance and replacement. That's why his Swedish company have gained a 20 per cent global-market share in an apparently old industrial commodity – spherical metal things.

INFORMATIONALISM AND COMPANIES

Nokia has (until recently) proved very good at managing the future.

Managing the future is largely a matter of seeing it. The reason Nokia saw the potential for different phone covers and ringtones to personalize its mobiles was that a high concentration of their staff carried phones, much earlier than that became common in society in general. Whenever a phone rang, or was left on a table, there would be confusion about whose phone it was. They recognized that this would become a problem.

If this doesn't sound 'smart' it's because looking back on it, it's such an obvious good idea. But looking forward to these ideas is much less easy. Otherwise Motorola would have launched them. We are all prisoners of convention.

With typical prescience, Nokia sat around at the *end* of the 1980s to discuss what the New Economy would mean for them. They realized that, in order to compete in the markets of the future, they'd have to raise productivity steeply.

So they did. They increased productivity by 20–30 per cent every year, throughout the 1990s, which is an achievement in any industry. But they were dealing with separate technologies converging for the first time. And with all the old-economy problems of labour relations and distribution too. And they made really neat phones.

Nokia has reinvented the way that they think about doing business, to manage this step change. They put the learning process at the centre of their company and organized everything else around it.

One concept I liked a lot, when I saw their CEO, Ollila Jorma, talk, was that 'products now behave like knowledge'. He was mainly talking about economics – it costs a lot to develop the product concept, but very little to produce extra product units. But I think the same goes for marketing: what we are branding is the knowledge, not the object. Do people 'buy' the concept? For WAP phones that turned out to be a rather sticky question.

Managing the future well means that you need to turn your attention from tangible to intangible assets.

Tangible assets are what the business is worth at present. They are the company's possessions, cash, land, equipment and so on. Intangible assets are some 'measure' of the company's future ability to make money.

As the information economy took hold, it became apparent that tangibles don't measure the company's true value. So, in the early 1980s, companies started being valued by capital markets, as worth more than the stuff they owned. Coca-Cola, which had a good fifteen-year run, was valued by the markets at $160 billion

in 1998. Whereas its tangible 'book value' was only $8 billion. At
the time this looked quite a low multiple – only twenty times,
compared with some of the tech stocks like AOL.

The key difference between tangible and intangible assets is
time. Tangible assets are what you own now. Intangible assets
give you the potential to earn money in the future.

I've been sitting on a UK government (DTI) advisory group
on 'Managing and Reporting Intangible Assets' (project MARIA).
As a result, I've come to understand the different streams of
value which exist in companies, as a result of the shift towards
Informationalism.

The DTI conducted research into how excellent UK companies managed intangible assets. The headline conclusion was
very simple. Intangible value derives from two classes of asset –
knowledge and relationships.

If you discover a new wonder drug and own the patent
(knowledge) then your company has the potential to make a
great deal of money in the future. When tiny biotech companies
do make discoveries like this, their stock goes sky-high. But that
knowledge is not the full story. You also need a strong network
of relationships (like the pharmaceutical companies have with
hospitals, doctors and pharmacists).

Knowledge and relationships are the raw materials of intangible value. This value is only realized when the company does
all kinds of things well, to extract this value. The research found
that there were six key multipliers.

Raw materials	• Knowledge • Relationships
Key multipliers	• Options and flexibility to change • Processes and systems • Skills and competencies • Culture and values • Reputation and trust • Networks and partnerships (DTI)

Fig. 13　*Raw materials and key multipliers*

Knowledge and relationships combine, in the natural form of organization for the information age, which is the network. The key shift in thinking was to see the business universe as a connected ecosystem, rather than as discrete blocks. Some quotes from the companies illustrate this point:

> We gather intelligence from suppliers, machinery manufacturers, consultants and academics to understand better the trends and developments which will influence the development of products and services which meet customers' needs.

> Networks help to feed the systems and processes which make value creation possible. They feed in knowledge, fuel innovation and create the context for valuable relationships.

> We need to remove the 'silo mentality' which destroys value and replace it with more open relationships between product areas and a joint commitment to corporate goals.[18]

In an open network of shared information, without 'silos', the role of branding changes. Rather than being stuck in its own silo of customer segments, the brand plays a broader role, shaping the minds and behaviour of: employees, partners and suppliers – and investors.

To build intangible value, the brand also needs to move from the current tangible objects, to become an envelope for future development. That's why it was a great idea to call Amazon something heroic and non-specific. They could have been called 'E-Books'. But that would have stunted their development into new markets, like CDs and household goods. And 'E-Books' doesn't inspire – it doesn't sound like the leading pioneer in the Internet space. The media, investors and employees saw Amazon as amazing. It was the Sony Walkman of the Net. They *owned* e-tailing.

Each of the following key multipliers has implications for marketing.

Options and Flexibility to Change

A company's future value derives from its ability to change and adapt to the markets of tomorrow. These days, this means much more than 'R&D'. It means an ability to invent whole new business models, markets and strategies. Companies that do this well tend to develop future options which they then put into action if the conditions are right. Having a spread of possible future options is a far better future-proofing than developing just one, in today's changeable environment.

Marketing has a vital role to play in this process. We need to understand how to turn a complex bundle of new business features into a compelling idea. So that we can contribute at the start of this process, not at the end when an ad campaign is needed.

I've been involved in a lot of new business models over the last two years, when helping dot-coms to write business plans. I was usually called in to write the marketing plan and add my name and credibility to the team. But what I ended up doing was rather different – helping to put a human concept at the heart of the business.

I helped one high-tech start-up frame their revolutionary voice commerce application. They had designed a system which allowed you to access all kinds of personal and public information: e-mail, news, call-divert, share prices, voicemail, weather, fax relay services, entertainment bookings and even your own diary . . . using voice recognition from your mobile phone. It's a complex bundle of new features and revenue streams. But the actual concept, I persuaded them, was simple:

This was a *virtual secretary*.

Inspired by this insight, one member of the team went off and started negotiations with the James Bond movie producers to license a virtual 'Miss Moneypenny'. She would be featured in the new movie and with a revenue sharing agreement would be exclusive to us as merchandizing.

This was now a *great* idea. Unfortunately they missed the 'dot-com funding curfew' by a few months. Otherwise I'd be writing this book from my own island in the South Seas!

Processes and Systems

If one person in a company does something well it has little lasting value. The whole company must make doing things well an ingrained habit, 'the way we do things'.

The processes and systems that can add value are wide ranging. People are of paramount importance, so the way that a company does recruitment, appraisal, training, motivation and remuneration is key. As are the processes through which a company 'thinks' – processes of communication and reporting, systems for gathering, storing, and retrieving information, processes of research and development, risk management and analysis processes, innovation and design processes etc.

The old rule-book way of doing all this was to work a minimum standard. But knowledge-value companies get their edge from giving people the freedom to think about what they are doing. So managing these processes and systems is far more about helping workers to consciously adopt habits and routines which create quality and value; like learning to give and receive honest, objective feedback. The whole 'Learning Organization' movement reflects this new way of working.[19]

The way companies do things is another new focus for branding. An obvious case is service, where the staff's way of dealing with customers *is* the product. First Direct, Southwest Airlines and Saturn Cars were all built on a different style of conversation, both internally and with customers. How you do things may be the most tangible sign that your future products and prospects will be good. Future branding is a leap of faith, and increasingly people will 'trust the process'.

Skills and Competencies

Almost all the companies in the DTI study recognized the value in building the abilities of their people and the ways in which the business makes the best use of their various talents. Workers need the capacity to respond to leadership, and the framework it provides for taking decisions, dealing with conflicting priorities, breaking the rules in order to achieve strategic aims, 'doing the right thing versus doing things right'.

How long will it be until a major consultancy – maybe McKinsey – IQ tests its people and publishes the results? Consultancies like Pricewaterhouse Coopers have already publicized their testing and accreditation of all employees on e-business. If knowledge is the source of your major added value, then the talent of your workforce is a key selling point.

One option I am exploring on a project to brand the country of Sweden (on behalf of their IT industry) is to emphasize the competence of the population as a whole. As one member of the working group said, 'we're born mobile'.

Culture and Values

Culture in this context means: ways of working, attitudes expected from people and the environment created to maximize value creation. This is often the most powerful and unique thing about a company.

The companies in the DTI survey agreed that the most productive culture was one where individuals had the freedom to perform. Employees are expected to take responsibility and act swiftly. Building an understanding of the core purpose, and an empathy with a clear set of values is the best way to set a course, with micro decision-making delegated.

Again, as value migrates into the future and intangibles, what is branded will more often be the purpose and values, rather than the current actions. I was involved in a project to communicate IKEA's ethical and environmental policy. Point for point this policy sets one of the highest standards in the world. It's already being used by campaigning organizations like Greenpeace as a reference point to help persuade other companies to follow the company's lead. IKEA's vision is to improve everyday life for the majority of people. This ethos is reflected in people's attitudes to the company. So the initiatives are readily accepted, almost expected. When we trust someone, we trust their intentions.

Reputation and Trust

This key multiplier includes brands. Although the research sounded a note of warning: do not mistake a 'trapped customer' for a 'loyal customer'. Both may appear to act in the same way but a trapped customer will head for the exit as soon as an opportunity arises. The research also found that *brand inflexibility* can be an intangible liability.

Businesses with or without consumer brands recognized that their corporate brand, or reputation, can be equally significant. It may influence customer decisions. It may also be the key to attracting the best people to work for the company. It may be a company's reputation that determines whether they are selected as business partners.

This is a general trend. More and more brands are pitched at the company rather than product level: Virgin, the Body Shop, MUJI ... Because the action is in whole new markets and concepts, not in flogging a single product line.

Networks and Partnerships

Few companies in the research believed they had a monopoly of knowledge, or the power to operate entirely independently of others. Many were therefore seeking partnerships. Increasingly companies see suppliers, customers and networks, inside and outside the business, as essential for business success. Examples in the organizations visited were found both on the buying and selling side, particularly in technology, links with academia etc.

The six multipliers are not mutually exclusive. On the contrary the DTI report described them in terms of a single prism, where the different streams of valuable knowledge and relationship combine. So there are networks of multipliers to deal with.

The overall picture is one of companies in a new higher level of development; networked, enlightened, attuned to the future and in constant flexible development.

This presents a very complex and fast-moving target for branding. I keep finding a general paradox – brands work best when they make things simple. But this doesn't mean we can pretend that *business* is simple.

Branding needs to step up a level, or it is in constant danger of oversimplifying. We see this again and again in corporate advertising. How often have we seen a manifestly excellent and progressive company, working at the leading edge of its industry, present itself in a facile way through advertising?

Of course there is no room in short television commercials to convey what really makes a company tick. But perhaps allowing the ad space to dictate the marketing is the tail wagging the dog? The Medicis had much better corporate marketing than most telco's (and probably with similar budgets!).

INFORMATIONALISM AND THE WORKER

The key asset in most businesses is people. Because knowledge, ideas and relationships drive value (rather than capital and plant), a good person can be disproportionately valuable, compared to an 'average' one. Bill Gates famously said that if the wrong twenty people left Microsoft, the company would be finished, and he founded an institute to attract the best brains in advanced research, to drip feed the business with new insights and ideas.

Most of the debate about 'the war for talent' centred on how to recruit the best people. This was a healthy stimulus for companies to think about, which led to the creation of more free-range working environments; the kinds of places people would love to work at and hate to leave. An extra stimulus was the brain drain to dot-com's. And this also made mainstream companies think about ownership, modern office designs and so on.

But as my friends at the Talent Foundation point out, it's dangerous to see the workplace as a 'transfer market'. In business, as in football, the best results come from growing your own talent. The hire-and-fire mentality actually works against creating a strong team.

If such a select few are so important to the organization, what's to stop them finding other ways to realize their value? By forming break-away companies, that sell their talent back to the big companies at a premium? Many people who create value (for instance 'inventors') tend not to like big organizations. They prefer the freedom to explore, create, be chaotic, fanatical etc. They are happiest in little clans of like-minded pioneers.

A dramatic example of the power-to-the-people trend happened in 1999, when a disgruntled IT department in Silicon Valley sold itself off to another company, by auction, on e-Bay. Quite a wake-up call, to the management of that company, I should think. They had thought they were the lords and masters of all they surveyed. Now it turned out they were just running 'a tourist destination' for employees. Poor service, bad experience, or an unfriendly ambience can kill off a 'resort' overnight.

In this context, the company brand is key. Companies used to offer long-term job security. But this went out of the window some decades ago. Most people don't even want a 'job for life' anymore. They choose their next employer (or to stay with the current employer) for a variety of subjective as well as objective reasons. The company brand – standing for the ethos and culture – can play a big role in this.

Companies also have a broader role, in attracting talented people to work in their industry, in the first place. Look at how technology careers went from being seen as dull, 'nerdy' backwaters to being seen as super-cool 'geeky' adventures. Which brings us back to customer learning. Where does the industry culture come from, if not from consuming passions turning into careers? Sun, Oracle and Unix have all benefited in recruitment terms from a generation of teenage hackers and Nintendo nuts.

Who in the world wouldn't love to go and work for Sony?

INFORMATIONALISM AND WORK

> Learning is what most adults will do for a living in the twenty-first
> century.
>
> PERELMAN

There has been a shift in employment; away from farming,
followed by factories, to 70 per cent of jobs now being in the
'service sector'. Which is fairly old news. But starkly true. And
probably the best indicator of how society has changed in the last
200 years:

%	1800	1850	1900	1950	2000
Services	3	17	28	45	70
Manufacturing	4	23	26	37	27
Agriculture	93	60	46	18	3

Social pessimists say that most of the service sector jobs are
low-skilled, boring 'McJobs' – waiting in fast-food chains, or
answering the phone in a call centre. But the pessimists are
wrong. In 1991, 55 per cent of the labour force were in skilled
jobs. In 2000 this figure was estimated to have risen to 65 per
cent. It is forecast to rise in the next few years to upwards of
85 per cent.[20]

Skilled jobs are knowledge intensive. You have to train and
retrain to get the 'know how'. The knowledge you are working
with, whether you are a doctor, lawyer, plumber or counsellor
. . . keeps changing.

Then there are the more obvious knowledge workers (or
symbolic analysts as some economists now call them). With their
open-collar dress code and clever-looking glasses, they make up
about 30 per cent of the workforce. These people are in desperately short supply, with education struggling to keep up with
demand. In the US the number of graphic designers grew 30 per
cent year-on-year in 2000.[21]

There is a strong case for employers investing in workplace learning. Studies have shown that a 10 per cent higher level of education in a workforce has two-and-a-half times greater effect on productivity, than a 10 per cent higher capital investment.[22]

Corporate training budgets have grown; from $50 billion in 1994 to an estimated $63 billion in 1999. There are 2000 workplace 'universities' and this number is increasing all the time. Working life is punctuated by courses these days. Volvo were one of the first companies to give Internet-ready home PCs to all employees. This, they hope, will nourish their evolution – or 'ReVolvolution' as they now brand it – from building solid cars, to building smart cars, using IT.

Training is no longer just an employer priority. Quite the reverse. Training is in high demand by employees. In a UK survey, 77 per cent of adults agreed that: 'I'd prefer to work for an employer who provides time, money and support for my training than for one who gives big salary increases but little opportunity for training.'[23]

National Express, the UK coach company had a big success with a drop-in education centre at their main terminal in London's Victoria. Here, a driver waiting for a return journey could develop a new skill – for instance learn a language – rather than just sit around for hours drinking endless cups of tea. This was strategic for the company (coach drivers should ideally speak other languages). It was beneficial for the workers, alleviating boredom and giving them better future prospects.

The reasons why training is important to today's workers are fairly self-evident.

The OECD put it this way; the average adult leaving school now will have five different jobs across their working life, with major retraining for each.[24] Since this report was published in 1994, it has also become clear that most people need major ongoing training *within* each job. A recent survey showed, for instance, that 42 per cent of UK workers have 'updated their computer skills recently'.

Learning is also regarded as a life-changing tool – to kick-start your life in a new direction. There are echoes of, in a previous era, sport and music being seen as the way 'out of the ghetto'.

Most people now believe that education is the key to getting on in life.

There was a desperately bleak documentary on British TV about a couple, recently released from prison, struggling to keep off the drugs and get one foot back on the social ladder. They eventually split up. And the man became homeless. But then the credits at the end of the programme told us that – after several false starts back into work – the woman in the programme had enrolled on a degree course to become a social worker. Where there's learning, there's hope.

No-one reaches eighteen now and thinks, 'I now know all I need for the rest of my life.'

People's choices are guided consciously and unconsciously by the potential benefits. There is clear evidence that learning increases earning power, and that gap is widening. In 1980 American graduates earned, on average, 50 per cent more than high school leavers. By 1999 that figure had reached 111 per cent.[25]

Successful organizations have changed to accommodate knowledge work rather than supervised manual work. This was described in *The Individualised Corporation* as a 'once in a lifetime management revolution'.[26] Empowered, self-directed employees and teams set the pace on their own projects. Hierarchies have been flattened – expensive suits, corner offices and many signs of status driven out, in favour of a flatter, 'free-range', creative work 'Antiarchy'.

I believe that the next essential step is to change the nature of workplace training. Too much of this still targets the application of routine knowledge, whereas what is really needed is development of initiative and fluid thinking to tackle unprecedented problems and opportunities.

In a recent project for the Cabinet Office my friend James Parr and I proposed that British workforce development should shift its focus from helping people be more industrious to helping people become more ingenious. With 'British Ingenuity' as a great asset to develop (and brand), to strengthen our twenty-first-century productivity and competitiveness.

Knowledge workers – along with young people still in education – also make knowledgeable consumers. This group are especially important for new concepts and markets. Their confidence and openness to change makes them the early adopters, even if they are not the main market in terms of spending power and scale.

Let's summarize the Informationalism chain reaction:

- businesses create new value by creating whole new business concepts
- this requires a new enlightened management, focused on intangible assets
- and this in turn requires a highly educated, motivated and flexible workforce.

The next section explores how the same trends to learning, self-direction, networks and flexibility now infuse society in general.

SECTION TWO

APOLLO RISING

Apollo was the Greek god of knowledge. 'Apollo Rising' is a trend – away from leisure life-style concerns – towards learning and self-development. Modern culture has become more serious and studious, as surveys of young people show. But this is not a move back to conformity and rote learning. It's a new self-directed, flexible, network spirit. It's about people working things out for themselves, individually and collectively. In this new culture, knowledge and passion are fused to create a new learning ethic.

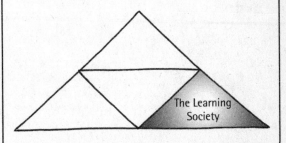

The Learning Society

3

LIFELONG LEARNING

Learning is the main source of future economic value for companies and regions. It is also a consistent thread through life, for individuals, as other roles, relationships and identities will be variable. Learning is a means to becoming, to developing as a human being. When we learn, the connections in our mind change and we change, usually for the better. What does not kill us makes us, not stronger, but in some sense more knowledgeable – a more complete human being.

We used to assume that we'd reach adulthood, and then not need to learn any more. Now this couldn't be further from the truth. It's like there was a rusty switch in people's minds saying 'learning' and it's just been thrown. People have quietly changed into curious, questioning, learning agents.

Learning is one of those activities, like exercise, that tends to be self-reinforcing once started. The more you learn, the more you get into learning. So what started as vocational learning, has spread to many other areas of adult life.

THE SILENT EXPLOSION

I do not believe that it is possible to understand the persistence and appeal of the lifelong-learning agenda, without recognizing the fundamental underlying shift in the behaviour of ordinary citizens, who increasingly regard the day-to-day practise of adult learning as routine, perhaps so routine that they give it little explicit attention.[27]

John Field is the UK's first professor of lifelong learning. He points to a much wider range of activities than are usually considered – like health clubs and self-help books – as 'implicit education' so routine it's barely recognized as learning.

There has been a tendency among many academics and market analysts to recognize only 'instruction'; learning that looks like school. Only recently has *any* learning which increases people's knowledge and changes their mental models started to be counted. If you look at it this way, lifelong learning is already the biggest social trend to emerge in the last fifty years, both in the number of adults participating, and in the knock-on effect on their values, lifestyles and attitudes. It has been, as Field points out, a silent explosion.

To see this picture fully, you have to shift your attention:

- from education (the supply of formal learning experiences)
- to learning (the much larger set of informal experiences).

When you look at the world this way, everything is a potential learning experience. Even soap operas. The educative role of soaps was recognized by a government/Demos think-tank. Which pointed to the way that soaps enable people to absorb and reflect on social change. Soaps routinely deal with questions such as:

> what if your daughter took a bad ecstasy tablet?
> what does divorce do to a family?
> what if there was a suspected paedophile living on your estate?
> what if your teenage daughter became pregnant?
> what if your next door neighbour had AIDS?
> what if your partner had an affair with your best friend?
> what if your son fell in with a bad crowd and stole cars?
> what if both you and your partner lost your jobs?
> what if there was an attempted murder outside your local pub?

It's sensationalist stuff. With ratings driven by pungent 'tabloid' stories. The conventions of soap opera are artificial. A lot of people these days don't know their neighbours, let alone live their lives in a conversation-rich network of local community and family. And the murder rates per thousand in soap operas make Lagos look safe!

But none of this detracts from what the think-tank suggested: that soap operas are used by people to understand modern life – what the 'news' of objective social change could mean for their subjective lives, giving them a chance to rehearse their own reactions for a life of unprecedented events; events for which there are no traditions to give guidance.

Looking at how people learn 'implicitly' from entertainment media and informal settings creates a much bigger view of life-long learning. Here's a 'map' I developed for the digital learning company, K-World, when we were rethinking their TV schedule. The figures in the chart below refer to approximate participation rates:

	Informal	Non-formal	Formal
Practical	Keeping up with news 90%	Life management IT, health, money 60%	Training work courses 60%
Social	Absorbing soaps 80%	Self-help books, magazines 50%	Self-development courses/counselling 30%
Aspirational	Lifestyle, travel, wine 70%	Quality of life hobbies 70%	Tuition courses, classes 30%

The three columns are based on Field's division of learning into three types:

- informal, which is so implicit it isn't recognized;
- non-formal, which is largely self-instigated and self-taught and
- formal, which involves some form of tuition.

The three rows are my own common-sense division of the types of learning people are going in for, based on their underlying needs:

- practical, to do everyday things
- social, to get a handle on relationships and the changing society and
- aspirational, to change your life for the better.

As learning en masse enters society and everyday life, it changes too. Just as sport changed – as the keep-fit craze spread – from elite competition, to jogging. We're not moving to a classroom society.

The drive to 'keep up' and develop one's self conflicts with an older (now eroding, but still potent) view that learning is boring and not much use. Culture had to find a way around the hang-ups. Jogging is quite a good analogy for how popular culture does this.

Jogging offered a new acceptable form of 'keep-fit'. A type of exercise that was nothing like physical education at school. It was individualized. It became a culturally supporting craze. Jogging in the early 1980s was exciting. Jogging was functional (don't feel sluggish all your life), achievable and even enjoyable.

Hobbies are a prime example of the implicit learning trend. Hobbies are increasingly knowhow- and skill-rich; PlayStation, home music studios, yoga ... Many enthusiasts set up their own websites. And also use the Internet to swap, for example, tips, kit and stories with other buffs. People tend to migrate from hobbies and training, such as a computer course at work, to more challenging sustained projects of learning.

Hobbyist 'how to' shows on TV, for cooking, gardening, DIY and even sex, have exploded in recent years: more evidence of the new relevance and popularity of lifelong learning. They are now a primetime staple along with another great implicit learning genre – and still the most popular single form of television – the documentary.

THE DISCOVERY CHANNEL

The name says it all. The Discovery Channel. It's a sign of the times. Discovery was initially launched as the Learning Network. But changed its name after a year – because research said the word 'learning' was a turn off, for most people, because it reminded them of school.

The founder, John Hendrix, was a fundraiser for Maryland University. His big insight was that there was 'never anything decent to watch on TV'. His passion was for documentaries. So he set up a small-scale US cable channel to plug the gap. Joyce Taylor, the European managing director of what is now the Discovery Network, started out as a teacher (although she always wanted to be in television). I met Taylor at a corporate learning event and went on to interview her about the Discovery story.

Discovery has become a 'network' because it has nine channels including: Health and Leisure, Kids, Travel and Adventure as well as the original Discovery Channel. In a rather American view of 'Europe', it spans thirty-three countries, from the UK to Israel and Kazakhstan.

The average viewer is male, over twenty-five years old and very loyal.

The biggest show in mid 2001 was *Forensic Detectives*. Other hot topics include angling (the most popular European hobby) and health (the 'medical dictionary' factor). Discovery also owns and promotes big knowledge events – digging up a whole mammoth was a past coup. Their current big event is the Space Station. If you go on their website you can actually look around the Space Station, which is pretty absorbing. Their positioning is 'entertainment that tells you something'. Words like education, learning and knowledge are avoided, as major turn-offs.

There's no denying that, in a fragmenting media universe, Discovery stands out, like very few others. It has even been immortalized in a recent pop hit:

> You and me baby ain't nothin' but mammals
> So let's do it like they do on the Discovery Channel.

You might think this lyric is funny, maybe, but no big deal. But try to imagine a (positive) lyric that mentioned Sky, Nickelodeon, CNN, or even MTV these days.

Discovery is where it's at:

- individual not institutional
- creative ('ahah!') and participative
- self-directed, following my interests
- implicit
- *entertaining*.

I know it helps that they're best known for showing 'nature's pornography', animals killing and mating. But this is the point. Discovery always finds the passionate, entertaining angle in the science, the history and the geography. It's entertainment that tells you something, indeed.

Interestingly, what a programme is called is a key to gaining audience share. Especially given the way programme guides work nowadays, where all you have is the title to choose from. The perfect name is specific but sparky, Taylor told me: 'You can't just call a programme "Horses" but they should know there's horses in it.' When Channel 4's *Scrapheap* programme was renamed *Scrapheap Challenge* for its second series, the viewing figures shot up by 30 per cent.

This question of how to *categorize* something in people's minds is a central issue for 'branding knowledge'.

PEOPLE SWITCHING ON TO LEARNING

How do you stimulate people, for whom education is a turn-off, to take up some form of adult education? That was the advertising brief from the UK Campaign for Learning that I worked on in my last months at St Luke's. The idea we came up with was even more implicit than 'Discovery'.

Each of our ads (on poster sites around London transport and outside colleges) featured a picture of an everyday item. For instance a pair of shoes, or a bunch of tomatoes. And had a headline, which started to give you a fascinating fact, but got cut off just before the punchline.

My favourite example was this ad (I've still got the t-shirt):

Tomato plants grow almost twice as fast when

That's a little infuriating isn't it? (Unless you already know your tomatoes.)

No-one at the Campaign for Learning will ever tell you the answer. You'll just have to go and find out. You could look in a gardening book. You could ask an expert friend. You could search on the Web. You could even pop along to an evening class.

I bet that if you do any of that, you'll end up growing some tomatoes of your own. Once you have some knowledge about 'how to', it's very tempting to try it out. Giving away knowledge keys is a great lever for market development.

Our idea was to avoid 'talking people into' learning. This would only have hit the 'learning is not for me' barrier. And we didn't trust the 'remember to do something later' approach. We wanted to hook them there and then. Curiosity, we argued, is one of the most powerful human motivations. Once you've got a curiosity itch, you can't help scratching.

The ads only had a tiny budget for public media. But the campaign eked this out by giving the artwork to local colleges to adapt for their own courses. It apparently worked pretty well, especially at the grassroots level. The Campaign for Learning have become one of my best sources of fascinating contacts and useful information.[28] Through research they gave me, I've discovered that:

90 per cent of UK adults think 'learning is important to me personally'.

The main 'reasons why' it's important to them were split equally between vocational/career prospects and self-improvement/quality of life/confidence.

60 per cent of adults participated in taught learning in the last year.

57 per cent of adults undertook some self-directed learning.

And 91 per cent of these stated reasons as 'for a current or future job'.

THE NEW LEARNING ETHIC

An ethic – in the sense of 'Protestant work ethic' – is a central principle, which organizes a whole system of values and behaviours. I think learning is becoming an ethic in its own right. This would be a kind of Copernican shift. Learning would no longer be the by-product of work, or a means of gaining power and status. It is an end in itself, against which other activities and outcomes are measured.

Pekka Himanen calls this the 'the hacker ethic'. 'Hackers', in his usage, are expert coders or computer gurus (not to be confused, he says, with 'crackers' who wreak havoc with computer viruses, worms and virtual break-ins). Himanen's book describes the 'hacker' ethos, not just as a way of computing, but as a general approach to life.[29] He identifies the key values of this new spirit as:

- Passion – 'some intrinsically interesting pursuit that energizes the hacker'
- Freedom – 'Hackers do not organize their lives in terms of a routinized workday, but in terms of a dynamic flow between creative work and life's other passions'.

As Himanen notes, this is not just a coder's way of life. It is increasingly becoming the new work ethic. It bursts from every seam of publications like *Fast Company*. It is how people live for their hobbies, their small business, even their garden. Learning is central to this 'hacker ethic'. And the way Himanen describes hacker learning fits very well with the themes of this book:

> A typical hacker's learning process starts out with setting up an interesting problem, working towards a solution by using various sources, then submitting the solution to extensive testing. Learning more about a subject becomes the hacker's passion.

I recently visited Sony Computer Entertainment in London. The programmers there described how – working exactly this way

– they'd get stuck on something and work on right through the night (fuelled by Coca-Cola and Mars bars) just to crack a solution. You can see why employers would reorganize a few management structures, just to stand out of these learning heroes' way! It's passionate work like this, and also the open sharing of ideas among people who care about getting a great solution rather than any status, credit or extrinsic rewards, that makes companies with a learning ethic so awesomely prolific.

If that sounds like an apology for a new workaholism, bear in mind that a passionate absorption in challenging tasks can also be very rewarding. Psychologist Mihalyi Csikszentmihalyi after thirty years of studying what is most likely to produce happiness, concluded that:

> In the course of my studies I tried to understand as exactly as possible how people felt when they most enjoyed themselves, and why . . . I developed a theory of optimal experience based on the concept of flow – the state in which people are so involved in an activity that nothing else seems to matter.[30]

A report on 'Generation X and Work' by Demos in the early 1990s detected strong hints of this new self-directed, passionate project spirit among 18–35-year-olds.[31] What they wanted from work was projects where they could achieve results within months (not years) without supervision or control. Contrary to the 'slacker' stereotype, they were highly motivated under these conditions.

The learning ethic is a central principle, to which are attached a lot of secondary values and behaviours – by-products of approaching life this way. Farmers learn to be patient because things grow slowly. They value family and community highly because harvests are based on effective teamwork and neighbours helping each other. In a similar way, people who have the learning ethic become independent of judgment, resilient, passionate – and ready to network with other people on similar journeys.

We can define these side-effects a little more closely, by looking at the learning ethic in a number of different contexts:

graduate students; entrepreneurs and creative production companies. All of these have a learning ethic in common, which is a good fit with that described by Himanen as a 'hacker ethic'. This suggests that it is self-directed work rather than computer usage which is responsible for this new approach to life.

MEET THE GRADS

An American study of graduate student values gives us an (extreme) indication of what a concentrated period of self-directed learning can do to anyone's values:

- **SACRIFICE:** in contrast to other surveys of Americans (a society constituted for the pursuit of happiness) graduates showed a high propensity to sacrifice time, money and even personal relationships in pursuit of their goals.
- **ACHIEVEMENT:** asked about what sparks their motivation to study, they cited intellectual achievement: a great paper, a high grade, affirmation by a mentor.
- **IDEALISM AND RELATIONSHIPS:** their top-ranked 'dreams for the future' are being known for integrity (87 per cent), having close friendships (81 per cent), being married (59 per cent), having children (52 per cent) and influencing lives (37 per cent). Material ambitions ranked low in this list: high-paid job (10 per cent), fame or recognition (9 per cent), own a large home (5 per cent). This is an inner-directed and intrinsically motivated group, in other words.
- **SELF-RELIANCE AND RESPONSIBILITY:** a key characteristic of the group is their self-reliance, forming their own objectives and concentration on their achievement. They gravitate towards challenges with responsibility. They regard having a driven personality as a positive. And nine out of ten when asked who they turn to for emotional support said they rely upon themselves for growth and stability and turn inwards to handle pressure.
- **SCEPTICISM:** the researchers linked this to an education process, which teaches them to challenge everything and take

nothing on trust. 'They are too intelligent and inquisitive to accept dogmatic statements without further scrutiny.'

- **SERIOUSNESS:** leisure activities were largely considered a waste of time that could be spent studying. They devoted little or no time to 'frivolous activity' (in marked contrast to the public image of students!). Their average fifteen-hours-a-week leisure time was spent on music, sport, exercise . . . Honestly. That's what the research said.
- **STRESS:** nine out of ten students said that stress and burnout were key concerns and they also worry about the balance of their lives and their health in general.
- **INTELLECT FIRST:** the research found the students were 'motivated by knowing rather than being' – and by the respect of others for their intellect, drive and goals.[32]

Of course it's not new for graduate researchers to fall passionately in love with their field, to be high-minded or sceptical. But what *is* significant is the sheer numbers of people going into higher education.

In the UK 32 per cent (1998) then 42 per cent (2001) and soon 50 per cent (2004) of young adults are going on to higher education – that is, university.[33] This is an astonishing shift: from 16 per cent of school leavers in the early 1980s, or nearer 2 per cent in the first half of the century. The government plan is that the remaining 50 per cent should have access to vocational-skills training, a bit like the old apprenticeship schemes.

As time goes on, one in two adults you meet ever, anywhere, will be a university graduate. And most of the rest will have a developed skill that they are constantly learning to maintain and update. This will create a very different kind of society.

Four out of every ten university students are over the age of 24 (43 per cent in the US – figures may be slightly higher in Europe).[34] This figure has doubled in the last thirty years, turning 'mature students' from a rarity to almost the norm. This creates a very different dynamic in lecture halls. Most students are there at great personal sacrifice. And many are older and more experienced than the 'teachers'. University as a last spurt of rote, regimented learning is increasingly an untenable pedagogic model. It's already changing into a continually assessed, individualized journey of discovery. This means that undergraduate higher education is installing the learning ethic.

THE ENTREPRENEURS

Plato said 'necessity is the mother of invention'. You don't have to be a classical philosopher to realize that the father was probably an entrepreneur.

A Demos report on media and arts-industry entrepreneurs studied outfits like *Aaaargh!* (the animators). The report was summarized by the title, 'The Independents'.[35] Much of what they found is in good agreement with the values described in the previous sections of this book.

Entrepreneurs tend to be well educated: on average 43 per cent have higher education qualifications – this is even more marked amongst those under the age of 34, where 77 per cent have a degree.

Their most important characteristic is their independence. They are almost allergic to the idea of working for a big organization: They are wary of subsidies and grants and even overdrafts ('too many strings attached') and are determined to make it on their own.

This independence is vital to their way of working, which is predicated on having great ideas, an end which tends to suit a 'structured chaos' approach to a degree which few corporations could understand or tolerate. Their independence is offset by their fluid collaborations and drive to network with a larger community of peers; providing ideas, contacts, complementary skills, venues and access to the market.

The Demos study was into a specific group of 'creative industry' entrepreneurs. But I find them to be a good fit with the entrepreneurs I have met in many other industries. The media tends to emphasize the macho, risk-taking bravado and rashness of these characters. Which is a stereotype that some live up to and others don't. Bill Gates is hardly a mountain man.

What you tend to find more consistently, if you scratch the

surface is a questioning spirit. These are people who have been caught on finding the answer to some simple question – like the founder of Discovery who simply wondered 'why is there never anything good to watch on TV?' and who have set out to find an answer.

VALUE AND VALUES

In the consumer society epoch, we valued lifestyle, status, glamour, class and the trappings that went with them. Education was subsumed to these central issues of social standing. Subtle cultural markers of taste determined where you stood in the world, and education was therefore a means, with the resulting 'status' the ultimate end.

Now we value learning. Which is key to both individual development, and also the creation of new wealth. It's like the difference between 'physique' and 'health'. One overt and all for show, the other innate, implicit, a basis for a way of life.

I see the learning ethic as an algorithm. It takes the data of experience and crunches it differently from the old routines. And it transforms as it iterates.

What was a branch, or some foliage, is now the tree trunk. It's the central vector that drives people's journey through life, the measure of progress, the yardstick of relative value:

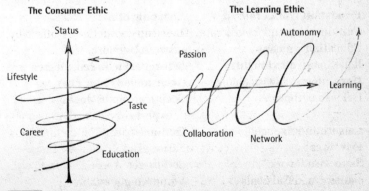

Fig. 14 *The Consumer Ethic versus the Learning Ethic*

This has everything to do with new forms of company and marketing.

Max Weber showed how the Protestant work ethic was a central organizing principle, which aligned individuals, companies, communities and societies. It was the lynchpin of capitalism. It's possible that the learning ethic represents a challenge to much more than consumer lifestyles and brand image. It may be the key to a new kind of society, politics and economics. Linux, which is one of the first examples of this ethic acting on a large scale, certainly represents something other than 'normal' capitalism. As do consumer goods which align more with learning than with the status vector – like home computers.

Across all those niches of society where the pure learning ethic is active, we've seen the same two key strands, of independence and interdependence:

- Self-reliance/self-direction/creativity/passion
- Network/collaboration/conversation.

THE NEW CULTURE

An algorithm produces some new result. The result of the Protestant work ethic was consumer capitalism. The learning ethic seems to be taking us somewhere new:

Protestant work ethic	Learning ethic
Tuition	Discovery
Education = means	Learning = end
Rebellious individualism	Self-reliance, independence
Uncomfortable with change	Accustomed to big changes
Defer to authorities	Sceptical versus dogma, experts
Leisure-indulgence	Optimal-flow
Frivolous	Serious fun
Supervised work	Self-directed work
Value = material goals	Value = higher values
Grounded in community	Networked

Protestant work ethic	**Learning ethic**
Passive, visual spectacle (eg TV)	Active learning experiences (eg Net)
Knowledge = boring	Learning = power, passion, entertainment
IMAGE	INTELLECT

This may look like just another 'new zeitgeist' theory. But there is stark evidence that the trend has spread very far, well beyond students and entrepreneurs, into the whole population, as this survey of 1000 UK adults shows:[36]

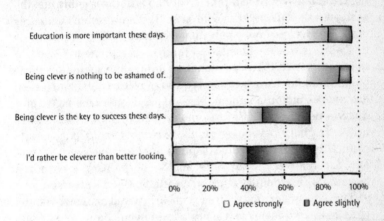

Education is more important these days.

Being clever is nothing to be ashamed of.

Being clever is the key to success these days.

I'd rather be cleverer than better looking.

0% 20% 40% 60% 80% 100%

□ Agree strongly ▣ Agree slightly

Fig. 15 | *Results of an education survey*

THE LEARNING FAMILY

Here's a familiar tale, the story of a typical middle-English family, at the start of 2001.

Paul, the father, is recovering from a heart by-pass operation. Paul and his wife Ursula are now experts on his medical condition. They are impatient with any doctors and nurses who aren't up to speed. In the early recovery phase, they plotted Paul's twice-daily vital signs, on a spreadsheet on their computer.

Before this calamity, Paul was enjoying an active retirement;

a packed schedule of French classes, local charity work and the golf club. While recovering, Paul enjoyed reading up on the latest popular science books. A new laptop computer (at 800MHz, a supercomputer the size of a coffee table book) has arrived.

Ursula is similarly occupied with learning; ranging from local history, to languages and bridge. Ursula also continues her role as matriarch. Recent news and views are distributed in all-family e-mail bulletins. Paul and Ursula lived abroad for years and enjoy travel, especially as a getaway from the drab winter. The latest bulletin writes up their trip to Madeira for Mardi Gras.

Mick, the oldest son, is a rural police sergeant. This demanding job still leaves time for the great hobbyist loves of his life: the gun dogs, the DIY and the computer (key applications being his dog-breed website and a new digital camera).

Claire, the next oldest is a creative entrepreneur. Based in the north east, Claire has managed to juggle bringing up three children on her own, with a portfolio of roles as make-up artist, beauty consultant, photographer's rep and studio manager, production manager, stylist, art director and much besides. Claire is into 'self help' psychology, to the extent of encouraging 'family council' meetings to resolve disputes at home. She's also a fan of new-age remedies. Claire has made a foray back into formal learning with a foundation course with the Open University.

The next sister, Katy, lives with her two daughters. Having chosen not to go to university at nineteen, Katy, in her late thirties, took a degree in history and is now working part-time for Camden Council, while also lecturing at the Open University. Katy's big cause in life at the moment is the treatment of refugees in the UK and she's been involved in a charity which offers them support.

The youngest brother Mark went to work in the City of London straight from school, selling government equities. He saw his future prospects dwindle, because of the changes looming in the financial markets (moving to European equities). So he left. First he finished his investment banking exams. Then he switched career tracks – he's now selling financial IT systems to corporate treasury departments.

By now this is starting to sound like one of those 'family of the future' case studies, an unconvincing fiction. How could one family be part of nearly every current lifelong-learning trend: from mature students to 'self help'; from the expert patient to vocational retraining? But it's not. There were five children – and I am the second youngest.

In the last five years my family has probably done more learning than in the previous thirty.

4

A PASSION FOR KNOWLEDGE

HOW APOLLO, THE GOD OF KNOWLEDGE, SMILED ON A CERTAIN TV EXECUTIVE

In the year 2000, *Who Wants to be a Millionaire?* became the biggest TV show in the world. As one American network chief put it, it was 'the biggest British cultural invasion of America since The Beatles'. And it's not just a hit in the UK and America. 'Phone a friend' is now a global catch-phrase.

Why is this show so successful?

It's hard to pin it down to just one reason. The astronomical prize money helps. So does the immaculate formatting and staging. The catch-phrases. The name. The way the show invites the audience at home to ponder the question or to shout out the answer. The clever interplay between the presenter and con-testant ('Is that your final answer?'). The panic-stricken looks. All the glimpses into contestants' lives and characters.

All of these would just make it a good TV show. But it has something else.

Who Wants to be a Millionaire? signifies that in modern life it is your knowledge (and how you apply it under pressure) that could propel you to sudden, dramatic fame and fortune. This mythologizes a bigger trend. Look at America's five richest men in 1999, the year the programme was first screened:

America's wealthiest people

1. Bill Gates	software	$85 billion
2. Paul Allen	software, cable	$40 billion
3. Warren Buffet	stock market	$31 billion
4. Steven Ballmer	software	$23 billion
5. Michael Dell	computers	$20 billion

Even more visible, that year, were the new dot-com millionaires. It suddenly seemed that all it took was some new thinking, to add seven zeros to your bank balance. It gave the lie to the taunt from another American era: 'If you're so smart, why ain't you rich?' It's a rewriting of the American Dream. It used to be that anybody could go from rags to riches through hard work, discipline, perseverance, leadership and insidious networking ... Now it's not how you work, or even who you know, it's *what* you know.

It takes repression to make an explosion. The most startling thing about *Who Wants to be a Millionaire?* is that we have grown up in a generally anti-intellectual culture: a teenage culture; a glamour culture; a leisure culture; a consumer culture; a dumbed-down, 30 second attention-span culture – an image culture. Compared with which an hour-long TV programme which asks questions like 'Which British king was the husband of Queen Mary?' is an anomaly.

Who Wants to be a Millionaire? is making a new equation:

Knowledge = Emotion, Passion and Entertainment

- it's a show that sends the viewer's heart and mind racing
- it's like a cross between a multi-choice exam and the gladiatorium
- it combines extreme 'death row' ominous styling with extreme gloss
- it alternates between moments of utter concentration and levity
- it delights in people's everyday ordinariness but presents them as celebrities.

Just to prove that wasn't a fluke – and that it wasn't just about the prize money – along came stern Anne Robinson with *The Weakest Link*. Another show that fuses deep general knowledge with human emotions. This show (at least in the UK) didn't even have a big prize. The knowledge fused with sadistic putdowns, tension and infighting were plenty to carry the viewers' interest. NBC's version went to the top of the US TV programme chart within three weeks.

WHO WANTS TO BE A DUMB BLONDE?

Once upon a time, *Baywatch* was the biggest TV show on earth. It made Pamela Anderson a global pin-up and launched her movie career. It stood for everything 'blonde': sunshine, melodrama ('hurry, my kitten is drowning!'), pneumatic fake breasts and perfectly toned abdominals, one-dimensional characters. All woven together with story lines, that made other many TV soaps look post-doctoral, by comparison.

It was the ultimate dumb image-youth-glamour-aspiration TV show. A half-hour advert for a lifestyle. And people all over the world loved it. And, in its own way, it was great.

Baywatch has just been cancelled, after years of declining audience ratings. Intellect is eclipsing image. The new passionate-knowledge culture is displacing everything *Baywatch*. 'Dumbing Down' is dead.

Consider another piece of evidence. Every year, 3000 UK adults are asked to vote for 'the world's most beautiful women'.[37] Blondes used to sweep the board, but not in the latest survey. There were only three blondes in the top ten. And one of these was Joanna Lumley, actress and star of the smartly observant comedy *Absolutely Fabulous*. Dumb and blonde go together like ham and pineapple. And the brunettes were not just chosen for their looks. Top of the chart was Andrea Corr (of Irish pop group, the Corrs). Also featured in the top ten were Carol Vorderman (celebrity high-IQ presenter) and Nigella Lawson (broadcaster and author of *How to Eat*).

As *Blow!* magazine said on its front cover earlier in the 1990s,

'It doesn't matter if you're 32A or 34EE – Intelligence is *the* new accessory.'[38]

ADVENTURES IN POPULAR SCIENCE

'Popular' and 'science' were not two words that went together, twenty years ago. Back then I was a science student. I enjoyed the subjects. But it wasn't a path through life that grabbed me. Being a scientist was just so *nerdy*.

Then, in the 1990s, Stephen Hawking's *A Brief History of Time* became an international bestseller. The topic was cosmology, which is quite a picturesque field of knowledge; covering black holes, white dwarves, neutron stars and, of course, the big bang. But the public didn't seem to have maintained any interest in the actual subject matter. It was the story of the man, rather than his theories, which most caught the public imagination.

What does this modern myth tell us? Hawking signifies a powerful intellect trapped by a limiting physical condition. (Physical deformities are powerful symbols in mythology; for example, 'Oedipus' means 'swollen foot'.) This is a victory of brains over brawn. And this myth makes an equation, similar to *Who Wants to be a Millionaire?*

Knowledge = Transcending Your Limits

Hawking represents hope. His story illuminates the otherwise dry world of theoretical physics, with human passion and courage. This fusion of knowledge with great stories like this is *how* science has become popular again – it equates knowledge and passion.

That was the formula in *Longitude*, another popular science bestseller. This is the true story of a humble clockmaker from working-class origins, rejected by the academic aristocracy of the Royal Society, who made a great discovery against the odds.

This story highlights another facet of the modern knowledge culture – it's a great leveller.

The Internet and general spread of education has put

knowledge, which equates to power, in many more hands. A patient who knows more than their doctor, a computer hacker who knows more than Microsoft . . . these are unsettling times for those who hold positions, through former monopolies of knowledge. And that's why it's also so exciting for the rest of us. Power, transformation, success, passion . . . it is knowledge that helps us stretch for them.

HOLLYWOOD WISES UP

Hollywood, sensitive to the zeitgeist as ever, have picked up the trend. They have been infusing their passionate stories with a little bit of knowledge. It's like the yeast that makes the dough rise. A visit to the cinema now is often a visit to some domain of specialist knowledge, rather than just a fantasy escape:

Jurassic Park and genetics
Shakespeare in Love and literature
Gladiator and ancient history
Titanic and modern class history
Saving Private Ryan and the Second World War.

APOLLO'S CHILDREN

Many social trends spread fastest among 15-year-olds. Not because this age-group are especially innovative. They're usually not. It's art students, computer hackers, entrepreneurs, gay activists, rap artists, eco-warriors, cult followers, and other pioneering niches that create new social ideas. It's hard to contribute to a culture until you've fully absorbed and partly rejected it.

15-year-olds are the fastest to change simply because they are the most open to it. They are tuned into adult society, unlike the younger age-groups, but they are still forming their identity. They are pure imprints of what's 'now', whereas us old-timers are also repositories of past trends and phases.

And the big change in this group, compared with our teenage

years, is that 15-year-olds have become meeker, milder and more studious.

Surveys show they get on well with their parents and live at home into their mid 20s. (Their parents aren't even 'old'. There's nothing to kick against when your parents wear the same trainers, talk the same language, use the same phone, listen to the same bands . . .) That they favour monogamy. That they are ambitious and studious, from an early age (especially the girls). But, above all, surveys reveal that they are not very rebellious.

In the early 1990s the idea spread among teens of 'staying on' (at school). There was a bitter recession, particularly in the old industrial regions. Staying on at school made sense. At least it delayed the no-hope, no-jobs dole queue, while the recession blew over. So the number of kids staying on at school leapt up in just a few years. And the idea took hold that, to survive in life, you needed good exam results.

A classic study of working class boys from the 1970s contrasted the official culture (academic, studious, docile) with the more effective counter-culture of working class lads (physical, 'having a laff', boisterous).[39] Kids were choosing to 'succeed' in culture terms, by 'failing' in academic terms. But the tide has turned, albeit faster among girls who are today's model students and exam achievers.

Global surveys of young people reveal that this new zest for education is part of a broader shift – to more serious, goal-setting, conforming but sceptical, mature attitudes:

- 68 per cent favoured marriage as providing security for children. 90 per cent favoured carrying on learning after leaving school.[40]
- 'This is a very pragmatic group, at the age of 18 they have 5 year plans' – from a survey that also found that '100 per cent believe they will achieve their lifetime goals'. Attributes most admired were honesty and integrity.[41]
- Generation Y are 'well-informed, pragmatic and increasingly confident'. 82 per cent think 'computers at school are a good idea'. 71 per cent think 'products that are bad for the environment should be banned'.[42]

- In the USA, two thirds use computers regularly, at least half intend to attend a four year college, most have divorced parents, but – far from being disenchanted rebels – most rate their parents' generation positively.[43]
- 'It doesn't matter that Michael Jordan endorses Nike' – Ben, aged 13.[44]

Adolescence was, and still is, when people develop many of their social values. The generation that is growing up serious, principled and self-directed now is the adult population of tomorrow.

POPSTARS: FROM REBELLION TO AMBITION

Teenage rebellion was by definition anti-intellectual, because it was anti-school. As the Pink Floyd anthem, 'Another brick in the wall', says:

> We don't need no education.
> We don't need no thought control.
> No dark sarcasm in the classroom.
> Teachers leave them kids alone . . .

Popstars is another recent international hit TV show. The premise was to open the audition process for a new band, to the public, the media and the show's own cameras. In the hope that the sheer exposure would guarantee a hit.

In Britain, the show's band – Hear'say – went straight to number one in the singles chart. In the TV show, pop culture was allied to career ambitions. *Popstars* is another myth of the new zeitgeist:

Success = Passion + Application (Learn, Practise, Compete)

There's nothing new about role models. But the idea, at the age of 15, that 'I want to be a big success in life' is something of a revelation, compared with our own youths of slacking, hacking and backpacking.

This changes the meaning of Pop culture; it's turning into a career guide. What we keep encountering – from TV programmes to youth attitudes – is diverse examples of the same cultural remix:

Learning + Passion

There may be a new zest for knowledge. But it has a dark side.

The learning boom is set against general anxiety and uncertainty. People are adapting to a situation where they have to learn. Not just skills to apply in a routine way, but the ability to be flexible and 'live on your wits'.

THE POST-TRADITION AND -CUSTOM SOCIETY

The insight, from sociologist Anthony Giddens, is that late modern societies are *different*, in that the traditions and customs handed down from past ages are in question, and subject to revision.

An example I use to illustrate this is that, when I was growing up, I thought English food was great. My reason for thinking that way was that everyone I knew ate English food. My illusions were shattered when my parents moved to France when I was ten. Here I learned that French food – while bearing some similarities to the food I'd grown up on – was better. Not in some acquired taste, cultural way. It just tasted really good.

The fusion of different local cultures – through travel, imports and the media – is one cause of the post-traditional age. We are aware, through direct and indirect experience, that there are other ways to live. This applies, not only to food, but to many things, like relationships, fashion, design, architecture, politics, schooling and religion . . . As soon as you are aware that there are different options, you are post-tradition. Traditions blinker you to other possibilities, tradition = no choice.

Continuing the culinary theme, another of life's tricky questions these days is: what to have for breakfast.

I grew up with a 'traditional' English breakfast: fried egg, bacon, sausage, toast and so on. But 'what to have for breakfast' now is a problem.

Should I eat salad? Probably not. Why not? Because this is not an 'accepted' alternative that I know of. Should I eat bread? Maybe. Maybe French bread and café au lait. Maybe fruit. That's a popular choice these days. Should I have fried fish and pickles? They do in Japan. Perhaps I should skip breakfast and have a Starbucks latte on the way to a meeting?

I have a choice of 'surrogate' traditions to replace my original real tradition. There is not one accepted way of doing things. But nor is there an infinite choice, there are still some 'accepted' options. We don't tend to decide these questions completely from scratch, which is why branding still has teeth. It's 'acceptable' to pick up a breakfast from Starbucks, but perhaps not from a fishmonger.

What I actually did today was have a banana and a cappuccino.

Knowledge trends play a role in our decisions. My decisions are informed by new knowledge – my breakfasts, broadly, are getting healthier. And the other impetus, to change this most basic habit, is that my life circumstances keep changing. Different relationships have brought different options and compromises. Working from home has changed the place of breakfast in the day, so has the (annoying) practice of early meetings, with breakfast en route and working abroad on long business trips.

Along with 'what to eat for breakfast' another great uncertainty is what to wear? When I started work at a big ad agency in the 1980s there was no question. I wore a suit. Most people in business did. Now things are much more open. There are many choices, but again there are some 'accepted' options, which I can choose, mix and match. We would like to think we can choose freely, creatively and without any limits. But all of us follow conventions; even the most radical drag queens and fetishists work from fixed options.

Claude Levi Strauss, a pioneer of modern anthropology, introduced the concept of *bricolage* to describe these kinds of choices. *Bricolage* is French for do it yourself. Like the DIY enthusiast, people don't choose from an infinite range of options. They have a limited set of cultural tools for thinking and behaviour, and have no concept of making their own tools as an engineer would.

Our minds have not evolved beyond this *bricolage* way of putting together our lives; out of meaningful units of behaviour, meaningful objects, or ways of thinking. But we now have many more options. There is more than one accepted way of doing everything. We are constantly re-stocking our personal *bricolage* toolbox. And we go through 'spring-cleaning' exercises, adopting whole new sets of procedures, at times when our life changes course.

The Network Society has created a context where people have to constantly update their knowledge. But this is set a against a broader context of uncertainty in how to live. The two together are *why* we now go through life updating our knowledge.

This presents a double challenge to companies. They compete in a fast-moving environment, where if they don't innovate competitors will. But they also need to help customers who are already stretched and stressed with uncertainty to keep up.

The winning ideas close the loop, by coming up with not just innovative, but also simpler, more 'manageable' ways of life. They solve life's problems, rather than adding to them. That's why 'killer applications' win – not just 'killer technologies'. It is ideas like e-mail that will inherit the earth.

RETHINKING BRANDING

Brand image has been in trouble for ten years or so. Many brands have been 'found out', or simply been left behind by progress in industries and society. The successes have come from branding higher-level concepts. To understand this kind of branding, we need to draw on cognitive science and recent discoveries about how the mind works. Here we find that a brand is just a type of mental model. The mental model framework gives us a landing strip for concept branding. And also ties marketing in to learning, which is the same thing as changing a mental model.

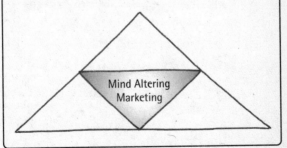

Mind Altering
Marketing

5

THE BRAND-IMAGE CRISIS

Branding is everywhere. We have moved from its origins, in the branding of throwaway goods such as soap powders and soft drinks, to branding political policies and lifestyle choices. This is partly the result of the increasing influence, sophistication and reach of the media, and partly a testament to the fact that branding works and that it does so because it is grounded in some innately human ways of making sense of the world. But all is not well in the land of branding. Over the last ten years it has been through a crisis. The kind of branding which links the image of a product or service – its 'personality' – with social aspiration has been under attack. As a result branding is changing.

GOOD RIDDANCE

'How do I justify spending millions on creating an image. That's millions my customers have to spend when they buy from us,' said Tim Parker, CEO of Clarks shoes, philosophically as we supped our (unadvertised, but rather good) Costa coffee.

The economics of brand-image building do leave much to be desired. It's a point I once tried to impress on a group of IKEA marketing managers. They asked St Luke's to produce a 'brand book' to guide the efforts of ad agencies in their other markets.

What we produced instead was the IKEA 'not-a-brand book'.

The not-a-brand book was made out of cheap photocopied paper and corrugated cardboard. Inside was a polemic against the 'American Dream for Profit'. At the start of this book were simple illustrated formulae like: Trainers cost $10 to produce, $40 marketing, $100 ticket price. IKEA's is a different way – we try to get the lowest possible price, not the highest.

Alongside these case studies in the questionable economics of brand image was a picture of IKEA founder, Ingvar Kamprad, with a speech bubble saying: 'thou shall not worship false goods!' Another page showed pictures of Michael Jackson over the years, with the caption 'It's always possible that if you keep changing your image to please others, you may end up forgetting who you are!'

Our suggestion was that consistency in IKEA communications should be achieved through sticking to their core values: anti-conventionality, co-operation, humility and so on. If everybody's minds were engaged with these, they couldn't go wrong.

A year later Nike's brand image collapsed. A newspaper in the States reported that in police crime-scene investigations, the most common footprints found were from Nike Air Max. It was suggested that neighbourhood kids were being led into crime, just to pay for their sneakers. This exploitation of American youth, through image and extortionate prices, became linked in people's minds with Nike's exploitation of youth on the other side of the world, through child labour. Not a great 'image'. Nike's sales plummeted. And its 'cool' rating among American teenagers halved in just twelve months.[45]

Even more dubious than charging people for your advertising, perhaps, was the effect that image branding had on society cumulatively. It may not have caused the consumer society, but it certainly fanned the flames. John Berger described the key driver of the consumer society as *envy*.

Glamour is a modern invention. In the heyday of oil painting it did not exist. Ideas of grace, elegance, authority amounted to something apparently similar but fundamentally different. Mrs Siddens as seen by Gainsborough is not glamorous, because she is not presented as enviable and therefore happy. She may be seen as wealthy, beautiful, talented, lucky. But her qualities are her own and are recognized as such. What she is does not depend on others wanting to be like her. She is not purely the creature of others' envy which is how Andy Warhol presents Marilyn Monroe.[46]

. . . and which was how Nike presented Jordan, Woods and Ronaldo.

Little wonder that as the consumer society took root, between the 1950s and 1990s, crime statistics in America, the heartland of brand image, rose year, by year, by year. If your society is based on the status glamour and attractiveness of the objects you acquire, is it any wonder that those shut out from wealth take matters into their own hands? And this is now reversing; US crime figures started falling in the mid-1990s.[47]

DESIGNER LAGERS MUST DIE

The beer market in the UK, in the early 1990s, went through a paradigm shift. As did the markets for fashion, music and other 'youth' products. It's a smaller story than Nike's titanic hubris. But it was even more indicative of a run on the 'image' bank. This was a reality check – people suddenly realised that, even with a slice of lime in the top, most designer lagers were not worth the high price.

The big 'brewed in the UK' draft lagers were also in trouble. Throughout the 1980s, they had the funniest, most awarded advertising in the world. The theory was that this advertising became part of 'lads' social life. They knew they'd be accepted if they drank 'that one with the brilliant adverts'. The ads even became part of their conversations, especially in the peak lager summer season, when there was no football on!

But the sad fact was that anything on tap and brewed in the UK tasted bland at best, and all were indistinguishable. Even my clients in a brewery marketing department could not easily tell their own lagers apart in blind taste tests.

The brewers panicked. Out went the funniest ads ever made. In came serious commercials, which tried to sell a product proposition (for example, 'brewed with Czechoslovakian yeast'). Which was a retreat from 'level two' to 'level one' marketing. None of which did much good. Lager lost its lead to the tastier and more authentic British ales. Only the near-monopoly on distribution enjoyed by the breweries held up individual brand sales. In the shops, lager prices went into free-fall.

The only winners among lagers were those brands that had kept a low profile, had some genuine quality and had 'stood the test of time' as people in research groups put it. Becks was a prime example. It has a distinct 'German', sulphury taste. And had confined its marketing to imaginative event promotions and tie-ins with the arts.

Budweiser was another beneficiary. This was long before *those* 'Whassuuup?', TV commercials but it had the same ring of authenticity (True). In 1991 Budweiser sales in the UK were growing at 150 per cent a year.

THE LEVI'S TEST CASE

Levi Strauss, the clothing manufacturer, is currently embroiled in a dispute with Tesco, the UK retailer, which has reached the European Court of Justice. However the ruling goes, Levi's have already suffered considerable damage to their public image.

Levi's in Europe were cool. Twenty years of sublime advertising has groomed the brand into an icon of seductive, rebellious glamour. The TV commercials are so popular that many of the soundtracks have become number one hits. One of their first TV commercials, 'Launderette', featuring model Nick Kamen taking his clothes off, used 'Heard it on the Grapevine' by Marvin Gaye as its soundtrack. This was the starting gun for the mainstream American Retro trend in the early 1980s. In 2000, it was the turn of 'Flat Eric', a weird glove puppet and a Europe-wide number one single.

Levi's in America are a commodity. Whereas in Britain a pair of 501s costs £50 (about $72) you can pick up a pair in America for as little as $30. The difference is pure image.

Then along came Tesco, who bought their supplies direct from an international wholesaler. Which allowed them to charge just £25. This outed an issue Levi Strauss were bound to face sooner or later – European consumers are increasingly well-travelled, brand suspicious, and Levi's in the US are much cheaper.

Whatever happens in their court case, Levi's have been found out. Once people can see that they are 'just paying for the image', a brand is in serious trouble. As a *Financial Times* article about this test case concluded, '[any] global brand is worth a lot less now than it was a year and a half ago.'[48]

THE TRUTH ABOUT BRAND IMAGE

The truth about brand image is that it was a pack of lies. A brand, on one definition, is 'a promise'. And brand image was usually promising something that wasn't true.

The brand lie	The dawning truth
Chanel makes you seductive	Chanel makes you smell like your mum
Fosters lager makes you a good bloke	Fosters makes you loud and sweaty
Häagen-Dazs makes you sexy	Häagen-Dazs makes you fat
Nike makes you a hero	Nike makes you $100 poorer
Ferrero Rocher makes you an aristocrat	Ferrero Rocher gives you cavities

How did people get taken in for fifty years by these fantasies? It's like the fairy tale of the 'Emperor's New Clothes'. When the Emperor paraded up the street in his 'birthday suit', everybody applauded and admired him, because everyone else did. It only took one little boy to **point** out that the Emperor had no clothes on, for the whole crowd to change their attitude from admiration to mirth.

The brand image fantasies were *half-true* when people believed them en masse. If your hot date believed that Chanel perfume made you sexy, glamorous, seductive, then it did. If your friends down the pub thought you were 'one of the lads' for drinking Fosters, then you were.

The problem came when the house of cards of brand image started to collapse. In some ways it was more than a house of cards, it was a pyramid scheme. People wanted brands to be true because they had already invested time, money and a little piece of their identity in buying them.

The collapse of this pyramid came about when people – especially the younger and more media literate – started rejecting brand image. Once post-modern ironic distance arrived on the scene, then image brands were in immediate trouble.

BRAND IMAGE STOPS PAYING

During and since the 1990s we have seen, again and again, that a 'strong brand image' can be a liability. Just ask Nike, Marks & Spencer, Rover and British Airways. Even Coca-Cola, the strongest brand in the world is losing its grip. Coca-Cola's share price between the start of 2000 and mid-2001, fell by 30 per cent.

The whole point of expensively investing in a brand was supposed to be that it would add more value than it cost, that it would create a stable long-term loyalty, beyond any product cycles and that it would justify a higher share price by valuing a company's brands.

It's noticeable that the biggest, most successful brands got hit the hardest. This tends to be true in evolution too. When the environment changes rapidly it is those animals that adapted most successfully to the previous ecology that get wiped out. That's why we are here, and the dinosaurs aren't.

The main problems facing these Tyrannosaurus-Rex brands have been:

■ BUSINESS PACE AND SCALE OF CHANGE: IBM had a great brand image for a bygone age. It stood for everything 'corporate'. As their ad campaign proudly proclaimed: 'No-one ever got fired for buying an IBM'. As business culture changed this image was dragging it down. In the mid 1990s they seemed to have finally fixed their brand image problem. But the computing market is in continuous revolution. Re-branding IBM as *the* e-business company must be a lot less attractive now than it was a year ago. Apple meanwhile has pinned its brand to i-Mac and G4. That's gone well. The problem is that Steve Jobs also canned the Newton. Desk PC or handheld? I know which business *I'd* rather be in, in 5 years' time.

■ **VISIBILITY:** High profile = high exposure to risk. Coca-Cola took a tumble in 1999, for two reasons. Firstly, the worldwide economy was stumbling and ostentatious American lifestyles were going out in many markets, like South-East Asia. Secondly, a product safety scare in Belgium rocked European sales. The problem with being a strong brand in a bad place is that it makes a great media story. It's like when a celebrity gets caught doing something wrong, rather than just an ordinary citizen.

■ **CULTURAL WEATHER:** Any true fashion cycles left are very fast. This creates problems on the way up (capacity, delivery) and problems on the way down (over-capacity, huge overheads). So adidas can go sky-high one year because of a hip-hop revival. And then get caught by a backlash to rock. And it's not just fashion that swings violently. Marks & Spencer and British Airways got caught out by a swing away from 'middle England'. As Alvin Toffler said in a recent interview, 'it's hard to think in terms of brand loyalty when the culture behind it is changing so fast'.

■ **MEDIA COSTS:** According to a venture capitalist at the height of the boom, the cost of establishing a national brand in the US is now $100 million.[49] I'd question this – Hotmail and Amazon, Napster and e-Bay spent almost nothing. What he meant was that the cost of national brand-image advertising was $100 million.

■ **FRAGMENTATION:** The shrinking size of fragmenting niches makes it very hard to find any decent bedrock of genuine 'following'. And brands only really make sense if they are fairly big and stable, because they cost so much money and effort to establish. A few brands have worked these niches really well, like Red Bull, but only as a smart way to become the fastest growing drinks brand in the UK.

6

BRANDING'S NEXT LEVEL

The science of advertising is so far advanced, it is impossible to foresee further developments.

SAMUEL JOHNSON, 1776

Marketing is not just a collection of ideas, tools and practices. It is an institution, with its own mental and business models. All of which had evolved – by natural selection – to create optimum marketing for the times. Samuel Johnson's approach to advertising was probably ideally suited to business, media and society in the eighteenth century, just as brand-image advertising was ideally suited to the last fifty years.

Business strategy now is concerned with whole new models and markets, rather than simply products and services. Society now is concerned with learning, self-direction and new ways of living, rather than fitting in with a fairly fixed social ladder of aspiration. Brand image is out of step with these new realities, and brands built on image have been failing. But a new form of branding has been taking its place – one which works at a higher level of new concepts, surrogate traditions, or ideas to live by.

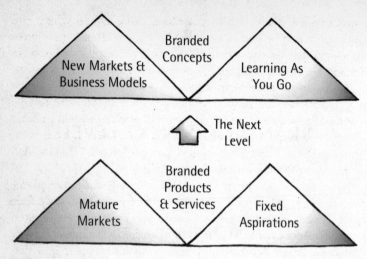

Fig. 16 | *The next level of marketing*

MIND THE GAP

Gap in the 1960s and 1970s was a casual clothes store, like many others. Its main product line was Levi's. They also sold records and tapes. In the late 1970s a change in American law meant that Levi's couldn't set their retail prices; this led to a huge drop in prices, which devastated Gap's margins.

In the 1980s, Mickey Drexler joined Gap, and in 1984 the basic Gap range of simple classic clothes was introduced. All other brands were de-listed. Around this time the classic Gap brand logo was introduced. The retail concept was new to the mid-market. This was a spacy, calm, refined place to shop. The staff were trained to be ultra smiley and nice. The changing rooms were really roomy.

The key business concept was *ubiquity*. Driven by a Coca-Cola-of-clothes ambition, they left retailing conventional wisdom behind and would open as many as three branches, just up the street from each other.

While many other brands and styles came and went at the extremes, Gap stayed at the centre as the blank canvas, the simple white, black, denim and chino base around which you could accessorize and improvise. Because of this it may have appeared that Gap was being conservative. Actually they were driving a clothing revolution, but in workwear, not casual wear.

There was a general shift towards Gap-style clothes, as the new workwear, for 'casual or dress-down Fridays', and for the 'open collar workers' (as *Wired* once called its readership). Later most of corporate America dressed this way. That's not a revolution in fashion. But it felt like one in people's lives. What the hell do you wear to work on a dress-down Friday?

Put yourself in the place of the average American office worker. They have spent years wearing a suit. Suddenly they can't wear it on Fridays and – because American offices are often quite sensitive to this kind of issue – they are left wondering what will be seen as 'business appropriate'. Gap stepped into that gap. There were three stores in your high street. Everybody from the CEO to the receptionist seemed to have Gap-like clothes on. Problem solved.

Which is a next-level branding strategy:

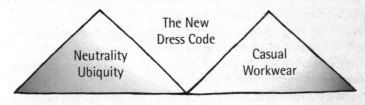

| Fig. 17 | *Next-level branding*

By the late 1990s casual workwear was old news. Everybody felt more comfortable judging what they could and couldn't wear to work. Gap took it to the next level. They launched Khakis.

The fashion magazines had already said 'brown is the new black'. But the mass market don't read high fashion editorial. Gap came out and said 'it's okay to wear this stuff too'.

They were the last to stock it. But the first to proclaim to average Joe that 'everyone's wearing it now'. Which was their second big concept innovation. They also did some near perfect advertising for this content message – with people dancing in Khakis, and the message 'Khakis rock'. So once again they had the perfect next level strategy:

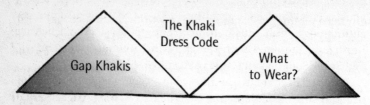

Fig. 18 | *Gap Khaki's marketing message*

It would be easy to conclude from the success of Khakis: 'I see. So we did these great TV ads and sales just went through the roof.' That's true. But the TV ads were not the prime cause. The sales sky-rocketed because they were giving 'permission to wear' brown, *not* because they had a great brand image.

Breaking the new dress code into the mass market is a strategy that relies on a whole network of other influences, advertising being just a catalyst: word of mouth, media coverage, store displays, what everyone else is wearing . . . You can't just head off in your own direction in an ad.

Since then Gap have proved this. They have done more 'great ads', Broadway musical-style dancing extravaganzas, which won lots of 'creative' awards. But unless I missed something, they didn't get the next dress code question. While the rest of us went back to sports, Gap went pastel. What they now seemed to be saying, in a loud voice, was 'we are no longer with it'. And the rest is dismal results history.

THE SONY PLAYSTATION

In 1999 PlayStation made over 40 per cent of Sony's profit, so it must have done something right. It's not just about being in a profitable market – far from it, consoles make a huge loss. It's the games which repay the investment, if you're successful. Sega pulled out of consoles in 2001. PlayStation succeeded by promoting a bigger concept, which was the 'gamer cult'.

Their business-model innovation was open source software. Letting third-party developers make their games opened the doors to really innovative, cult products. 'Wipeout' from Psygnosis, combined cool graphics, high-speed rocket racing and cutting-edge club music from groups such as the Chemical Brothers. Compared with the childish Nintendo (Super Mario) and Sega (Sonic) games, this was radical stuff.

The social context was the cyber scene. Techno music had been pulsing through the raves of the early 1990s. While parents struggled to programme their videos, the chemical generation embraced technology and graphics, the Internet and cyberculture, pagan cultures, the underground, more technology and peak experiences. PlayStation gave them the lot in one package.

This was a cult, underground scene. PlayStation marketing set about joining this counterculture. They placed consoles in cool venues. Their first advertising was in gamer and technology magazines – reinforced with fly-posting. It was all a bit like the film *12 Monkeys*: futurist, paranoid and underground – right on the money.

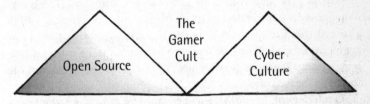

The
Gamer
Cult

Open Source

Cyber
Culture

| Fig. 19 | *The Sony PlayStation 'cult'*

Nintendo didn't stand a chance. It was stuck in the old paradigm of teenage bedrooms. PlayStation was on the next level – a veritable cult, or at least something to belong to.

Sony's media strategy here was creating a community. Diverse media were used to draw existing communities of ravers and geeks into this fold, which has not only been powerful, but cost effective. Once it was established, they went even more underground, often using just the four control pad symbols as a sort of Masonic code:

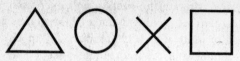

Fig. 20 *Sony PlayStation symbols*

David Patton, marketing director of Sony Computer Entertainment in Europe, says they deliberately make even their mass media communications challenging and hard to get. Because their media strategy is to 'reach the 97 per cent, through the 3 per cent'. This conveys 'cult' complicity to the few who knew. And they tell the rest.

THE BODY SHOP

I once asked Anita and Gordon Roddick, 'what was your original business idea?' I expected them to say something like 'challenging capitalist models with eco-principles'. What they actually said was, 'we put the money into the product, not the packaging'.

This is very smart (as well as being eco-friendly). The packaging costs are a fraction of those of 'glamour' cosmetics, which allowed them to create a new price point, attractive to the key segments of green consumers, who happened to be teenage girls and young mothers – two groups without high disposable incomes for luxuries.

The 'concept' branding was eco-politcal campaigns and activities:

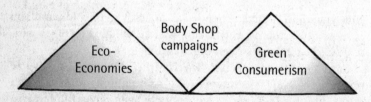

Fig. 21 *The Body Shop concept*

They have never advertised (another colossal saving in the toiletries market!). They focus their marketing money not on the Body Shop products, but on campaigns which customers and staff support and which the products reflect.

The Body Shop is not just a retailer, it is a cause! Over the years their campaigns have included beauty without cruelty (against animal testing), trade not aid, fat is a feminist issue, alternative therapies, hope not dope (hemp-based not petroleum-based) . . . and their 'media' plan includes a diverse mix of window posters, petitions, even demonstrations.

None of this is to detract from the fact that the Body Shop is genuinely committed to its cause. It's just to say that good business can be great business.

What is actually being 'branded' in these cases?

Gap branded a dress code
PlayStation branded a cult community
The Body Shop branded a series of causes.

It's not the product or service that is being branded, it's on a whole different level. New concepts are being introduced – new ways to live our lives.

These concepts have some similarity with branded products. They are luminous, emotionalized, simple to grasp and visualize, media-friendly . . . but they stretch the notion of classical branding to some kind of breaking point. They are not concentric layers built up around an inner product and service core. They are 'something completely different'.

We badly need a new model of branding, capable of explaining how cultural ideas and concepts can be branded. Otherwise we will be caught in 'the Gap trap' (applying the old assumptions to a new level of marketing).

7

A NEW MODEL OF BRANDING

In the 1960s, the theory of brand image was derived from psycho-analysis. Now we can turn to cognitive neuroscience, to help us understand what makes next-level brands tick. This provides a 'grand unified theory' of branding, based on how people formulate mental models. This is quite useful in understanding *any* brand – and invaluable in understanding level three and branded concepts.

WHAT, IF ANYTHING, IS A BRAND?

'Brand' is a mysterious term. Business people are expected to buy into it. 'Branding is key' I kept being told during the dot-com frenzy.

Branding is also a mysterious art. All too often 'a brand' is defined as whatever the advertising or design agency is trying to sell you, and they all use different systems. Here is a selection of statements from various experts in a single magazine report.[50] It aimed to explain to dot-com entrepreneurs what a brand was:

- brand is an 'aura' that surrounds a product
- brand is a 'symbol of quality' plus some 'attractive values'
- brand tells people 'what business you are in'
- brand 'humanizes' commerce with emotional appeals to 'allegiance'

- brand is a company's most valuable business 'asset'
- brand 'translates' into strong sales and an enduring market 'presence'
- brand is 'what aligns a company's business plan with its products and services'
- brand means you can 'cover a company's logo and still have a distinctive feel for its product'
- brand is a 'foundation' on which to build every experience a customer has
- brand is 'instant recognition'
- brand is a 'deep psychological affinity to a product or service'
- brand is 'deep psychological energy' and 'penetration'

The authors of this *Red Herring* report admitted that they got confused themselves. When they talked to advertisers, marketers and venture capitalists they found that 'these people see branding in much the same way that Supreme Justice, Potter Stewart, described obscenity in 1964 – he couldn't define it but he knew it when he saw it.'

Meanwhile management schools, of course, do try to define 'brand' rigorously. But the trouble with these scientific dissections is that they kill the subject. Marketing professor, Peter Doyle, for instance, defines a brand by a precise-looking formula:

Strong Brand = Product Benefits × Distinct Identity × Emotional Values.[51]

That's true if you want to define 'brand' that way, and it's mercifully clear. But what use is it? The implication of the 'equation' is that these are objective measurable quantities. But then how do you define and measure these? And how do these relate to people's decisions and behaviour? Especially at our third level, where what is being branded and emotionalized may be a new intangible concept?

A big part of the problem is that 'brand' can be all of these many splendid things and more, because it is not grounded in anything. The set of ideas like 'recognition' 'aura', 'emotional values' . . . do not relate to any robust theoretical model of how the human mind works, what culture is, and how people make decisions.

Brand-image theory was originally grounded in Freudian ideas of unconscious identification, fetish and desire, but these links are long forgotten, and the practice of branding has left them far behind.

So 'brand' has become a folklore theory.

A COGNITIVE-SCIENCE APPROACH

Cognitive science is the branch of psychology (linked to linguistics and anthropology) which deals with how our minds work, from the inside. It looks at the mind as revealed by language, logic, perception, culture, artificial intelligence, and neurology. It's not philosophy or social pseudo-scientific waffle. It is based on experiments.

In cognitive science, 'what is a brand?' has a simple answer:

> We make sense of the world through mental models.
> A brand is a type of mental model.
> Brand image is a (debased) mental model that emphasizes metaphor.

The beauty of the cognitive science view, for the purposes of this book, is that it automatically fuses branding and learning:

> Learning (by definition) is when someone changes their mental model.

In cognitive science, the base unit of thinking is the mental model. Think of a mental model as like an architect's scale prototype. It approximates to something in the outside world. Or as cognitive scientists say, a mental model is a 'representation'.

According to George Lakoff, linguistics professor at Berkeley, there are four distinct elements which make up a mental model.[52] They come in two pairs. One pair deals with the basic ingredients of representation – coding – the two types of code being sense impressions and propositions. The other pair deals with selecting and linking these codes – mapping – and the two operations here are metaphor and metonymy.

I've invented a diagram to show these four elements. Each element is shown as a cog-wheel ('cog' acts as a mnemonic for 'cognitive').

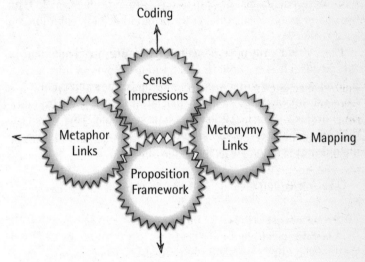

Coding

Sense Impressions

Metaphor Links

Metonymy Links

Mapping

Proposition Framework

Fig. 22 | *Key brand ingredients*

Let's explore these four elements, which are the key mental ingredients of any brand.

Proposition Framework

A proposition is a unit of belief. And that sentence is one example.

These tend to be rather simple, deep-rooted ideas such as 'the book is on the table', but they need not be perceptual. Human beings' main domain of thinking is the social world they share with other people, so many of our propositions are social concepts, for instance, the feminist slogan 'all men are rapists'.

Propositions need not be 100 per cent true or false.

Cognitive scientist Rosario Conte uses artificial intelligence to model human thinking.[53] Conte found that we have a spectrum of beliefs along the true/false axes, like the notion that 'politicians *tend to be* liars' – and certitude is just one dimension of belief. Others include retractability (how likely a belief is to be modified), and connectivity (how much it ties in with other beliefs). Conte also points out that there are many kinds of belief with different status in the mind, 'superstition, creed, faith, postulate, axiom, principle, conception, idea, view, opinion and many others'.

Propositions are pure concepts. They are not dependent on the words chosen. Beliefs exist independent of language. It doesn't matter whether you say 'the book is on the table' or 'le libre est sur la table' or even 'the latest thinking on brands is on your desk' – you're still saying book-on-table.[54] To reflect this difference between thoughts and their expression in language, cognitive psychologists developed a notation:

On (book, table)

Propositions combine into more complicated sets, and the notation is designed to reflect this by 'nesting' propositions within each other. For example:

Cause [hit (mary, john, chopsticks), upset (john)]
= Mary hit John with chopsticks and he was upset

This example highlights another important finding from cognitive science. Our beliefs are based on large amounts of prior real-world knowledge. To understand the proposition you have to know not only what chopsticks are, but also what typically happens in a situation where they are used. This system of prior knowledge is called a 'frame' or 'script'. This is because it tends to be a narrative: usually, you go into the restaurant, are shown to a table, sit down and are handed menus etc.

These 'scripts' are powerful channels for thought, because, as experiments show, everything else is forced to fit into them – unless a conscious effort is made to understand anomalous information and form a new mental model (= true learning).

Sense Impressions

Sense impressions are also known in the cognitive trade as mental images. But these 'images' can come from any of the senses, not just from sight. One of George Lackoff's contributions to cognitive science is the recognition that mental models are 'embodied'.[55] All our abstract notions of physics, art, politics and relationships are grounded in simple intuitions that tie in with bodily experience ('grounded' is an example of this).

This realization came from experimental studies. How we categorize the world at the most basic levels, starts with our experience, our bodily functions, our perception.

One famous study showed that the basic emotions (anger, fear, happiness, sadness, surprise and interest) have the same facial expressions and physiological responses in all human cultures.[56] The concepts of emotion build on these physical foundations, for instance 'anger = heat' is a universal metaphor. Because, physiologically, anger does indeed make us 'hot under the collar'.

The basic set of body-sensed concepts is universal. But the further we go into abstract ideas, the more variation there is in what is 'rooted' in what, and this makes a big difference to how people from different cultures think.

For instance, the Japanese concept of TV (and all media) is based on the concept of *trajectories* which is part of the category of 'long thin things' (or, in Japanese, *hon*). Whereas our mental image of *broadcast* is more like dispersal (sowing seeds in a field). So it's natural for Japanese people to see television as more 'direct'. If you watch Japanese TV, you notice that a lot of it is presented directly to camera – almost as if it was a videophone. Whereas our TV programmes are structured more for onlookers, as if in the theatre, for example.

Propositions and sense impressions are the two types of code we take in from the outside world. Often at the same time – when we are exploring the world of sensations and at the same time keep hearing propositions such as 'dangerous' and 'don't touch,' for example.

Coding simplifies the world in the process. As when you make an architectural model, you don't include every brick. A 'mental model' is a balance between accuracy and factors like speed and ease of memory.

Cognitive science has also found that the two forms of coding – sense impressions and propositions – are quite separate in the brain. This is called 'dual coding theory'.[57] We think in 'stereo', combining these two types of code. That's why, in my diagram, these two 'cogs' don't touch, see Fig. 23. They put different 'spins' on reality.

These codes are derived from the outside world – from your lived experience. If you have a different domain of experience from someone else, you build up different codes. If these domains of experience are very different, fundamental disagreements can arise. One example of this is animal rights. The very different domains of experience, education and indoctrination create two irreconcilable worldviews:

The Scientist Position
Proposition – different (people, animals)
Sense impressions – sterile, data, experiments, laboratory
    and medicines.

The Animal Rights Position
Proposition – same (people, animals)
Sense impressions – furry, hurt, pleading eyes, wounded and
    caged.

The other axis is not about the content of our memories. It concerns the way in which the contents are linked, internally and externally, like the hyperlinks on the Web.

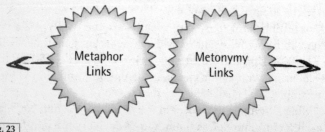

Fig. 23

Metonymy Links

Metonymy is when something is used to represent some bigger set of ideas of which it is part. A classic example is the use of the term 'the White House' to stand for the whole institution of American government. This is a cognitive streamlining device. We use it to make things easier to think about, or to communicate, or to remember.

Being 'part of a bigger set' is a very common device in everyday language, as this list from George Lackoff demonstrates:

The part for the whole:
   Get *your butt* over here!

Producer for product:
   He's got *a Picasso* in his den.

Object for user:
   The *buses* are on strike.

Controller for controlled:
   Nixon bombed Hanoi.

Institution for those responsible:
   You'll never get *the university* to agree to that.

The place for the institution:
   The *White House* isn't saying anything.

The place for the event:
   Let's not let Thailand become *another Vietnam*.[58]

Metonymy is one of the most influential thought-shaping devices in the human mind. It exists to make thinking simple and fast. But what it chooses to highlight (and leave out) has a great impact. It is why, for instance, stereotypes have such a powerful role in culture. Metonymy applies to our animal rights example, in that each side sees vivisection as part of a completely different system:

The 'scientific' worldview
Animal experimentation is part of developing medicines that save
   lives.

The 'animal rights' worldview
Vivisection is part of the abuse of the natural environment by people.

Metaphor Links

A metaphor, in cognitive terms, is when one model is linked to a totally different one.

'The car beetled along' links 'car' with our ideas about 'how insects move'. Metaphors have a sting in the tail – 'beetles' explicitly describes a type of slow, idling movement, but implicitly brings hidden baggage. It's unlikely you'd say, 'the Rolls Royce beetled along', because insects are low status animals in our culture.

Metaphor enriches thought. The choice of metaphor colours a discourse with emotion, nuance and resonance. But whereas metonymy pares it down to selected essentials, metaphor clouds it slightly.

Metaphor is the lynchpin of 'brand image'. Through associative 'personality' media forms like TV advertising, products were linked metaphorically in people's minds with other more emotional spheres of life. Here are some classic examples:

After Eight mints linked the product – and by extension the consumer – with upper class dinner party hosts.

Sugar Puffs linked the product with a mischievous make-believe monster – and by extension conveyed a sense of childish fun and enjoyment.

Häagen-Dazs linked the product with sexual imagery – and by extension conveyed an experience of sensual indulgence.

Metaphor is where the emotion and passion is added to the dry argument. In the animal rights conflict, emotionally charged metaphors are used to reinforce each position:

The scientific key metaphor:
The animals are being *sacrificed*

The animal rights key metaphor:
The animals are being *tortured*

Metonymy and metaphor conflict with each other – one makes things simpler, the other fuzzier. Out of the tension comes subtlety of meaning, language and communication. Cognitive scientists have come to the conclusion, based on studies of brain damaged patients, that just like the two kinds of mapping, metaphor and metonymy are separate in the brain. Which is why these two cogs don't touch in my simplified maps.

Linguist Roman Jacobsen, who discovered this separation, described metaphors as 'poetic' whereas metonymy tends to be used in logical 'prose'. The split extends throughout human thinking and its cultural products. For instance in art – surrealism is metaphorical (it substitutes something seen for something suggested), whereas cubism is metonymic (it selects only parts of what is seen).[59]

Metaphor and metonymy tend to dominate each other at different times in history. Theodore Zeldin reports that there was a swing in the style of conversation in America in the nineteenth century, away from romantic and rhetorical floweriness (metaphor) towards plain speaking and scientific concepts (metonymy).[60] I believe that the Apollo Rising trend brings a similar swing from image (metaphor) to intellect (metonymy).

THE BRAND IS A MENTAL MODEL

It's obvious really. We have mental models of everything in our human experience. In our minds, all the 'Budweisers' are similar and belong to a single model. Just as all the 'Persian cats', 'dance records' and 'goat's cheeses' form single mental models. Thinking about well-known brands, we'll see they have the four basic cog ingredients.

Let's start with cars.

One of the main examples quoted by those 1960s psychoanalysts of marketing was the motor car. It was perhaps more obvious that people chose cars for 'non-rational' reasons – because Americans love their cars. This, plus the Freudian leanings of the analysts, was where notions like the 'sports car as mistress' came from.

Strong car brands have tended to be different in each of the four cogs:

- car brands include distinct **sense impressions** – such as a distinctive car shape, feel or even sound ('you can hear the clock ticking in a Rolls Royce at 60 mph')
- they have related **proposition** beliefs – such as 'Volvos are safe family cars'.
- they are subject to **metonymic** selections, of the most salient features – like 'German engineering' or 'Italian styling'.
- and, above all, classical car-marketing has emphasized **metaphor** – such as the Renault Clio, which was apparently like a leggy French girl ('Nicole?', 'Oui, Papa!').

Branding has been so successful because it draws on innate human ways of thinking about the world. In this sense marketing has always been viral, inhabiting the information processes of the host, to reproduce its own information.

THE VW GOLF GTI (1980s)

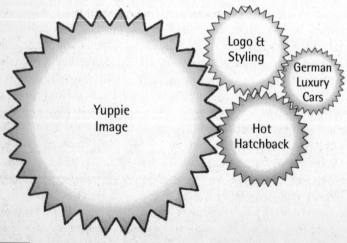

Fig. 24 *The Golf GTi mental model*

Proposition framework: 'Hot Hatch'. The car created a new category to consider when buying a car – sports-car performance with hatchback affordability and accessibility.

Sense impressions: the VW logo was already iconic. The Golf (Mark I) body shape was new and unique, you could tell at a glance this wasn't a Ford Fiesta. It had a great grille and wicked sports-car headlights, and there was the speed!

Metonymy link: Germany was key. This car came from the same place as Mercedes and BMW, so it was credible to think of it as 'a poor man's Porsche'.

Metaphor link: a Golf GTi driver was like the glamorous woman in the advert who stormed out on a rich lover, throwing away the fur coat and pearls, but keeping the car. Or like the guy in the other early UK commercial, who lost his shirt at the casino.

It was this metaphorical 'brand image' that got the GTi into trouble later in the 1980s when it became a target for joy-riders and gained a (negative) image as a 'yuppie' purchase.

VOLKSWAGEN 30 YEARS EARLIER (AND 50 YEARS AHEAD OF ITS TIME)

I worked on Volkswagen advertising when the GTi-backlash happened. It was hard not to notice that there was an older VW tradition. Compared to which, the GTi's high-status image was an aberration. Perhaps something of 'good old VW' could be revived?

Volkswagen is a brand with a fantastic heritage. In Europe it was the original 'car for the masses' – affordable, easy to maintain and easy to drive. Hence the name 'Volkswagen' – the people's car. In Mexico they call it 'the belly button' because everyone has one!

The old VW mental model was almost opposite to that of the GTi;

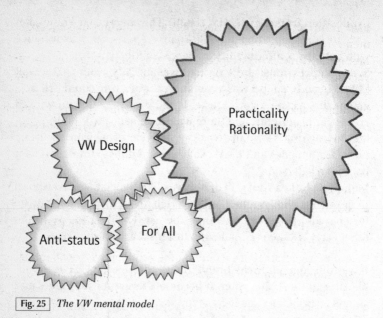

| Fig. 25 | *The VW mental model* |

Proposition framework: a car for all people. At a time when other cars were elitist.

Sense impressions: the VW Beetle had one of the most distinctive visual designs in the history of marketing. It also was unique in its feel . . . It had the engine in the boot. And the VW logo, the sound of the engine, and everything sets this marque and car apart.

Metonymy link: A focus on mechanical performance – it starts even in snow, it's economical, it's durable . . . This may look natural to you now. But then it ran against every idea marketing people had about why people bought cars – for status.

This metonymy made the VW a durable, authentic brand. It was used by everyone – from police forces, to housewives, to beatniks – as a cheap reliable car. Other cars were presented as 'aspirational'. VW was a 'friend' – a link the *Herbie* films reinforced.

The car became an emblem of the new spirit of the 1960s. The anti-image stance was made into an anti-status icon, a symbol of the new zeitgeist. But, unlike the GTi, VW wasn't tied to any user group or moment in time, because it did not make a statement.

Metaphor link: Volkswagen made car marketing history. It was sold on the basis of *no image*. The early VW advertising always featured a simple shot of the car and a deceptively simple headline, backed up by some 'no nonsense' copy. Here is the text from a vintage (but rather 'postmodern') VW ad. With the headline . . .

'*How to do a Volkswagen ad*'
- look at the car
- look harder. You'll find enough advantages to fill a lot of ads. Like the air-cooled engine. The economy, the design that never goes out of date.
- don't exaggerate. For instance some people have got 50 m.p.g. and more from a VW. But others have only managed 28. Average 32. Don't promise more.
- call a spade, a spade. And a suspension a suspension. Not something like 'orbital cushioning'.
- speak to the reader. Don't shout. He can hear you. Especially if you talk sense.
- pencil sharp? You're on your own.

Volkswagen's early advertising is living proof that it is possible to avoid the excesses of 'brand image' and still make creative and engaging communications.

VW – WHAT HAPPENED NEXT

By 1990 the VW Golf, in silhouette, looked like every other hatchback. Its famous reliability claim had been eroded by quality revolutions in other countries, notably Japan. In tests Toyota actually made the most reliable cars.

One thing still set VW cars apart from their rivals – their solidity.

In qualitative research, people described the VW build. One owner described how the car felt like it was made by 'pouring molten metal into a mould', it was *that* solid. Key mental images from past advertising were the car being dropped from a great height, and the slow, deep clunk of the door closing.

One of our TV ads caught this quality. In this commercial (by the brilliant John Webster), the driver keeps hearing squeaking. He checks all over the car. But eventually discovers it's his wife's earring. We also used it to launch the new Golf saloon, the Vento. Our poster, featuring the car and a female body builder, said 'Kimberly. Built like a Vento.'

I wanted to take it much further. I wanted to build on solidity as a virtue. As in 'a solid citizen'. Not through 'image making', but through action such as car sharing schemes. This would have been level three marketing – driving the culture with a brand, not just dressing up a brand with culture.

José Ignacio López de Arriortúa, the VW CEO at the time, planned something even more revolutionary. He wanted to take the business concept back to VW's roots, by producing a $1000 car. To be manufactured in his beloved home Basque region, creating huge savings, thousands of jobs, and hopefully some great little motor cars.

Neither idea happened. But later VW brought back the sensory difference, in the new Beetle. Which was a very successful launch and a good step in the right direction.

CATEGORIES, BASIC LEVELS AND PROTOTYPES

Studies in linguistics have shown that there is a basic level, at which children acquire ideas about categories of things in the world.[61] This tends to be in the middle – between very general stuff and very specific stuff. Basic level ideas are favoured by simple words, which create easy communication and definite mental images, with characteristic shapes and interactions – just like good brands.

Basic level concepts, for example, 'dog', are the level at which we think and communicate most easily.

'There's a mammal on the porch.'
versus 'There's a dog on the porch.'
versus 'There's a cocker spaniel on the porch.'

This is important in branding new cultural concepts. 'Organic' would still be on the starting blocks, if it had been called something like 'chemical-free horticulture'. To become a basic-level idea, and not some minor quirk, you need to be simple.

Within any category, there are prototype examples, which are more representative than all the other members of that category. When I say 'tree', you'll probably picture an oak tree if you are English, a fir tree if you are Scandinavian, or a maple if you are Canadian.

Prototypes affect the way we reason. For example, an experiment has proved that:

> If I tell you that the robins on a certain island have caught a disease you are more likely to think that the ducks have caught it too.

versus

> If I tell you the ducks on the island have caught a disease you are less likely to think the robins have caught it too.[62]

Why? Because robins (or sparrows) are prototype examples of birds, while ducks, penguins, chickens, ostriches and others are less central, and we tend to think outwards from prototype examples in our 'logical' deductions.

The value of a brand is greatest when it is the prototype example, which people think of whenever they think of the category. For instance, if they draw up a shopping list of alternatives to consider, it is more likely to include the prototype.

Being a prototype can mean – as in Microsoft's case – that you have a dominant market leadership position and are, in reality, the main example. But it doesn't necessarily mean anything of the sort. For example, IKEA usually has less than a 10 per cent share of even its mature markets. But it is often the 'reference' brand or prototype. Being the prototype means being the most salient example, not necessarily the most common – it's a form of metonymy.

Strong brands are prototypes. It's hard to think about fast food without thinking McDonald's or soft drinks without thinking of Coca-Cola or Internet retailers without thinking Amazon, or camera film without thinking Kodak, and so on.

Strong brands hold this prototype position in *some* people's minds. It's a common misconception that you can measure brands through the average public perception. What does it actually matter what non-parents think of Pampers? 90 per cent of computer users have not much idea about Apple, but for 10 per cent of us it is almost a religion.

The strongest brands establish their own category, at least at the outset of their success. Which is why so many prototype brands were 'prototypes' in the other sense – of being the first instance. Some brands lose their monopoly (but not their special-ness) to hundreds of clones: like Starbucks and Napster. Others, like Disney and Virgin have used the fact that they transcend categories, by crossing many categories to stay in a class of their own.

THE PROTOTYPE TRAP

If you are in the position of becoming a prototype brand, the general advice you'd get from any branding consultant is don't rock the boat.

'New Coke' (a disaster that had to be withdrawn) is what happens when you change something at the heart of people's classification of the world. In this case, they missed the charac-teristic taste. This kind of change is deeply unsettling, almost like a moment of insanity. Imagine you woke up this morning and all dogs had two legs!

That's also the cost of classical branding. It's a straitjacket of fixed expectations. You are stuck with that mental model. If sugary drinks become outmoded, then the taste expectation could take Coca-Cola down. Diet Coke is no substitute, because it's not the prototype. It takes 130 years to become Coca-Cola. And then it can be a curse in disguise.

I believe that you should not tinker with the nucleus of your brand but that there is plenty of scope to create some movement, elsewhere. The reason for doing this is that static brands can become a liability in a fast-changing culture. Remember what happened to the GTi when the 1980s ended. And in the 'level three' view you can leave your product brand where it is and move into redefining the market, culture, knowledge, habits, communities and so on, instead.

To be fair, Coca-Cola has worked on this level for many years. Back in the 1930s they invented the modern icon of Father Christmas (yes, that's why he's dressed in Coca-Cola red-and-white). In the 1970s they used 'I'd like to teach the world to sing' – a chart-topping song (that happened to come from an ad) which took them away from being 'American' towards being the first truly 'global' brand. There's nothing new under the sun. Level three is the space that all truly great brands have played in, in that they have shaped the way we think and how we live. Sony, Starbucks, Amazon, Disney, Apple and even McDonald's ... have always been about much more than their 'brand images'. They are what archaeologists in the distant future would use to describe our way of life.

COGNITIVE BRANDING: A SUMMARY

Definitions of the term 'brand' are notoriously imprecise. So I have used a model from cognitive science to explain what branding is and why it is so powerful. Every brand is made up of four distinct elements, which are what we think *with*, when we think about brands.

Any brand will have these four elements. A better brand will have more appealing and distinctive elements, compared with others in its category – a unique and attractive appearance, a unique and compelling set of beliefs ... Stronger brands still, tend to be the 'prototype', i.e. the first one that people generally think

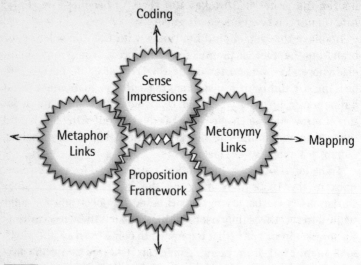

Coding

Metaphor
Links

Sense
Impressions

Metonymy
Links

Mapping

Proposition
Framework

Fig. 26 | *Mental model of a brand*

about and to which others are compared. The strongest brands that are the most defensible and most adaptable to new social trends are in a category of their own.

This has all been true throughout the history of branding because it is based on how the mind works and not some property of modern media. What's changing now is the level at which brand mental models are built, from branding products to branding concepts.

8

CONCEPT BRANDING

It doesn't make a difference, unless it makes a difference in people's lives

JOSEPH SCHUMPETER

REINVENTING YOUR MARKET

What is a market?

Say you were a baker. You could decide that:

'We're in the groceries market.'
'We're in the breakfast market.'
'We're in the fast-food market.'
'We're in the diet market.'
'We're in the special occasions market.'
'We're in the delicatessen market.'
'We're in the traditional English food market.'
'We're in the snacks market.'
'We're in the home-baking market.'

These decisions affect the whole shape and focus of a business, and also figure in customers' thinking and behaviour. Cognitive psychology and business use the same word . . .

A market is a *category*.

Reinventing the market means *redefining the category*.

The market is more basic than the brands it contains. Changing the market means people have to change their ideas about a whole domain of their life. This is obvious in the examples I used earlier: What to have for breakfast? What to wear? How to be a man . . .?

It is possible for brands to invent new categories. Past examples include:

- Starbucks
- CK One
- Viagra
- *Big Brother*
- Gap
- the Ministry of Sound
- Amazon
- the i-Mac
- Pokèmon

Metaphor is not enough. In fact it can cloud the issue. Most category redefining brands tend to be very simple, at least at their launch:

- unique and rigorously worked out design format (sensory codes)
- a new underlying belief system (proposition codes)
- disciplined selection and repetition – a few elements that stand out (metonymy).

This goes back to how children learn. Look at any 'picture book' – cat, sat, mat, hat . . . For the first time in history the majority of people are experiencing a lifelong childhood, when new shapes, names, tastes . . . have to be learned at a basic level, just to keep up.

Companies that define categories create a unique parallel universe. But they don't stay unique very long. When they become successful they are quickly copied. But they often retain a massive advantage as the prototype in their category. Anything else is always just 'me too'.

It is also possible to create higher-level category concepts, which are 'brands' (in the mental model sense) in their own right. These are often 'authored' by a company brand. Which creates strong (prototype) claims to ownership. And also leaves the company freer to roll through successive innovations, as times and business models change.

Past examples of categories authored and/or owned by company brands include:

- the Walkman = portable, pocket music players, invented by Sony
- upper class = mid-way between business and first class, from Virgin Atlantic
- Internet share dealing = lower cost, accessible stockbrokers, notably from Schwab
- New Man = soft-edged, groomed identity, invented in the 1980s by Arena magazine
- MP3 = a music format, taken to its logical conclusion by Napster
- Sloane Ranger = another 1980s identity trend, part-owned by Barbour
- Internet e-mail = like ISP e-mail, but free, web-based, owned by Hotmail.

Anyone can invent a new category. All it takes is a brilliant, visionary idea and radical new inventions and designs to deliver this vision! Most concept branding will tackle something slightly less ambitious, which is *redefining* the category . . .

TWO WORDS: 'INTEL INSIDE'

The mental model built by Intel is a great example of how concept branding, as opposed to product branding, can work to devastating effect. It isn't about 'our chips', although this is a knock-on effect. Intel is the definitive processor, because it is the prototype. It's on the next level. Intel have created a mental model about *how computers work*.

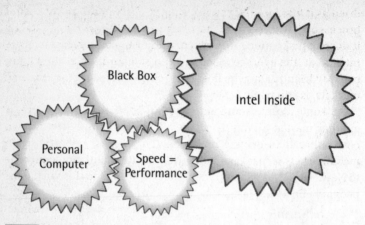

Fig. 27 │ *A computer's mental model*

The *sensory* experience of a modern PC is that of a black box. In the 'good old days' people using computers had a good idea of how they worked. You had to know how programming languages worked, from the moment you booted up. Some commentators worry that hiding the command line impoverished our long-term prospects for working with computers – that we should have taught the world to code. I don't agree.

The *personal* computer is a powerful metaphor. It has the side-effect of making us our own 'IT person'. Whereas mainframes were looked after by people in white coats, many of us now chose which computer to buy, set it up and deal with the glitches and crashes. This, in a market where computers are now black boxes, creates a learning need, for simple concepts for amateurs to navigate by.

The proposition capitalized on by Intel is that 'faster' means 'better'. That's generally true in the long term. It's certainly what computer engineers like to think. Thanks to Moore's Law (which says that the performance of microchips doubles roughly every two years), affordable computers can do things we couldn't dream of ten years ago. Our Apple G4 runs my wife's professional-quality music studio and also recognizes her voice, so that she can write without typing.

But for most uses, this 'speed' proposition is not as cut and dried as it first looks. If you use your PC for home accounts, word processing, Web surfing and e-mail (like 90 per cent of users) it doesn't make much difference. And even computer games are pitched at 'the average machine' and so gain little at the higher end. My friend Kim, who does hard-core C++ coding for the stock markets, is still using a 286 PC.

At some point, someone is going to realize that there is another market driven by Moore's Law – one that drives down cost rather than driving up speed. The biggest opportunity in most markets is 'package holiday flights to Spain', not 'concorde to New York'. But perception is what matters. And, for now, most people believe that faster = better.

Intel Inside is a metonymy. The part stands for the whole. Clever Intel has succeeded in defining computer quality as depending on their latest, fastest chips. We buy into this because it's 'easier to understand, remember, recognize or use somehow'.

The truth is more complicated, even if you think performance matters. RAM determines 'how big?' and 'how many?' for applications. And until recently was one of the most expensive components. Within processing, speed in MHz is not the only issue. Apple's G4 runs at slower frequencies than Intel Pentium, but performs more calculations per second. But that in a way is the point. The truth is complicated. People like to have a simple yardstick. It's easier, and Intel has used metonymy to become phenomenally successful. People happily accept IBM clones, but they are still brand conscious when it comes to having Intel inside.

IKEA CHANGES PEOPLE'S TASTE

In 1995, through focus-group research, I discovered that the real problem facing IKEA – in their plan to expand into Middle England (Thurrocks, Nottingham, Bristol) – was that most English people at the time preferred 'traditional English styles' of décor. Our solution was a TV ad, which told women to 'chuck out your chintz'. There's no way to account for this kind of strategy in traditional brand diagrams, because it's not *about* IKEA. It's about redefining the furniture category by shifting tastes.

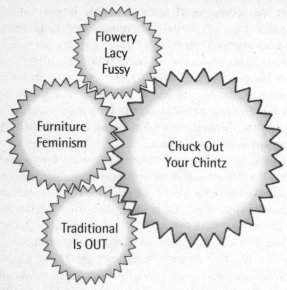

IKEA's mental model

The advertising had a very distinctive *look* and *feel*. It was deliberately dowdy. We even took out insurance against there being sunny weather, because we wanted it to be drab, and in this world we put the most horrible flowery curtains and lace doilies we could find.

In my research groups, people were very confused about what styles were 'in' – 'I think it's the modern traditional look if you know what I mean?' We left no doubt. Chintz was out. Modern was in – a pure *proposition*.

The metaphor which lent emotion to this piece of 'style news' was feminism. Women were shown working and marching and singing together to rid the world of this chintz. The whole idea was to establish 'chuck out your chintz' as a political slogan: like 'burn your bra'. The commercial trod a perilous path between being funny and obnoxious. There were complaints, but fewer than we expected.

The payload was making chintz stand for the whole of tradition; a metonymy. It worked through implied criticism. A (true) story that explains how it worked was this. When I was quite junior, my boss gave me a lift home in his car. It was quite a long way out of his way, so I invited him in for a cup of tea before he continued his journey. When he got into my living room he burst out laughing, 'You haven't still got *dado rails* have you?' At the time I hated him for saying this. How dare he come into my home and criticize my taste? But a few weeks later I found myself checking if the offending dado rails (left by a previous owner, I rationalized) would come off. A few weeks later and the room was redecorated. We don't like criticism, but it does wear us down. At least those of us (nearly all of the people in my research groups) who aren't really that sure what we like.

And it worked. IKEA's sales doubled within a year. And a later survey showed that only a third of adults now have traditional English tastes. They have taken this new mental model on board. And the homes of the shires will never look the same again.

How it worked was that the 'chuck out your chintz' concept became a talking point in British culture. It was used by politicians in New Labour's election campaign to signify Old Britain – which had to change. 'Tony Blair; tough on chintz, tough on the causes of chintz' said the *Evening Standard*. It was quoted in hundreds of articles. So people came to believe that this must be what everyone else was thinking.

HEATHROW EXPRESS: FAMOUS FOR FIFTEEN MINUTES

There were already train and tube services to London airports. But Heathrow Express's look and feel was so much more modern, efficient and futuristic. It had onboard TV, mobile phone connection (even in the tunnel) and great styling.

The driving concept is 'fifteen minutes'. It takes fifteen minutes to get to the airport, and the trains arrive every fifteen minutes. This is *metonymy* at its best – the ruthless selection of one feature to stand for all others.

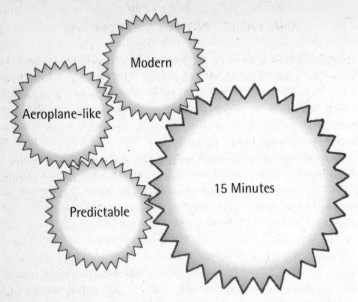

Fig. 29 *The Heathrow Express mental model*

The underlying **proposition** is reliability. This train runs like clockwork, so I can be far more relaxed about making my plane. Which is a huge relief.

The **metaphor** is that it's like flying, usually fairly efficient, rather than like other trains (a nightmare in the UK). The inflight media (screen and magazine), décor, seating shape, and staff uniforms, all support this implicit metaphor.

A concept brand can play a powerful internal role if it presents a core purpose, as when NASA strained every sinew towards being the first on the moon.

'Fifteen minutes' did just this. An attendant who helped a wheel-chair passenger to fix a puncture, before arrival at Heathrow. This is second nature to a company focused on getting people there on time. The wheel-chair owner turned out to be on the way to the Paralympic Games in Sydney, which made it a great public relations story.

ANALOGIES AND THE SPOT MARKET

Metaphor plays a key role in helping us understand our world. Metaphor takes something unfamiliar and says 'it's a bit like this'. This property was misused by brand-image makers to attach brands to untrue fantasies – untrue because they were unattainable. But that doesn't mean that all level three brands have to be denuded of metaphor.

Properly speaking, metaphors used for the purposes of understanding something tend to be analogies (A *really* is like B, not just in a poetic way). These are a standard teaching tool. When we first learn about electricity at school we are introduced to electrical current as a form of flow – like water in our central heating at home.

One of my 'almost'-projects last year was with a property company. They were developing a new type of temporary/flexible office space for Europe, based on a concept called 'Tech Space' in the US. Given what has just happened to the tech companies, I imagine that there are good reasons why we didn't get past the starting line.

But I am philosophical about all the projects that don't come to fruition. Because they are such a great way to rehearse for the ones that do. And I did have an idea, which illustrates how a metaphor can be used to build a whole new concept.

My idea was to create a spot market for office space.

A spot market is a real-time exchange (as opposed to a futures market). It's the system used, for instance, in the energy industry. Spot markets are very cost efficient, because they match a buyer's daily needs to the available supply. Supermarkets in the UK were able sell petrol more cheaply than the oil companies, because they bought their petrol on the spot market.

Say I was a tenant . . .

I could pay an annual membership fee, which would give me access to the general 'club lounge' style facilities and meeting rooms etc. on the ground floor of the building. When I needed an office, I'd book this on a daily, weekly or monthly basis to exactly fit my needs. Right now I need a desk and some privacy. In a few months' time I might be putting together a project team of four freelancers, with clients dropping in, or running a series of workshops for thirty people, or hosting an exhibition/event for hundreds at a time. Most information-age small businesses are like mine. We still need all the varied resources of a big business, and these needs vary (in size and use) on different days.

The spot-market concept would also suit the needs of corporate over-spill, for awaydays or creative breakout space, and spin-off project teams.

The company and its office locations would be branded 'spot' (a single dot). You can't get more basic level than that. These would be minimal, modern, attractive, funky offices. Compared with most normal serviced offices, which are fussy and uncool. This minimal modernism would form the key sense impressions.

We'd create a spot market site. Which would be the metonymic front end of the whole office. The real and the virtual office would work together seamlessly.

The site would take bookings for rooms and facilities. First come, first served, but we'd manage the membership and building capacity – and hold an emergency reserve – to avoid people getting stranded at key moments. Obviously the space available would have to be highly flexible – I imagined most of the furnishings would be on wheels.

The cost per square metre per day would be high, compared with other office space, but both sides would be able to manage space costs more efficiently. A tenant could cut space costs altogether in a tight month or buy premium space just for new client wooing moments. And the property company could manage and optimize their yield, room by room.

The resulting mental model we'd build for the spot concept looks something like this:

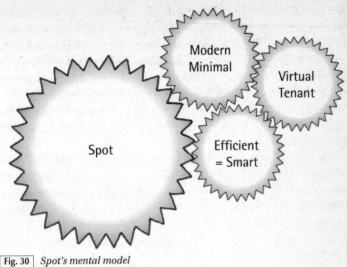

Spot's mental model

COMPANY BRANDING CONCEPTS

How do you create a consistent identity for a company which is flexible enough to remain meaningful, as the business evolves? This was the challenge I faced on a project last summer for Capco – known at the start of this exercise as the Capital Markets Company.

I found one answer, which is to base your identity in archetypes – a deep form of mental model unearthed by Carl Jung. Archetypes are deep metaphors that represent our development, and conflicts, as human beings. They go by slightly Marvel comics names such as the 'shadow' and the 'anima' etc. These are the figures that recur in ancient art and myths across the world. Don't be put off by their antiquity, you can find them in the celebrities who inspire the public imagination:

- basketball giants, like Michael Jordan = Hercules
- Madonna and her children = *the* Madonna and Child
- Princess Diana = St Joan

Capco specializes in finance. They combine deep financial insights with business consulting, IT systems and components. Their projects range from building back office systems for major global financial institutions, to mergers and acquisitions.

Unlike their main competitor, Accenture, Capco focuses purely on finance. Half of their people come from financial backgrounds – which balances out the IT, consulting, venture capital and marketing. It's an unusual blend of skills, working styles and knowledge.

Culturally, Capco is a very heroic company. Their founder, 37-year-old Rob Heyvaert, sets the tone. He's a snow-boarding fanatic. And he founded a hugely successful IT consultancy, Cimad, in his early twenties. Heyvaert is a visionary. He is passionate about leading change in the finance industry, and that's what has attracted his activist people. They come to Capco, often from key positions in much bigger firms, because they have a fire in their belly about building the future.

'Capco the Hero' was the only identity which would fit. Being a hero in the summer of 2000 meant e-finance. Now it's more about mergers and acquisitions. Wherever the charge is headed, Capco is at the front. 'Hero' was flexible enough for the company's needs. We got to that base camp in the first few weeks. The next question was: what kind of hero?

Jung saw 'hero' as a complex idea.[63] It is universal because it relates to the transition from child to adult, and it proceeds through a number of stages – four to be precise.

Up until then Capco was best described by the third kind of hero listed by Jung:

Red Horn – The hero who conquers nature. A reckless thrill seeker. Jung's examples include Superman and Gilgamesh (an ancient Babylonian tough guy). A corporate example would be Virgin. Or Jim Clark, the stunt plane-flying founder of Netscape.

But to lead an industry, rather than just challenge it, they needed a more grown up, mature and rounded personality that was more 'McKinsey' and less 'dot-com'. This kind of hero is better described by Jung's fourth archetype in the series:

The Twins – The hero achieves adult maturity, by splitting their instinctive core into two opposites. In mythology, twins threaten old orders and build new ones. Jung's examples were Cain and Abel, and Romulus and Remus the founders of Rome. Modern examples include Gates and Allen, Marx and Lenin, Watson and Crick.

The weird thing about archetypes is that, if you get it right, you find that you are discovering an inner core which was always there, not 'adding an image':

- Rob Heyvaert had just twinned. He'd brought in a co-leader, Michael Enthoven, to counter his own rash energy with maturity and stability
- the partners of the company work in pairs, to bring complementary expertise
- their work is all about duality; thinking and doing; strategy and execution.

The more we looked, the more the Twins theme already ran through the company, like dual stranded DNA (another Twins archetype).

The concept of the Twins has now been woven into the new brand design and all of the communications. The proposition is 'future founders'. The look and feel is 'Neo-Classical', which goes with this sign. So the mental model we set out to build for the company brand is this:

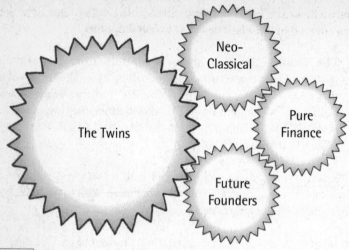

Fig. 31 | *The Twins mental model*

CAPCO AND L3

As befits a company based on 'twinning', the strategy we developed for Capco had a second prong.

'Twins' was the company concept. But we also created a concept brand, called L3, about the future of finance. It's based on a new theory of liquidity developed by Capco.

Liquidity is the amount of value freely circulating in an economy. For example, your current account is liquid, your pension is not. A public company is liquid, a private company is not. L3 is the third time liquidity has gone through a step change. The first was with the invention of coins, which kick-started the intellectual flowering of ancient Greece. The second was the development of new paper money (bills of exchange) which was the catalyst of the Renaissance. The theory with L3 was that electronic money would cause a similar spread of wealth and a consequent flowering of culture.

If L3 is right, we're going to go through a step change in the amount of wealth in the system. Capco's initial estimate was $13 trillion; this is double the equities boom of the 1980s–90s. Not only will wealth increase, it will also spread. Both of these factors are covered by a metaphor – it's like a floodplain.

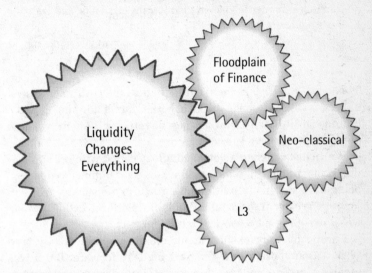

Fig. 32   *A pure knowledge brand*

This is a pure knowledge brand. What is being 'sold' here is a theory.

Big theories do sweep through this market like real option value theory, which goes something like this:

> We can regard the capital employed in immature companies as possessing some sort of option value. In a mathematical sense two components are necessary to create option value; an uncertain state or underlying variable and convexity of the final pay off in that underlying variable.[64]

Compared to most finance, L3 is really simple.

MESSAGE IN A MOBILE

Nothing is harder to change than human behaviour and nothing's more valuable.

HERMAN HAUSER

This says it all, but then could educating consumer tastes, beliefs, habits ... have been a better target for the dot-com billions, in 1999, than 'brand-image advertising'? Ah, the wisdom of hindsight.

We've just watched a new technology called wireless application protocol (WAP), which companies paid billions to develop, being hung out in an indifferent market, to die slowly. While in Japan a greatly inferior mobile-phone platform called i-Mode was a sweeping success.

Europeans were excited about mobile phones already, and WAP was supposed to be the next big leap forward. But it was lifeless, bloodless and brainless; where is the learning adventure, or the cultural exoticism, in getting weather forecasts and stock updates? What thrived in Europe instead of WAP was short message service (SMS).

SMS, or text messaging, is a good basic product. It's more private than old style paging as no-one can read the messages en route, and it's very cheap too – especially, given a flat global rate, for sending messages abroad. The total number of messages sent leapt up from 2.2 million in April 1998 to an estimated 200 billion in 2001.

But more than this, SMS is a rich and playful field of customer knowledge.

In SMS you have a limit of 160 characters. It's a truncated medium. Just like haiku (3 line Japanese poetry), the lack of space is a spur for creativity. Here are just a few of the many SMS 'codes' that have sprung up (the reader can test their culture quotient by checking how many they know):

ATB, B4, BBL, BCNU, BTW, XLNT, F2F, GR8, L8, LUV, LOL,
NO1, OIC, PCM, RUOK? SPK, THX, TTYL, 2MORO, WAN2,
WOT.

Two books of SMS codes have been in the UK top ten non-
fiction book chart, which, for the time being, makes SMS even
bigger than cookery.

Hits don't happen by accident, even if they don't often happen
by design either. There are a number of key ingredients in this
case study that should have been part of WAP's thinking very
early on:

- the value of technology is in the end-user-experience
- ideas that spread are sparky, playful, social catalysts, very
  close to the customer
- co-creativity and a flow of ideas from all sides is the surest
  development process
- customers learning and teaching each other is the make or
  break step in adoption.

The key lesson of this case, and most of the other examples
in this chapter is that, if you're going to reinvent your market,
you have to reshape the culture around that market. As Herman
Hauser said, this is not easy. But it's also not something you can
side-step.

9

APOLLO RISING REVISITED

The Apollo Rising trend charts the rise of a new, flexible and knowledge-hungry culture. Now that we've explored brands as types of mental model, it's possible to be a bit more precise about what exactly is changing.

Brands used to colour in people's fairly crystalline map of the human world around them. They did this by linking existing cultural content to products and services, by using metaphors. The brand image linked people's aspirations with things that they could buy. If you wanted to appear a little more successful, sophisticated, macho or whatever you could switch alliegances to brands which supported this expanded view of yourself.

Now that this whole map is up for question and subject to constant revision, a new deeper role for brands suggests itself. Instead of colouring in your identity and habits, brands can help you *relearn* human culture, to keep up with a fast-changing world. That may sound quite philosophical, but in practice it's no more complicated than getting into text messaging, fine wines, or shopping on the Internet.

ONCE IN A LIFETIME?

There is a hierarchy within human knowledge, from the essential and general, to the optional and specific. Let's represent this

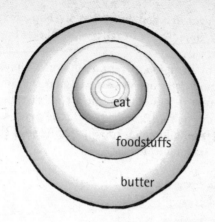

Fig. 33 | *The hierarchy of human knowledge*

by 'tree rings', with more basic (usually older) mental models at the centre.

Psychologist Henry Plotkin has studied how different sorts of information have different places in this hierarchy.[65] Simple information updates – the small-change of culture – are highly dependent on much more general 'memories and knowledge structures', he found. Just as in the tree, outer layers are built on all that's come before.

Understanding the news that a shop has a sale on depends, Plotkin points out, on our deeper structures of knowledge about what a shop is ('an aggregate, composite, abstracted characterization of places that one goes to where goods are on display which can become one's own property in return for money'). These structures are of 'much wider scope informationally and of much greater longevity, with transmission normally restricted to just once in a lifetime'.

But Plotkin's very example – the once in a lifetime concept of 'a shop' – is shifting. Amazon, Sephora, the Body Shop, e-Bay, Letsbuyit, Hotline and others have been reinventing the shop recently, in diverse directions.

Normally the way the human mind learns is that we get the deeper ideas – like shop – early in our development, and then modify some details as necessary. The human mind is not designed for a world when the notion of 'shop' changes half way through a lifetime. That's exactly what's been happening over the last fifteen years.

Our ideas of shop, job, parent and man . . . have been modified. A shop no longer has to be a real place. A job is no longer for life. A parent is less of an authority, more a mentor. A man no longer 'rules the roost', and so on. In the new era, adults have to revise their mental models, not just at the surface level, but at deeper more 'schematic' levels.

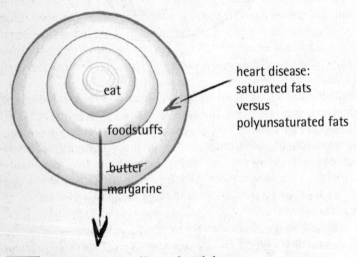

eat

foodstuffs

heart disease:
saturated fats
versus
polyunsaturated fats

butter
margarine

Fig. 34 | *Modified hierarchy of human knowledge*

And it's hard, but it is possible, and it is necessary. People are being forced to find the flexibility to take on completely new roles in life – in a new career, newly divorced, in a new country . . . Businesses are reinventing their markets and asking people to keep up. We had to learn to accept and use mobile phones, for telecoms to move forward.

The indications are that the ability to flexibly *relearn* throughout life is growing:

■ the rate of technology adoption has speeded up – the Internet as consumer medium spread quicker in its first ten years than television did in its first 30 years

■ the rate of adoption of new consumer habits in 'custom' areas like food and drink; for instance, Starbucks has dramatically increased America's caffeine consumption

■ the speed of fashion cycles and volatility of consumer 'crazes'.

The most direct evidence of this change in people's mental abilities comes from IQ tests. These show that while crystalline intelligence – the ability to reapply old thinking in familiar situations – has not changed much, fluid intelligence – the ability to think your way through problems you have not encountered before – has increased quite sharply.[66]

There are limits to relearning. The deeper the mental model is, within this hierarchy, the older it is likely to be in our development. In fact some of the deepest levels are likely – according to evolutionary psychologists – to be innate or 'hard wired' by our genes.

> Human beings' asymmetries of sexual preferences, our patterns of male jealousy and female adultery; the propensity of young men to form aggressive coalitions for war, children's play fighting; attachment (and grief) between carers and children; our tastes for salt, sugar, fatty foods and open landscapes – all these may, in principle, be understood as universally human, 'species typical' adaptations of hunter gatherer life.[67]

Evolutionary biologists have come to the same conclusion about *relearning* in a slightly different form.[68] They see the key change as moving from culture transmission across generations, to culture transmission within a single generation:

> In post-industrial societies meme transmission systems in humans ... (are) favouring horizontal cultural transmission systems. Modern culturally-constructed environments seem to be changing so rapidly that, increasingly, vertically transmitted information

between parents and offspring is too slow to be of sufficient adaptive value.

Every generation has its own challenges. The challenge of our time is to have the flexibility to change your mental models throughout your adult life. Lifelong learning in the formal sense is just one part of this. Much of the *relearning* is done in the context of everyday life experiences. Which is where brands come in.

In a world where people are 'making it up as they go along' we need a different kind of brand. Not one that helps us 'fit in' so much as one which helps us to 'work things out'. One implication is that (in contrast to the brand-image phase) the media will again become more valuable than the ads which they carry, and there is every sign that this is already happening. The latest UK series of *Big Brother* (from one point of view, an interactive training course in how – and how not to – win friends and influence people) netted millions in income, from the phone-voting charges alone.

MEDIA STRATEGY AND LEARNING

The media for brand-image building required passive attention and retention. The media for the next level of branding requires active learning of new concepts. Whereas brand-image advertising was very static and monolithic, the next level will mean building flexible brand 'molecules' out of ideas in multiple media. The interactive media are in their in-fancy, but some form of audience participation is essential. The best way to plan media strategies is to start with general modes (how it will work) not specific channels . . .

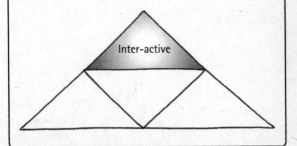

10

THE MEDIA REVOLUTION

There is going to have to be a revolution in marketing, for the ideas in this book to come to fruition. 'Revolution' is an over-used word in business. It's all too often used just to mean 'change', but I mean it in a more literal sense – a fairly violent struggle to overthrow an established order and replace it with new institutions that better fit the needs of society.

BEYOND IMAGE ADVERTISING

At the moment, if you are a marketing person who wants to do things in a new way, the hardest thing is to decide who to do it with. If you start with the conventional suppliers, you get the conventional answer – usually, a very expensive advertising campaign.

Advertising was a great tool for establishing brand image. Especially television advertising, with its seductive, emotional, personality-laden little films. At its best, advertising is something of an art form, but the majority of commercials are far from inspiring – for every 'Whassuuup?' there are a hundred bland 'Sowhaaats?'

What if you do not want to establish a brand image? What if you want to establish a deeper concept, to launch a new type of financial service, perhaps. Maybe a new kind of bank account, which gives people new ways of controlling their money and their lives?

The recent history of companies trying to do things like this suggests that advertising is not the answer. It may play a role. But it cannot be the main platform for your communications. This is because it is as bad at helping people to grasp new concepts, as it is good at building brand-image ideas. It is like using a poem to write a maths paper.

Banks have been very badly served by their advertising. After twenty years of working with the best ad agencies and spending huge amounts of money, by any advertisers' standards, most retail banks are still wildly out of touch with their customers. A survey in the 1990s by the Henley Centre found that the banks are the only high street retailer with an overall negative service reputation. Their advertising has failed them as an industry. And there are few signs that individual banks have improved their position, relative to the others, through better advertising either.

It has been a First World War of marketing, involving hundreds of millions of pounds. There has been some very creative advertising, judged solely on artistic or entertainment criteria. My own personal favourite was the campaign from Finland that said: 'We're boring, because you'd want it that way.'

But nothing much seems to have changed as a result.

Financial services have all the 'danger signs' of a difficult brief (from a conventional ad agency point of view). The business is complicated and fast-moving. The customers they compete for are increasingly informed and confident on the one hand, and hopeless with understanding and managing their finances on the other. The chances of producing a nice, simple brand-advertising idea in this context are slim.

If you think about it, the computer industry has the same characteristics and seems, on average, to have had far better marketing. Partly perhaps because it was so much less reliant on TV advertising. If banks, like the computer companies, had spent more time producing new business and customer concepts – such as the customization of Dell, the user-friendly interface and identity of Apple, the concept branding by Intel – then they might have been better placed.

The same failure of advertising to help complicated, fast, moving and intangible (or difficult to understand) categories extends to other retailers, media, utilities and services. And most of all, to the wave of dot-com advertisers who rushed into advertising like lemmings. These dot-coms often offered a combination of service, media and retailer and surpassed all three categories in the leap of understanding and faith they were asking customers to make. In the US, in 1999, dot-coms spent $2 billion on above-the-line advertising. The rest is history.

Come the revolution, it is very likely that advertising agencies will be first to the wall.

The battle is already on between ad agencies, design agencies, media agencies, Internet agencies, interactive agencies, event agencies, public relations agencies . . . not to mention the management and brand consultancies, to seize the new high ground. The new objective for all these parties is to take the lead in what is often being called 'total communications planning'. Here there are lucrative fees to be made from advice, and there is added security in being a close partner to the client, and not just 'another supplier'.

The in-fighting seems, if anything, to be pulling some agencies and consultancies back from innovation, towards lowest common denominators. I've seen reports on brands recently that claim to have *discovered* that people choose brands for subtle emotional reasons. An argument that was settled forty years ago – if indeed it is even still true.

What total communications planning should mean is some kind of holistic overview of the many possibilities, without any bias towards a certain type of media or creative production. Ad agencies are guilty of being biased towards advertising as *the* answer, following Buckminster Fuller's principle that, 'If all you have is a hammer, every problem looks like a nail.' But the others are not much better. Even the apparently neutral management consultancies seem to have a bias – towards customer relationship management and other technology-based solutions which, it's hard not to notice, are products which they can implement in-house for huge fees.

If ad agencies are set to play the royal family in the upcoming revolution, it may just be because they have lived in the palace for the last forty years and have the most to lose. Although the attitude of most ad agencies to change of any sort also does not bode well.

New approaches, interestingly, are more often being led by the more confident and adventurous clients. Who decide to leave behind the traditional media mix in favour of something a little closer to the action in their market.

Red Bull is a notable example. Its campaign encompassed painted jeeps at festivals and outside clubs, advertising posters inside a video game, an anti-supermarket distribution strategy and much besides. It is now the UK's number three soft drink, with sales of £500 million and it has only recently, and sadly, in my view, resorted to TV advertising.

Do-it-yourself marketers like Red Bull, Channel 4, Virgin and others have often worked closest with their media agencies. These were originally the ad agency media departments and just used to 'book the media schedule'. But now they are mostly independents and increasingly they have been coming up with their own ideas, and forming relationships with others who can execute these ideas, ranging from cricket festivals to TV series.

If I had to pick one group to be the Bolsheviks in the upcoming revolution, it would be the media agencies. Especially now that they seem to have become very much more sophisticated in their view of brands, business and media.

The reason why media agencies could well come out as 'the new ad agencies' is that they simply hold more trump cards. Media choices have increased dramatically over recent decades, with the Internet being just one of many 'new media'. This makes the choice of media platforms a vital first step, and a great source of fresh ideas.

If there is to be a revolution it will probably be triggered by the same causes as many social revolutions – an economic downturn. Soviet Russia was doing just fine in the 1960s and 70s, when its economic growth at times out-stripped the West. It was only when the bread queues started forming in Moscow that the pressure for change became too intense to resist.[69] We are now facing what could turn out to be a very deep recession.

When that happens companies tend to cut advertising and marketing budgets. It's such an easy cost saving. You can turn off the tap in a matter of months, whereas redundancies, mergers and restructuring take much longer to affect the bottom line and are anyway a much tougher course for managers to choose.

Once a company decides it needs to cut its marketing budgets, then cheaper alternatives to advertising become attractive. And new media, while they are often time-intensive and difficult to pull off, do tend to be much cheaper. Some of the most interesting media options available now – like making your own I-max movie, say – are based on investment, not spend. You pay for some of the production (usually 10 per cent) but are likely to recoup most of this later when the film (or whatever) is shown. New media also are often more accountable, because they tend to be planned in a less ethereal and more task-oriented way. That's why direct marketing made such a comeback in the early 90s.

THE NEW MARKETING APPROACH

In my last book I sifted through recent marketing campaigns and tried to find the current best practice. Many of these campaigns weren't arrived at by systematic theory and 'level three' marketing, but by an explosion of trial and error. This time of experimentation was a response to advertising saturation, spiralling costs and a new audience media literacy and cynicism, plus the profusion of new media choices in the Internet, interactive TV and multimedia, venue based experiences, viral and community marketing . . .

Some of the main principles that emerged from all this trial and error included:

- be intimate – get as close as possible to people's lives. Hence Nike's shift from heroic TV commercials to music CDs, Niketown, city runs, community facilities, and so on.
- be relevant – tap into the needs, changing lives and mentality of your audience. Like the Spice Girls, whose 'Girl Power' was perfectly attuned to the new teen girl spirit.

- be consensual – put the audience at the centre of your activities (not on the outside looking in) and make word of mouth your main medium; like the first New Labour election victory, which was proved to have been swung by word of mouth.
- be participative – allow the active and media-literate audience to get involved in engaging and creative ways; like hit TV show *Big Brother*, which drew in loyal viewers as voyeurs (Web cams), juries (voting) and gossips (tabloid coverage).

As time has gone on, I have come to see these principles as deriving from *both* the evolution in media possibilities *and* the evolution in business and society. They still hold true on every project I've worked on since. This is because they were the first signs of marketing stepping up to a new level.

MEDIA ENCOUNTERS OF THE THIRD KIND

The best way to grasp how media work best now is to change your perspective, from media broadcasting to individual reception:

My Sphere of Interest

Content On Demand

Mass Media Mess

Fig. 35 *Sphere of interest*

This perspective works quite well for level one – direct marketing on demand. Which is what I think Seth Godin was mostly driving at with *Permission Marketing*. Apparently the majority of car buyers in the US research the market online before they choose. So interactive brochures take on the role of the first dealership visit.

It also works quite well for level two. Like the Volvo S60 launch in the US, which used AOL exclusively. AOL members were offered special deals. The website allowed them to custom design their car from the many options. And even carried the advertising films. And guess what? This novel approach generated huge media coverage – the story was featured in over sixty mass broadcast media.[70] Which is a feature of new marketing. The campaign becomes the message, and you get your brand built for you.

The receiver perspective comes into its own in level three marketing. The plan here is to reinvent a market. By building new mental models or concepts in people's minds.

If a car marketer – like Volvo – wanted to build their business on this level, what could they do?

For a start they could move from claiming safety to teaching it.

- to blend skills transfer to customers with sales and service just as computer marketing does
- to build a deeper relationship with drivers
- to establish a venue for introducing new car models, new features such as on-board media
- to open a dialogue with a core group of enthusiasts, who would spread the word.

Volvo might provide driving lessons, to ultra-safe standards for learners plus annual top-up driving events, of the fun, race-track kind. On this basis they could provide much cheaper insurance as accredited safer drivers are a lower financial risk and they would achieve better safety figures for their cars as safer drivers have fewer crashes. They would also make some friends and do some good in the world.

None of which is likely to cost as much as global advertising. In fact, with the addition of insurance revenues, the company could actually come out in the black – car companies already make most of their money from financial services.

I know that all of Volvo's efforts have been focused on establishing a sexy image rather than reinforcing their safety image. But they may just be answering the wrong question. If you look at their 'image' data you could conclude that the brand is not sexy enough. But it may be that their original, very Swedish, mission to make driving safer is the right one for the times, it's just not the right strategy to make advertising that sells cars. Whereas as a concept for building relationships with drivers it looks great to me.

IF MENTAL MODELS ARE THE 'WHAT?' THEN LEARNING IS THE 'HOW?'

Rebuilding a deeper mental model is precisely what is meant by 'learning'.

Psychologist Gerhard Steiner points out that it is this process of modifying old, or building new mental models that distinguishes *learning* from 'merely noticing, understanding or remembering'.[71] When we learn something it has 'changed our mind'.

This is a direct contrast with marketing communications on level two. Brand-image building was all about attention and memory, but in didn't require any active cognitive involvement. True learning requires active involvement from the audience.

This immediately suggests a paradigm shift:

- level two – brand image suited passive reception and it had low cognitive demands
- level three – deeper concepts suit active reception and it has high cognitive demands.

The very word 'communication' is anti-learning. 'Communication' implies a passive receiver. Learning involves active not passive minds, often in some form of dialogue.

You have to turn media planning inside out, to engage people on this level. You have to plan a whole chain of events, experiences and interventions that your audience can pick up and use, to help them build their knowledge, concepts and beliefs in some new direction.

That sounds very demanding. But it's as simple as when Sainsbury's supermarket based their marketing on recipes. Their TV ads broadcast recipes. Their stores had leaflets which helped locate all the ingredients. Their promotions bundled a recipe's ingredients into special offers . . .

We are all updating our mental models, all the time:

What's safe to eat?

What's a good career opportunity?

How do people dress, for a second date, these days?

Do the lower interest rates mean 'saving isn't worth it', or 'save like mad' (because they wouldn't drop the rates unless we were in trouble)?

This kind of learning is informal and pervasive.

MAXIMIZING LEARNING (MEDIA) EFFECTIVENESS

If you want to optimize an attention-and-retention process, such as branding, then you need to ask questions about: impact; comprehension; repetition; enjoyment, which boosts memory; targeting and aperture issues – getting to the right people, at the right time, and so on.

Those are the right questions for brand image, but they are unlikely to work for learning, which requires a different sort of interaction, with a lot of active mental processing. It's more like 'doing the crossword' and less like 'skimming through the paper'.

What makes for effectiveness in learning?

Studies in cognitive education have identified four factors which aid better learning, which turn out to be identical to the 'new marketing' principles.[72]

Get Close to Life

What is remembered depends on the way it was received, compared with the setting in which it is recalled.

The closer the educational input is to the eventual application, the better the learning is recalled and applied. This has led to the development of learning modules based on real-life problem solving, rather than being based on exam regurgitation. It also implies that 'learning as you go' during problem solving will be highly effective.

Relevance

Effective education matches the receiver's existing knowledge.

It's no good giving people new information if their old mental models aren't right. They will just 'paper over the cracks'. Novices in a domain often have a set of 'folklore' ideas – conditioning from other areas of their lives. These beliefs and assumptions need to be tackled or they will persist.

For instance, a study showed that people often have a 'gas pedal' model of their thermostat which says 'the higher I set the thermostat the quicker the place will heat up'. Thermostat settings unfortunately are nothing like a car accelerator. The net result is that the room heats up at much the same pace but then overshoots. Traditional teaching methods, by ignoring these 'theories in use' and pouring on extra knowledge on top, fail to correct the underlying mistaken assumptions.

To help people get to a more expert level it is vital to find out what their existing mental models are, and then to encourage the correct ones and target the incorrect ones for change by instruction. Teaching methods that have taken this course have been shown to be the most successful.

Consensus

The most effective forum for school learning has been shown by studies to be one of classroom discussion, which is supported by the teacher, but which is directed by the students. Adult learning is much less 'instructed' and has strong social and self-directed components.

Active Participation

Good learners have a simple set of skills which bad learners lack. Teaching these simple skills – for instance when reading: summarizing, identifying 'difficult bits' and asking yourself questions about what was read – can greatly improve overall learning. Furthermore, self-awareness (of your thinking processes) has been shown to have an overall positive effect on learning too. Far from requiring the unreflective trance induced by watching long flows of television, learning requires people to be lively minded and aware of their own thoughts.

A fifth dimension of adult learning, which would not be so visible in a classroom setting, is *motivation*. How to start and to persevere with relearning? Changing your deeper models of how things work is hard work and more than a little unsettling. Experiences, for example those delivered by the media, which rouse, engage and encourage people, rather than those which make people feel chained to some impossible, or plain boring, task will be the most valuable.

A summary of those psychology studies would be: interactivity. I spell this out as two words, to emphasize that I do not necessarily mean interactive technologies, but rather the whole experience and involvement. Effective learning is inter-active, in comparison to, for example, rote learning to pass exams, which is passive and one-way.

The next marketing level has come just in time for the development of richer interactive networks, interfaces and formats over the next ten years:

- interactive TV
- interactive ambient computing (e.g. in ovens, cars)
- heads up displays and computing you wear
- true videophone
- shared virtual reality spaces
- co-creation tools . . .

The trouble with most interactive marketing I've seen is that it wears lead boots – it tries to work on the previous two levels. One major strand has been interactive direct marketing – click-through banners and interactive brochure-ware. The other has been interactive entertainment (for image).

Learning media need to be inter-active, somehow. It doesn't matter if buttons are being pressed or screens navigated. It is about the learners – are their minds active? Shouting the answers at a quiz show, chatting about the economy with a mate – these are highly interactive activities. It will take electronic media a long time to catch up with human communication.

There are two main meta-trends in media:

- Quantity – more media types carrying more ideas in more directions. Not just from broadcasters but also between people by e-mail and the other point-to-point media. The surface area of human communication has mushroomed. That's why we have information overload. If you get a hundred e-mails a day you'll know what I'm saying.
- Life-like quality – TV is more life-like than radio. Radio is more real to life than books. The Web may look more like books than TV, but the interactivity of even basic functions like searching makes it more like communication with another person; for example, sites like 'AskJeeves'. This moves it closer to the forms needed for learning. And with broadband and streaming, the Net will soon embrace all other media as content.

The Internet satisfies the four main learning amplifiers, but it's not good at motivation yet:

- it is used close to the application, researching a project while you're doing it
- it takes people on a learning 'random walk', so it is more likely to confront your old worldview, with very different mental models, than with one linear course of instruction
- it has high degrees of self-direction and opportunities for social interaction

■ it makes you aware of your learning process; when setting
  search criteria; following leads from one source, through
  links . . . it is 'sit forward', active and reflective rather than
  just a passive flow of content which you don't wrestle
  with.

'E' IS FOR EDUCATION

The Internet was originally (besides its military applications) a
network for educational establishments. The Web was invented
at CERN, to enable researchers to access each others' research.
HTML (the programming base of the Web) allows you to hypertext – go between texts no matter where they are stored in the
network – to follow trains of thought. Which is a dramatic advance, and it's also purpose designed for self-directed learning.

All of which should have made it obvious that a (or possibly
the) killer application of the Internet will be learning. John
Chambers, the CEO of Cisco Systems, put it this way: 'e-learning
will be so big, it'll make e-mail look like rounding error'.

Japan has the most advanced lifelong-learning programme in
the world. In the mid-1980s, the Japanese government formed a
Lifelong-Learning Division. A key objective was to encourage
individuals to take responsibility for their own development and
destiny (more self-direction). They also targeted the need for
greater creativity in the workforce and the need for an increased
understanding of information technology.

The result was a thriving local and regional programme of
adult training. When I was in Japan a few years ago I interviewed
Mr Taniguchi, head of Club 21, a business association with
800,000 member companies. He told me that the private sector
was equally active, 'the only people making any profits on the
Internet are the small- to medium-sized education companies'.
These were occupying thriving niches, like language courses.

Now China is leading the next wave of distance learning. At
a recent e-learning event, I met with a professor responsible for
distance learning in a province of China. He told me that his key
issue is keeping up with the growth in demand. Last year there

were one million university distance learning students in his region. This year there are two million.

Huge super-campus cities are under construction; like the University of South-East Asia, with a planned capacity of two million students. But even these are unlikely to keep up with demand or meet the needs of the population which is spread across vast geographical distances. So e-learning is key to the government strategy.

22.5 million individuals are online in China, but the number is still doubling every six months, while US growth has slowed. This fact led Accenture to claim in their corporate advertising ('now it gets interesting') that Chinese will soon be the main language of the Internet. Private companies have sprung up to meet the e-learning demand, like Sohu.com, which has just tied up a deal to give Chinese students access to US courses.

Sohu founder, Charles Zhang, has a powerful vision of the role of the Internet in bringing about:

> 'the Rebirth of Chinese Civilization'. The Internet makes people cleverer and more individual and allows them to form their own opinions . . . and this process is unstoppable.[73]

E-learning also has many advantages in the West:

- people are now familiar with the technology
- busy lifestyles make it a convenient alternative
- the potential for collaboration, but at the same time self-direction and autonomy
- you can learn at your own pace, in your own time.

Rich media could enable these learning encounters to have the autonomy of a free-flowing project, combined with the richness of a BBC documentary. Meanwhile, even on the good old Web, implicit, self-directed learning is already driving Internet usage.

As this survey of the main uses shows:[74]

% of Internet users, say they use it regularly for:

Research	92%
Communication with friends	88%
Product information	73%
Hobby information	70%
News	70%
Instant messages	56%
Entertainment	50%
Communication with co-workers	48%

A US Department of Commerce survey found 40 per cent of those using the Internet at home had already used it to 'take a course', but the bigger picture is day-in-day-out use of the Internet as the biggest source of reference information imaginable (unless God exists).

There's a lot of uncertainty about 'which medium will win?' and given the need for many diverse streams of stimulation and dialogue in learning this may be the wrong question anyway.

The best way to build media strategies for the new level while the media choices are so uncertain, is to work on the concept level. Media are like materials. They can be used in many ways, just as steel can be used for everything from a surgical instrument to a girder.

The key step – once you've worked out your core concept – is to work out 'how?' You can work on that question in a freeform, intuitive, creative way. But it's worth bearing in mind that there is a core set of learning modes – characteristic ways in which people can learn. A number of these are likely to be involved in transmitting any new mental model.

MODES OF LEARNING

The seven modes of learning I've identified will be examined in more detail in one of the following chapters.

All involve redirecting marketing budgets from building brand image to building new customer mental models. Most

involve a mix of formal media (which can be bought) and informal media (which can only be 'seeded' or 'amplified').

The modes do overlap, but each broadly involves different
sorts of media, used in different ways, for different kinds of tasks:

- **Knowledge** media
- **Reality** media
- **Dialogue** media
- **Memetic** media
- **Community** media
- **Story** media
- **Reputation** media

The first six are applicable to market-development-learning as
described throughout the book. The seventh is more about corporate branding – which still applies to consumer marketing in
cases (like IKEA, the Body Shop and Virgin) where the company
is the brand.

Although I'll deal with each mode separately, most initiatives
would draw on any number of these, together. Just as a classroom works best with a charismatic teacher (leader), tight-knit
classroom community, learning aids, computers, the word on the
playground, parents . . . it takes a whole mix of media to change a
mental model.

A good example of a mix of media that was close to the audience and the organization is the turnaround of BBC Radio 1. This
case is quite suggestive of the typical 'branding' campaign of the
future, and it features all of the learning modes.

'AS IT IS'

At the time (1995), Radio 1 was losing a million UK listeners a
year, because it had become, in the eyes of its 16–24-year-old
target market, out of touch with their culture. It was seen as
'naff'.

Radio 1 had already started reinventing their medium, under
the leadership of a new controller, Matthew Bannister. He had

sacked the forty-something, transatlantic cheesy DJs. And hired fresh talent; DJs from the rave scene like Pete Tong and Judge Jules, or from hip hop like Westwood.

These were people who were already breaking new trends in music. Radio 1 went from playing old classics to 'new music first' (Leadership Media).

The first big success was 'Britpop' (Community Media). Radio 1, rather than some regional or pirate station, was the first to play bands like Oasis.

They then hired a new anchor for the breakfast show called Chris Evans, the nearest thing the UK had to a 'shock jock'. He was the mouth that launched 1000 tabloid articles. Like the time he announced he was going to be 'gay for a year' (Mimetic Media).

Evans' shows were unusually interactive; using listener letters, calls, pranks . . . (Dialogue Media). He was fond of doing things like getting everyone in an area to switch their lights on and off at the same time.

That was the new internal reality. It was the AC Milan of radio. But the problem was that the 'image' held it back. It was thought of as more like Scunthorpe United. No listener was about to go back to Radio 1 and spend hours picking through the new schedule to discover that it had changed.

They needed to change the mental model of lost listeners somehow. How to do this was a fascinating question. Previous advertising had tried to project a more positive 'image' – whacky, brash, cheerful, and modern. But it didn't work, and it seemed that if something has a strong negative image, that trying to project a more positive image doesn't work.

The problem was 'prejudice', and the only way to tackle this is to confront people with the new truth, in the most realistic form possible. The first 'How?' was a behind-the-scenes documentary (Story Media). Documentaries were shown before the main movie in cinemas. Short documentary trails were shown on BBC TV.

Later Radio 1 took steps into people's lives, by meeting them halfway at music festivals (Reality Media).

The whole schedule for Radio 1 was published in the

Guardian newspaper, which is read by media opinion formers (Knowledge Media).

That total onslaught of thought-provoking, culture-shaping, mind-bending marketing worked. Within a year the decline was reversed. And it didn't even feel like 'marketing'. This sat very well with the BBC concept. They were in the process of rediscovering their commitment to artistic excellence and commercial independence. 'As It Is' (the slogan and spirit) was very 'politically correct' in this context (Reputation Media).

There is a kind of marketing reformation going on. The flashy image brands are being torn down, like the painted statues and finery of Roman Catholic churches. This move is linked with other movements, like the anti-capitalism protests, and it is right for a more switched on, educated and involved audience.

But 'As It Is' is far from being the only 'how?' Every brand should have some of the same integrity, authenticity and that lack of superficial 'image' metaphors. But there's more than one way to skin a mental model . . .

FROM ARROWS TO MOLECULES

It is ineffective to pour new content onto an old framework of propositions, when some of these old 'chunks' don't fit.

I've found that in order to get my head around branding and media on the third level, I have had to change my own mental model. So just in case you don't already think this way, as the cognitive jargon goes – I'm 'targeting this for intervention'.

'Arrows' is the old communication-model of branding.

A sender has a message, which they want to put into the minds of their audience. This message might be a selling point, it might also be an image (the poison on the tip?).

They do this by firing the message at the receiver, which is why we call it 'targeting'. Media are the 'air' through which this arrow flies. The branding is accumulative, like the scores in archery. A bigger number of direct hits creates a stronger brand. The brand is tracked by measuring how many arrows have 'hit the target'.

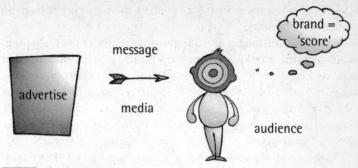

Fig. 36   *Targeting a customer*

All of which fits scientific selling very well and brand image-building quite well. But it is a very limited framework for the development of deeper mental models.

The problem with 'arrows' is that it describes the process of *creating* marketing messages far better than it describes the effects in people's minds. And it misses so much of the subtlety of human thinking, learning and communication, that it blinkers you to bigger possibilities.

The advertisers that hold this model end up in long meetings about 'quiver designs and shafts', when they really should be thinking deeper about whether shooting arrows at people is the best way to win them over!

'Molecules' is a different model altogether, which I find better describes how a diverse set of communicative stuff can result in people's minds changing. The fundamental unit (atom) of the molecule is an idea. The ideas, if they are coherent, stick together to form a molecule.

The molecule for the Radio 1 relaunch looked something like this:

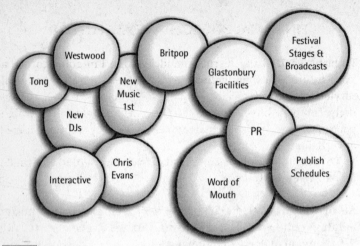

Fig. 37   *The Radio 1 marketing molecule*

Why is molecules a better model?

Firstly, it reflects the way the mind works, with masses of interconnected ideas; as one neuroscientist said, 'I link therefore I am'.

Secondly, it allows company activities and brand to be complex and multifaceted. With different people attaching themselves at different points. A hip-hop fan would attach themselves to Tim Westwood's show. A journalist to Chris Evans (tabloid), or the published schedule (media commentator).

One result of thinking this way is that your marketing planning becomes additive; 'what new atom could we introduce that would change our whole molecule for the better?' Rather than reductive in the insistence that one simple brand-image theme must consistently be reproduced in every setting. Brands built this way are organic. They have a satisfying richness and variation in what they are 'about'. Whereas brands planned on the 'arrows' model can be very synthetic.

Molecule planning is useful for media planning on any of the levels. But it comes into its own on level three, when the marketing is aiming to build a deep mental model. The best way of doing this seems to be to use the different learning modes in concert.

FINANCIAL SERVICES – A CASE FUTURE

To bring each of the learning modes to life I'm going to use a 'case future' – a hypothetical case study. I've chosen financial services as it is a typical information-age market, with a satisfyingly complex business and customer relationship and a high pace of change. It's also a market badly served by its brand-image advertising.

To bring the task into some kind of focus I've settled on a made up concept brand.

THE LIFE ACCOUNT

The life account is something finance has been groping towards for years.

My former First Direct client in their 'blue skies' moments had the vision of being a kind of financial 'butler', managing all their customers' affairs.

HSBC, another ex-client, toyed with the idea of offering sweeping discounts for customers, in return for a lifetime loyalty contract, which given the cost of recruitment and retention activities would be a win:win.

Capco had a vision of personal financial services offering benefits similar to those which public companies now enjoy. Liquidity would be released by using an investment (rather than lending) approach. Giving people freedom and capital, to develop 'Me plc'.

For my concept brand, I'm assuming a blend of these ideas and a few of my own. Let's piece together a mental model to work with.

The best cog to start with might be metonymy. This account is about *life plans* (not money). People find it very hard to make the link between a change in their financial circumstances and their lifestyle. Let alone to plan ahead.

The sense impressions therefore ought to be 'full of life'. Rather than seeing statements and policies, customers should be dreaming of their future. It's like sticking imagined family photos on top of the figures. People already do this in a crude way when they 'earmark' certain funds – for example, their kids' college money.

The proposition framework would include some generalities like 'plan life first, money last', and a lot of detailed reprogramming of people's naïve mental models of their personal finances (usually only a few steps above 'under the mattress'). Plus new elements special to the *life account*, such as services which increase liquidity.

One intriguing aspect of focusing on life goals, as numerous studies show, is that setting yourself goals in life, of itself, makes you more likely to be successful.[75] A new active type of bank emerges – one which helps its clients succeed. This is added value, compared with commodity bank accounts, which exist mostly just to process transactions. All sorts of ramifications occur for the business model, such as credit ratings. But working out the business model would get very messy. So I won't go there.

'Helping customers succeed' is different from the classic bank-customer relationship. Which despite the efforts of modern banks still feels like a Father-Child relationship, authoritarian and alienating. When I think of a bank, I think of the building (like a temple), not life. I think of the bank manager who told me off when I was a student. Empowerment is the last thing on my mind.

The role of metaphor would be to bring the empowerment to life.

It says something about our culture that we have many cultural ideas about Authority, but very few about empowerment. One that does stand out is mothering. It's a universal, close-to-real-life idea, of emotional and practical support. It's a clear contrast with banks who 'usually adopt the role of a stern father'.

According to Jung, the mother archetype in inner mental life is associated (in its positive aspects) with fecundity, protection, redemption, wisdom, change, growth and fundamentally with a great overflowing love.[76]

The concept of maternal love is a shockingly warm counterpoint to the cold, ascetic world of bank figures, stuffed in forgotten files in our attic. If finance was ruled by the Great Mother, what a different world it would be. To be this, authentically, we'd have to be dealing with New Age company culture. But, hey! – this is a hypothetical project . . .

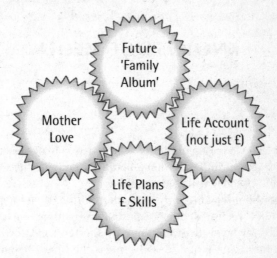

Fig. 38 | *Mother love*

So – with apologies to the excellent London agency of this name – let's say that our client is a Californian Self-Help/Banking cross-over called Mother. The product is the Life Account – as much about personal development (eg seminars) as cash.

This ought to change banking!

11

KNOWLEDGE MEDIA

Typical knowledge media include instructive books, factual TV programmes, online or CD-ROM courses, seminars, user-groups and venue-based learning experiences.

These should not be confused with traditional sales materials, like glossy brochures, press ads and even usage instructions because – for level three marketing – the knowledge would be fairly general, not brand-biased (unless the brand happened to be in a category of its own). It's the difference, in my earlier example, between selling people the features of a new Volvo model and teaching people to drive more safely.

Knowledge media will be useful in situations where people's lack of knowledge, expert concepts, skills and confidence are holding back the category. A good example was described to me by the marketing director of Boots as the key barrier to developing their business: 'If only UK women were as sophisticated in their beauty routines as French women.' As this example indicates, knowledge is not necessarily 'just the facts' – it can also include skills, standards, cultural concepts and values.

THE UK WINE MARKET

An example where the British *have* been playing catch-up with the French is wine. Twenty years ago, most British wine drinkers were limited to decisions such as, 'red, white or rosé?', to styles of wine like Leibfraumilch and to a few brands like Blue Nun. And the overall market was quite small, compared with beers and spirits.

Then the wine drinking revolution took hold, and we've progressed to buying a much more sophisticated, varied and knowledge-intensive range of wines. A typical purchase today is based on sophisticated information, for instance: 'Chateau Le Monestère, Cotes de Bourg, Appellation Controlée, 1999, Mis En Bouteille Au Chateau, Organic' (a smooth but powerful, full bodied red at £5.99 from Tesco's).

But however much the label tells you, you need some general knowledge. Some of it is objective; like knowing that 2000 was a great year for wines from the South of France. Or that Chilean wines have become overpriced compared with other New World wines. A lot of it is subjective, such as knowing that you don't particularly like Chardonnay.

Foreign travel, the growing mass middle class, food and drink TV programmes, a general shift towards gourmet pleasures, lifestyle magazines and newspaper supplements have together created a knowledge base for 'real' wines (not fake brands).

It was an acquired taste, involving people installing a more expert mental model of wine. They learned what went with what food and occasions. They learned to use words like 'fruity' and 'oak'. They learned to appreciate wine and the styles that suited them. The old idea of wine was bound by social class to the upper and (upper) middle classes. The new idea of wine was based on quality of life, like olive oil and country walks . . . With this in mind, wine was able to grow on a wave of enthusiasm, rather than etiquette.

While much of this was spontaneous and informal, in response to growing interest and demand, there were some very smart marketers at the heart of this movement.

None was smarter than Oddbins. This company started in 1963 by entrepreneur Ahmed Pochee. It was originally a niche business, delivering bin-ends and oddments of wine to the restaurants and clubs of London's West End. In the 1980s, now owned by Seagram, they developed their consumer retail business, opening over 100 stores in key high street locations, with a distinctive brand identity based on Gerald Scarfe cartoons.

Oddbins have preserved the wood-and-sawdust feel of a wine merchant. But are also accessible and informal. They have loaded the retail environment with information, right down to hand-written tasting notes with most wines. Their friendly staff, who come across as fellow-wine enthusiasts, willingly dispense advice. True to their bin-end origins they compete keenly on price and special offers. They hold wine-tastings in store, as well as annual wine fairs in London, Edinburgh and Dublin. In the late 1990s they launched a website, which not only takes online orders, but has helpful facilities for the wine fan, such as a geographical 'grape finder'.

Oddbins has played a strong role at the heart of the wine market boom. What they have managed to build is an environment that treats beginners like experts. No wonder they've been International Wine Merchant of the Year, eleven times in the last thirteen years.

The development of the wine market is a great example of the general shift away from brand image and towards more sophisticated interactions and customer learning. They started with branded wine, advertised on TV, which ensured that customers did not actually have to know anything about wine. These wines were mostly marketed as 'making you look sophisticated'.

But as real customer knowledge and sophistication increased this became untenable. The declining role of image brands like Piat D'Or coincided with a growth (not a decline) of market volume and value. In place of product brands came more natural innate knowledge brands like 'New World' and 'Pinot Noir'.

In a sophisticated and fast-evolving market, new kinds of competitors with different business models and cultures emerge. In computing, IBM (for so long marketed as the safe choice) struggled to keep its position against not just clones, but companies such as Dell, Intel and Microsoft, which branded the new knowledge-rich ingredients, not the old 'boxes', and threatened to take the lion's share of the profits.

Brand image was invented, in some ways, to keep people in the dark. It suited manufacturers in mature markets (with little to offer by way of true difference and added value) to use their brand image to reinforce loyal habits and protect margins.

But the world is changing. People are too switched on and markets are too fast moving to rely on old-style branding to protect your share. These days you have to work at your customer relationships, not take them for granted.

FINDING THE INSTRUCTIONS

There are two main trends in knowledge media. Both could be described as forming an instruction manual for modern life. One is how to live well, including new traditions in lifestyle. The other is how to keep up with developments, such as new technologies.

The quality-of-life media boom encompasses: cooking; decorating; travel; health and beauty; the gym; fashion; grooming products; leisure and entertainment . . . In many of these sectors a growth in knowledge, confidence and sophistication has been the key driver of both volume and value, and the knowledge needs have been met by a booming lifestyle-media industry, principally through the old media of TV, magazines and books.

Many of the tricks of brand-image building apply to knowledge media. These 'tricks' were innate to human nature. Hijacked by advertising, they have now resumed their natural role in human culture. A good example is the personality as paragon.

Personalities were often used in image advertising to connote certain admirable qualities, which would supposedly rub off on the buyer of that brand. Famous people that were already admired, like film and pop stars, created a short-cut to these values. But advertising also created some stars of its own like 'the Oxo family' in the UK. Now this approach has worn quite thin. Hiring a famous spokesperson for your brand is these days interpreted by media-literate audiences as little more than a ploy, and an expensive one at that. Only if they are properly connected with the business does it make sense.

Personalities in knowledge media assume the role of being 'master' to our apprentice. Like Martha Stewart's role as decor guru in the US. This goes beyond teaching explicit facts. It's the way they do things and talk about them that often matters more. Go to any bookshop and you find an array of differently positioned celebrity chefs – from the Naked Chef (= hip, rock and roll), to the Two Fat Ladies (= Victorian, traditional) and many points in between. Where brand image was, learning is now, not only replacing it, but also turning its sophisticated creative devices to new uses.

The other leading edge of knowledge media is helping people to keep up with progress. This learning curve is critical for success in launching new technologies. People already feel like they are stretched to the limit in knowing how to use the gadgets they have now. They had just mastered e-mail when along came mobile e-mail, instant messaging and other new communication tools.

The thing which I think many new technologies often miss is that, this is, if anything, more of a cultural task than marketing cookery. At least celebrity chefs, while introducing new traditions into our everyday lives, had a reasonable base of knowledge and cultural values to build from. We all knew what it was like to throw a dinner party.

If you look at the 'killer applications' in IT carefully, you find they share one key quality. They build upon accepted human cultural forms. The personal computer offered a desktop environment. E-mail took office memos as their template. The mobile phone took on the existing fixed phone handset and developed into something akin to the Walkman. The Web adopted the design template of magazines and newspapers. Napster took the record collection online. PDAs resembled the pocket diary. In this way new technologies can quickly become intuitive.

The branding of new technology devices is subject to the same constraints. Things which have friendly human names, such as Apple, Palm, the mouse and voicemail, have done generally done very well, when compared with things which haven't. However well-branded and packaged new technologies are there is a Catch 22. The more that they offer new, better and different functionality, the more they will also present a learning challenge.

Computers have been well-served by their spearhead applications being office-based (where you get training). But consumer electronics have all too often landed us with an incomprehensible manual and left us to work it out.

If people stick to using just e-mail, the Web, word processing and other basic applications, it's hard to see why they will upgrade to the next generation of hardware like faster PCs and broadband connections.

It's vital that the whole industry takes its cue from the downturn in hardware sales to promote new (processor and bandwidth) intensive applications. Apple have been active in this, offering free multimedia training and launching some great new free (bundled) software like i-Movie and i-Tunes.

But as a whole, the IT industry seems to be leaving this to chance, which is dangerous, not only for the healthy development of the market as a whole, but also because it leaves the door wide open to entrants coming out of the multimedia industries. So far, the trailblazing challenger for the new converged media space has been Sony . . .

GO CREATE

Sony are probably the best marketers of new consumer technology in the world. So it was little surprise that they got into true level three marketing before the last century was out.

Sony had been moving towards computing for some time. PlayStation, which I'll look at in a later chapter, launched in 1995 and cleaned up in the computer gaming industry. Then they launched their successful notebook 'video-audio integrated operation' computers or VAIO.

The acronym, video-audio-integrated operation, should have set off alarm bells in Silicon Valley. Sony were gunning for the converged computing and multimedia space.

Now they have third generation (3G) mobile handsets on trial in Japan and have signed a joint venture agreement with Ericsson. The IT industry should now be in full panic mode. They have already been outflanked. In five years' time it is quite possible that Sony will take over the consumer IT industry.

And they already have a knowledge-marketing strategy in place to do so.

Sony committed three years ago to a new business strategy:

The group will invest heavily in research and development, capital equipment and facilities so that our electronics business . . . can evolve to best meet the needs of a network-centric world. We are committed to creating new lifestyles and providing new forms of enjoyment to people in the network-centric society of the twenty-first century.[77]

Sony, with the launch of VAIO, is the only company in the world with the full range of products for a converging media world. They make audio products like the MP3 Walkman, video products like their Digital Handicams, powerful multimedia platforms like the PlayStation 2 (PS2) and computers like the VAIO notebook and mobile phones too. They also have a big stake in content, with film, music and games software all being produced within the Sony group.

For this range of products to fulfil its potential they firstly needed to ensure that all the products integrate into a single multimedia system. This process is well underway, with their cross-platform proprietary memory sticks and i-Link cables (but still has some way to go, in evolving PS2 from a gaming machine to a fully networked multimedia station). But much more importantly they need to educate consumers to use all these new and compatible digital technologies.

Sony has chosen to base its marketing on inspiring and educating customers to get the most out of their products. The slogan in Europe is 'Go Create'. This campaign was launched through advertising and followed through with interactive marketing, which allowed people to explore the possibilities and products online. It is this commitment to customer education, which makes it a great campaign.

The 'Go Create' concept is a true knowledge brand. It is introducing a new mental model about using digital technologies. It connects these technologies with the trend to individual creativity and self-expression (metonymy), which was already evident in everything from fashion to home music studios. Their campaign features people making their own videos, recording their own ringtones for phones and so on. It doesn't look anything like plodding through a computer manual. It looks accessible and fun.

This is a great end-to-end example of the new approach to marketing that this book is advocating. Sony have created a new business model and consumer market, promoted this with a strong concept, 'Go Create', that taps into social learning and lifestyle trends and uses a range of educational media to follow through the initiative.

If I have one regret for them, it's the actual ads. Learning doesn't sit well in such compressed and passive media. I wish they had spent the money on more interesting ways to help us all go digital.

If they had to use advertising, then I would have been tempted to stimulate learning (rather than actually trying to educate people in situ). I'd have made it a platform for real user creativity, not made-up 'image' versions. They could play the world my home-made videos on primetime TV. With an e-mail address for submissions for next week's TV spots and magazine spreads. *Show n tell tv? Let people see u whole series of live TV ads? know what it can do.*

KNOWLEDGE MEDIA AS SERVICE

The knowledge media I've been describing so far have played a 'snow plough' role in developing new markets. It is also possible to integrate knowledge media with your existing market, to create significant added value and change the culture from within.

I came up with a strategy to do just this for Eurostar, based on their on-board media. Planes were low culture, I argued, 'video films and popcorn'. Eurostar should be high culture, 'reading and cappuccino'. That would effortlessly communicate the travel experience – time to reflect, more civilized, a whiff of the golden age of steam . . .

The idea was to create a three-hour, journey-length read, a bit like Penguin 60s. But they would be original commissions from authors who matched the different traveller segments – a Tom Peters thought piece for executives in business class. A racy yet twisted thriller set in Paris by Will Self in economy. Obviously there would be French language counterparts, only adding to the sophistication. These books would add value to the journey and would also convey a different 'mental model' of travelling = leisurely, European, sophisticated . . . It would turn Eurostar into a 'Waterstones on wheels'.

Lots of companies have their own media. And most use some knowledge branding; like IKEA's inspiring catalogue, British Airways' travel magazines, Nike's *Book of Lies*. Learning is much bigger on people's life agenda and so there's value in offering it as a complementary service in both senses of 'complementary' – free and synergistic.

Just think how much you could learn about one thing on a long flight. It's an unusual media length and very suited to a concentrated short course of learning. The complete history of the city you're visiting. A crash course in wine appreciation. The next twenty years of space exploration. Or basic conversation skills in the language of your destination.

For airlines this could be a valuable atom in their brand molecule. The flavours of knowledge could help create a different identity. It could connect to the Airmiles loyalty schemes. With my stack of current Virgin points I could be learning Japanese at their online campus.

Loyalty and learning might turn out to be good friends. I switch airlines with few qualms. It's actually quite nice to vary the ambience and service if you do a lot of flying. But I'd be much less likely to switch to a new Japanese course halfway through.

KNOWLEDGE FREE SAMPLES

Knowledge intensive businesses, like professional services, have an established marketing tradition of what they call 'thought leadership'.

The *McKinsey Quarterly* is probably the leading version of this. It's a great resource for researching an issue or industry. If you are in finance, the *Capco Journal* is the one to get your hands on. These free sample ideas can be a powerful part of your branding in their own right. This is exactly what the Boston Consulting Group achieved when they invented and popularized the 'Boston

Grid'. This grid is a way of analysing your portfolio of brands and deciding which to invest in. It is a simple diagram tool. And every time someone in business uses it, the Boston Consulting Group gets a 'free advert'.

Transaction and other costs are tending towards zero, as friction is taken out of the economy by inter-company efficiency. How will companies make money in this context? Through the one component whose value doesn't decrease – advice, or education, which is the same thing in a more empowering form.

Warren Buffet became the richest man in finance by doing just this. He advises investors, both privately through his company Berkshire Hathaway and publicly through books, seminars and publicity. What he offers are simple rules, and they seem to work.

KNOWLEDGE ACUPUNCTURE

The knowledge ecosystem around a business is often complex. Involving many different groups with different needs and different levels of knowledge. 'Knowledge acupuncture' is my term for a strategy which pinpoints parts of this system, where knowledge interventions can do the most good.

The computing industry has been blocked by school-teachers' technophobia. It's vital for the industry that the next generation grow up on computing. And political pledges have been made in many countries – notably the US – to put a computer in every classroom. But the computer in the classroom is only one part of the picture; it's just a 'spear'. Someone needs to train the 'hunt leaders' to train the others.

And that's exactly what Intel is doing. They have pledged $100 million to a 'Teach the Future' programme which will train 400,000 teachers in twenty countries how to use technology to improve teaching. Microsoft have pledged $345 million of free software to the programme.

This is a great win:win. 400,000 teachers should conservatively reach 100 million children over the next ten years. That's a dollar a kid, for Intel – even before philanthropy tax write-offs. Each of those children will have grown up with Intel and

Windows, which is an important investment for those companies' futures. My first serious encounters with a computer were with Apple IIe. I'm sure this partly explains why I'm still using Apple, twenty years later. There's a kind of imprinting that happens with technology, like the way ducklings pick the first creature they see as their 'mother'.

Targeted-knowledge branding can do many different things, at many different levels of the business. The pharmaceutical industry is fairly typical, in having a chain of constituents with different knowledge needs: research and development people, marketing (and distribution) people, doctors and pharmacists as knowledge intermediaries and, of course, the patients.

Everybody in this pyramid is an *expert*.

This is an ecosystem of different actors with different knowledge needs. It is increasingly individual patient-centred, -sensitive and, with patient power, -controlled. Information used to be 'pushed down the pipeline' – but there is now a circuit of knowledge:

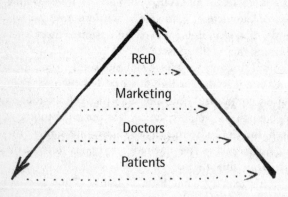

R&D

Marketing

Doctors

Patients

Fig. 39 | *A circuit of knowledge*

This creates all kinds of opportunities for targeted knowledge media:

- What if doctors each had their own website, where patients could check them out, make appointments, follow links to relevant education?

- What if R&D people could handle clinical trials over the Internet, making the process greatly more cost-efficient and also allowing drug effects to be tracked real-time?
- What if Web communities put patients with an ailment in touch with fellow sufferers?
- What if there was a toilet that could check your health and order your food accordingly?

All of these things have already happened, and there are many more possibilities.

SOME DO'S AND DON'TS IN KNOWLEDGE MEDIA

If you're going to do knowledge branding, think about how people learn best. One thing I've noticed about learning through my adventures with the music studio, is that no matter how good a manual or teacher is, it's far easier to grasp when you've received information from two or three sources, rather than just one. This allows you to look at the same thing from a number of angles and get a grip on what is really being described.

If you are packing an instruction manual with your computers, why not also ship the knowledge in different formats, such as videos of other beginners setting themselves up step by step, and lists of 'a hundred things to try with your new computer' so people can learn by discovery not rote? This would also allow for different people's different learning styles.

Knowledge branding is not a justification for producing yet more product- and company specific brochures and manuals. It's about sparks of genuine learning passing to customers.

From the point of view of trust and authenticity, it's vital to pitch your education at this kind of general wisdom level. Authenticity is the toughest issue in modern marketing. Because we've trained consumers over the last fifty years to be sceptical about the exaggerated claims, the image-building and the very motives of marketing.

There is a bar of authenticity for all marketing to leap over. This bar is raised especially high for education-as-marketing.

Education is about developing our minds, and we are very wary of being brainwashed. Several cases of consumer backlash, involving branded pseudo-education materials supplied to schools, have shown that this sensitivity needs to be heeded carefully. Marketing to children is a minefield anyway. With adults, a common-sense approach to what is acceptable should suffice.

Tea – an Example

Tea has some great medicinal selling points. For a start it contains theophylines. These relax the central nervous system. That's why shock victims are given tea not coffee.

Tea is also antisceptic. A dietary anthropologist discovered a few years ago that tea drinking nations (notably Britain) were the best placed to kick off the industrial revolution, because, in the days before modern medicine, there was a natural limit on the population of a city, before all kinds of nasty epidemics kicked in. In tea drinking cities, this limit is higher, because tea helps you ward off diseases.

Recent research has even shown that, of all the main ingredients in the English diet, tea is the most effective in preventing cancers, because tea makes DNA more stable, reducing mistakes in copying, which is a prime cause of cancer.[78]

It would be tempting as a tea marketer to take these facts and raise public awareness of tea's health benefits. But this would probably minimize their impact. It could even be counter-productive – tea is already more popular than medicine. The bigger opportunity is to use tea's medicinal qualities to place it at the heart of the growing New-Age culture. Rather than making tea seem like a hospital, make it seem like a yoga school.

If I were to advise a tea-brand now, I'd be inclined to wrap the knowledge brand up in a healthy living and balance strategy. Tea and calm go together. So why not teach people yoga, feng shui, even Taoism. Tea has been hammered in recent years by the advances of coffee drinking (just as it was in the 1980s). Now it could ride back on a wave of gentleness. Stress being public enemy number one, this could be a very big opportunity.

Knowledge branding can – and should, in my view – be much bigger than the 'facts':

- bigger ideas are more exciting and involving
- they create stronger cultural significance or 'brand values'
- they relate to people's motivations (eg to be less stressed) more fully
- they avoid the suspicion that you're just trying to persuade people to buy more
- they always contain the grain of truth anyway (eg that tea is healthier than coffee).

I can foresee all this having a remarkably positive effect on companies.

Educational establishments tend to have high principles and vision. Commercial organizations tend to have momentum and energy. A constructive fusion of the two would be a potent force for social change.

Just as education is a potent force for individual change. Did you know that in the UK, doctors are now able to prescribe education courses to tackle depression?

KNOWLEDGE BRANDING THE LIFE ACCOUNT FROM MOTHER

Karen Wendel, a partner at Capco, sat a group of us down at breakfast in San Francisco and produced a single dollar bill. 'What is this?' she asked. And she's right to ask. The more you think about it, the more intangible and strange money becomes.

A dollar is actually a number of different things: it's a unit of measure; it's a store of value; it's a unit of exchange. And things get even more interesting when it's an e-dollar, sitting in an account somewhere in cyberspace, or an even more 'virtual' dollar, like a share option. At this level, money is very hard to separate from other sorts of information.

The mental models of money we ordinary banking customers

have are, by comparison, in the dark ages. We still think of our dollars, pounds, euros as like the pocket-money coins we had in our 'piggy banks' when we were kids.

We don't have an intuitive notion of e-money, which is more like quantum money – a virtual entity made of potential value, with a number of 'energy levels' depending on context and liquidity. The same kinds of paradoxes and new laws involved in valuing companies also govern our personal financial lives. Or rather, they would, if we didn't manage our finances by old-fashioned 'Newtonian' rules.

The net result is alienation. We aren't in touch with what money means in our lives. We badly need ideas to integrate monetary value and other goods – quality of life, ethical values, future plans, security and knowledge. We need ideas to understand the world and which parts we can really affect and we need ideas to help us to make decisions.

People could get these ideas by a long and painful process of studying finance. When I started the Capco project, I bought several textbooks on the subject. Unfortunately they were too dry and detailed, even for a highly-motivated consultant trying to get his head around a project, and it takes at least ten years, I suspect, to get beyond detailed rote learning, to the kind of overview enjoyed by people like Karen Wendel.

At the same time, I also had a stack of books about money from a more imaginative point of view: a history of money; a book on how 'greed and fear' drive capital markets because they drive individual investor decisions; a book on the Internet-bubble phenomenon and a book on the psychology of money. These books were fascinating, for a specific reason – they linked money to other fields of human thinking.

That's what an idea is, a combination of two previously unconnected domains. It's how image branding worked (eg linking a car and the stereotyped personality of the country of origin: 'Nicole?', 'Oui papa?') and it's how knowledge branding can work too.

Here's an idea for Mother, our New-Age Bank and its Life Account . . .

Financial karma

Financial karma (FK) would aim to do for money, what feng shui did for decorating. Karma is a system of balances between people and the universe. If you do bad things you get bad Karma and this comes back and affects you negatively, if not in this life then in the next – what goes around comes around.

Karma is a knowledge system. It teaches you to quantify or at least objectify decisions and behaviour. Just like money it 'labels' human actions with value. To people's naïve models of money, FK could add simple, dynamic rules and structures.

This would have to be playful, fun, tongue in cheek, faux-hippy, rather than serious. FK in this context is a fun analogy to teach people to manage their finances. I see the Mother brand as having 'soul' but not being too mystical for real. At the end of the day it's a bank. Think 'Ben & Jerry's' not 'the Moonies'.

Financial karma makes an equation between monetary value and the human value which resides in: education; relationships; work; personal development; autonomy and helping others . . . If you were that kind of person it might also reside in status and glamour etc. but that kind of person is not ready for Mother.

FK would be a hub concept of Mother's wise teaching. You would start your relationship with the bank with a free financial karma seminar. From here you'd progress to planning your life and finances using a model which values what you value. Your account statements might include karma levels as well as money levels.

Over time people would become intuitive managers of their intangible assets and potential, as well as their current net cash flow. They'd learn to invest in self-development rather than to just 'save for a rainy day', and they'd also learn a lot about themselves. Financial-karma instruction would take people deeper into areas like how to match their financial strategies to their lifestage and goals. It's not a one-size fits all solution – it is intrinsic to the karma concept that every soul in the universe is unique, as well as connected.

Financial karma is an atom in the Mother brand molecule. It needs promoting in its own right. This could be done through teaching materials, seminars and so on, for customers. Which probably would generate huge word of mouth, but it might also need some kind of visible public launch.

Perhaps the same valuation could be applied to a published index. Which showed public institutions and celebrities' karma rating, based on recent news stories and judged by an advisory group with ethical credentials. The rating would boil down to a number – the 'FK' (like IQ). Imagine you bought a paper today and it contained the following scores: George W. Bush FK –93, Tokyo FK –16, Nicole Kidman FK +15, Tea FK +57 . . .

BRINGING KNOWLEDGE BRANDING TO LIFE – SOME STARTING POINTS

1 What's your best recent learning experience? What made it so compelling? How could you apply that to an activity that made a light go on in your customers' minds?
2 What one piece of knowledge, if it were widely held, would transform your market? This doesn't have to mean 'information'. It might mean something that experts value but us mortals can't grasp or perceive. Like the beauty of the simplicity of a piece of design? Or a taste we haven't acquired. Can you find a way to bridge this knowledge gap?
3 How can learning in your market be more self-directed, just-in-time and context-driven? Like those gallery audio tapes, with artists and critics discussing the work? Or the latest idea from Sweden, mobile society – sponsored phoneline numbers by every picture to call on your mobile if you want to know more.
4 Might other parts of life be a better learning context? If Apple taught people to think more logically and debug problems, that could help them in installing and using the software. And save a huge amount of money on unnecessary technical support. Why not teach these skills in everyday life contexts, rather than computing contexts?

There are some essential skills to debugging which are very generally applicable – like breaking the process into small steps to isolate the problem. These could form the basis of a great TV game show, or a series of intriguingly hybrid programmes: *Logical Cooking, Logical Parenting, Logical Soccer* etc.

5 Could knowledge be the added-value service that allows you to 'give your products away'? If your company was transformed into a school, what would you teach?

6 Could you add value to your existing customer experience by making it knowledge rich? Why don't supermarkets teach people while they buy? They could inform us about geography, economics, or ecology, for example, very easily.

7 What are the 'rules of thumb' that your internal experts know, but which customers generally don't? What if there were knowledge tools in clothes shops? What if they told me what proportion of my budget I should spend on shoes? What current fashions suit different body shapes? What colours work best on a first date? What else should I think about? If Oddbins can do it, why not H&M?

8 Who coaches your customers? How can you help them do it more effectively?

9 People learn deeply when they hit an anomaly or difficulty. Do you do *too much* to shield them from these opportunities? Do you let people learn, or do you take over with quick fixes? Every enquiry to a service line is an opportunity to teach deeper skills.

10 If people in the (near) future valued knowledge ten times as much as they do now, and image ten times less, how would they rate your current marketing programmes?

12

REALITY MEDIA

What role can design play on the next level of marketing? Certainly a very different role from the previous image era, when decadent 'designer' packaging gave the industry a bad name. To make the new role clear, I suggest 'reality media' as a heading.

This chapter is about building new mental models by shaping reality in people's immediate perception and experiences. Consider how man-made our everyday world is. It is estimated that there are twice as many 'species' of human objects now as biological species, and that a contemporary individual has to be able to distinguish between roughly 25,000 man-made items, in their immediate living environment.[79]

The man-made-reality around us is rich in meaning. Buildings tell us if they are impressive, friendly, modern, for children, or clinical, and buildings also programme daily life, forcing our thinking and behaviours along certain lines. If you want to change someone's mental model, the simplest and most direct way is to change the physical reality around them. That's why we have awaydays in business, after all.

As the phrase suggests, 'reality media' are useful in situations where you need to establish the reality of some concept. That can mean either developing your tangible differences, like the i-Mac. Or, turning an intangible concept into a tangible, vivid experience, like the Web browser.

GO FLY

I was in the middle of trying to explain my vision of New Marketing at a conference, when in walked one of the best examples in the world, in the form of the next speaker: Barbara Cassani, CEO of Go, the low cost airline. Cassani's talk worked seamlessly with mine because IKEA was where they got their inspiration for reinventing flying.

Go was launched in 1998 by British Airways, in response to the threat posed by new low-cost European operators like easyjet. After three years the business was sold off to Venture Capitalist 3i who supported the existing management team in a buyout. Go now flies to 25 European cities and after several years of investment in expansion, looks set to become profitable.

The Go concept is – just like IKEA – to offer high a value concept at low prices. To achieve this they took the standard airline apart and interrogated each element. Meals were expensive, and not that popular with customers either, so Go replaced them with what Cassani is proud to call 'the best coffee and cookies in the air'. The coffee (which costs roughly what it would on the ground) is served in cafetieres and is indeed good.

This is the value engineering approach done really well. Similar initiatives have covered the amount of time planes spend on the ground (very little) and online booking. Here, Go has one of the fastest websites in the UK (it downloads in only 0.6 seconds, on average). Why? Because people hate waiting more than they love all the flashy graphics and animation used by many airline competitors. Go has many other features which both save money and improve the experience. Like the fact it has no tickets, allocating seats at check-in (so you always get to sit with the rest of your party). As a result Go is exceptionally cheap. When I fly Go to Copenhagan, for example, it costs as little as £100, whereas the standard day return fare from other airlines can be more than £500.

But how do you sell something that's incredibly cheap (in cost) without appearing cheap (as in 'cheap and tacky')? In some countries that's not a contradiction, but in UK culture people expect to 'get what you pay for'. That's where reality design comes in.

Go have managed this through one of the best identity and experience design programmes I've ever seen. It's based on coloured circles that look a bit like Damien Hirst paintings. These give it a premium feel, while also offering the perfect platform for a fast website, great looking planes, complete with award-winning magazines (which act as destination guides). The identity is applied consistently to everything they do.

Go applies the same magic formula used by IKEA, MUJI, Zara, Swatch and others. In modern design, simplicity and discipline means not only style but also (potentially) low prices.

In any new concept, there's usually a blend of old and new. With a few elements that summarize what's really new and special. Making these new elements explicit, visible and *real* can create white space.

Other notable examples include:

- BMW which has revived its fortunes by making a better range of exciting experiences (i.e. cars). Like the Z3 sports car with it's menacing side grilles or the newly revamped Mini. On top of this it has created exciting media in which to meet this range in all its glory. The Z3 featured in a Bond movie in place of the customary Aston Martin. More recently BMW have moved up a gear and made their own movies – shorts directed by award winning film-makers like Ang Lee and Guy Ritchie. Needless to say, each film takes place in and around a BMW. These can be downloaded from BMW's website in the US.
- Pizza Express, which put the kitchen in the restaurant to emphasize that each pizza was hand-made, not just pulled out of the freezer like the other chains. In the process they have reinvented the eating out market in the UK by positioning themselves between fast food joints and formal restaurants.
- Apple, which created cutting-edge designer accessories that also happen to be computers, and brought them out in generations (eg G4). Their key audience are design and multimedia professionals. Apple understands their tastes as

well as their needs (like faster rendering of images, which is the really boring bit of design) like no other 'box' maker. Steve Jobs even went as far as to say, 'we don't sell computers, we sell design'.

CREATURES OF HABITAT

The sociobiologist, E. O. Wilson, spent a lifetime studying ants. One of his insights that I particularly liked was the idea that ants are 'agriculturists'. I'm used to seeing them as architects, soldiers and foragers, but I'd never thought of them as farmers. Just this one word completely changed my mental model of ant society.[80]

Ants, bees, beavers, nesting birds and others have another parallel with human beings. They encode their culture (biologists would say their protoculture) in habitats, and like humans, they have each re-adapted as a species to fit that habitat.

Beavers change the whole geography of a valley. But beavers are also the servants of their dams. Which is why they have wood-cutting teeth.

This circular process is called gene-culture co-evolution. Human physiques have altered in line with man-made artefacts – like clothing and housing (hairless apes), language (big brains), tools and fabrication (manual dexterity).

The rate of innovation in human habitats in recent centuries has left physical evolution trailing behind. Ergonomics, fitting habitats to our hunter-gatherer frames, has become paramount. Cars are designed with reaction times and automatic reflexes in mind. ABS brakes allow for our tendency to 'kick out' in reaction to danger. Conversely, changes in our artefacts are a key driver of changes in mind and society. Just having an Internet in the world moves us towards freedom of information, informality and networks.

Habitat, artefacts and other fabricated culture are vital parts of learning and thinking. Cognitive scientists put it this way: a lot of our thinking is done outside our bodies. That's why changing the immediate reality *automatically* changes mental models.

Technology extends our physical capabilities but also our mental capabilities. We have memory devices, like writing. We have calculating devices, like calculators obviously.

We have information processing devices, like diaries, and devices which encode our customs, like walls and boundaries which 'say' what should be kept separate.

Things that help us to think are called 'cognitive artefacts'. And they have their own IQ, in today's demanding and fast-changing human habitat; the artefacts around us can be very smart or very dumb, in their anticipation of the users' cognitive strengths and weaknesses. The classic example is the almost-impossible-to-programme video player:

> I have little difficulty interpreting the relatively simple procedures contained in the VCR's instruction manual. What I cannot do well, and the computer excels at, is to recall and consistently execute these programmes at later times when they are needed.[81]

Research into cognitive artefacts has looked into areas such as:

- how objects become part of memory systems. Expert bar-staff remember drinks orders by selecting glasses.
- how people offload cognitive demands into artefacts. Like pilots, who use 'speed bug' markers on the dials, to show critical speeds for takeoff.[82]

One of my recent projects was for IKEA Storage – an area which covers all the things which we use to put our belongings in (about a third of what they sell).

One concept we discussed was the idea of 'home as physical database'. The storage experiences in physical world are what's behind the 'desktop' and 'filing' and 'bin' in personal computing. The idea was to drive the analogy in reverse. The hypothesis was that IKEA could produce 'smart storage'. Using new Bluetooth technology they could create storage that remembers where you put your keys or notebook, or where you've put that tea-set from aunt Julia, who's arriving any minute now.

THE NUCLEAR FAMILY

Anthropologists think that the subdivision of human environments plays a fundamental role. It not only says 'keep these apart', but also says 'these two domains are distinct'. Many of the walls and fences in society are there to draw a distinction.

A modern social example, now under challenge, is the 'nuclear family'. The separation of mother, father and children, from the extended family of grandmothers, maiden aunts, and in-laws was a historical novelty. It suited the flexible, mobile workforce needed by factories. Whereas the extended family was ideal for a farm, embedding the social ties and teamwork needed when the household *was* the workforce.

The underlying distinction is home/work. The older notion of 'living place = workplace' was not just a farming thing. It extended into cities too. If you worked in a bakery, you lived in the baker's house, and a large part of your pay was the food and lodgings. This work-commune approach still applies to pockets of industrial age life; like the army base, cult retreat and university campus.

The home/work distinction is now eroding; 'taking your work home', 'working from home', even 'work-life balance'. Perhaps because the factory or office – separate from dwelling – is an overhead that has little to do with knowledge work productivity, and modern technology means you don't necessarily have to gather to communicate with colleagues.

We took advantage of this trend in the reality branding of St Luke's. In our office we tried to make things as homely as possible, with project rooms full of sofas instead of personal desks and offices, plus rest and stimulation areas with table-tennis, pool tables and a communal garden area. We had special days when everyone would redecorate the space, to increase the sense of personal connection with and ownership of the space.

MAKING THE INTANGIBLE TANGIBLE

When Al Gore called the Internet 'the information super-highway' he was making a metaphoric link for something hard to visualize and harder to love (at that time). It was a canny connection, given the love affair between Americans and the big open roads.

But the actual Internet experience at the time, was still a bit distant from life, until the World Wide Web came along. In this Web we had lots of familiar sights – and a *home* page.

Too often design in company websites has been used to try and project an attractive brand image. Like on the ill-starred boo.com website where every page seemed to take aeons to load, because it was so festooned with graphics and animations.

Contrast this with the elegant, functional simplicity of Amazon.com. Where the design of features like 1-Click™ ordering and reader recommendations add tremendous value and make the difference between this and your local bookstore manifest.

Although people can make abstract sense of the virtual, we are grounded in the physical. We are designed to physically interact with each other and our environments. This is our primary means of 'grasping' the world.

There is huge scope for computer-human interaction to reflect a much fuller range of our bodily experiences and interactions. The desktop-and-mouse environment was a good first step, but in many ways has now become a limit on this evolution. Interesting new peripherals and interfaces have started to emerge, like the vibrating feedback on some computer game handsets and some sound design tools that respond to hand movements. No doubt many of the breakthroughs to come will tackle specific issues at first, like wearable mobile computing, disability applications and robotics. Aural branding (for instance the sound that your computer makes when it boots up) has been a hot topic in design for several years, and the potential for advanced voice recognition systems (such as have been developed for jet fighter pilots) will hit the consumer markets and quite possibly do away with the keyboard for good.

There is a connection between graphics and brand image that runs deep into what visual perception is – a place where illusions as well as visions can be created. In culture in general, we have seen a growing emphasis on the other senses: massage, gourmet food, aromatherapy, body piercing, new fabrics, music rhythms . . . It may be that many of the opportunities for reality design are just 'out of sight', in these other areas.

REALITY BRANDING THE LIFE ACCOUNT FROM MOTHER

Until recently, giving someone your money to look after was a big leap of faith. In financial crises there could be 'a run on the bank', with people queuing down the street trying to get their money out, before a collapse. That's probably why the traditional bank branch uses such classical architecture – to imply permanence. Unfortunately this is also very paternal in overtone, reinforcing the negative view that banks look down on us.

Bank branches also have certain practical considerations coded in. Like the security screens we have in British banks. Or the security doors in French banks. They don't seem to have prevented armed robberies. But they certainly add to the customers' feeling of being naughty children, in the face of a stern, impassive father figure.

One option for Mother might be to do away with physical branches altogether. Go straight for the Internet. But, as I found with First Direct, the telephone bank, a lack of physical presence can deter people. A lot of people in our research found this 'absence' unsettling, and people have plenty of security worries about Internet-only banking.

Mother would need to create the opposite impression to the traditional stern bank, of warmth, welcome, a safe haven, a place to relax away from the stresses of modern life. Mother's role in life is to coach people, to enable them to make more of their life and funds. So this would be a natural new framework for their reality branding.

Instead of bank branches why not start with . . .

Karma Cafes

These would occupy cheap sites in the high streets, which many retailers are leaving in favour of out of town hyper-markets, Internet stores and so on.

A Karma Cafe would be centred on a lounge, with free entry to anyone with a Mother banking card. Here you could arrange to meet with advisors to discuss financial and life plans, if you wanted. There would be terminals for the usual banking services like cash withdrawal and deposit. But you'd be free to just relax and browse through books, multi-media and online terminals. Or just to relax, full stop.

At the front, and open to the general public would be the cafés. These would of course sell (vegetarian) food and the income from catering would probably at least partly finance these outlets. The cafés would sell tea (in many healthy varieties) but not coffee.

These sites would also double as natural health centres, yoga schools, de-stressing zones and so on (all out-sourced to excellent local providers). Alongside these would be hard-edged enablers of personal financial growth; career and education advisors, recruitment and management coaching specialists. There would also be conference facilities, for the many seminars that Mother would run.

PUTTING REALITY BRANDING INTO PRACTICE – SOME STARTING POINTS

1 Why not audit all the places your customer touches your industry? What do the structures mean? For instance, banking behind thick security glass means 'we don't trust any of you'.

2 What preconceptions do you need to shatter to build the desired mental model? BT after privatization demonstrated that they were no longer a slow-moving bureaucracy, by fixing any out of order phone boxes within hours (rather than weeks).

3 What adjacent possibilities could your market extend into? Voicemail 'takes a message'. Karaoke packaged 'singing along'. Amazon formalized 'comparing notes'. Yo Sushi – the conveyer-belt sushi bar – lets you see what other diners are eating, before choosing your own food.

4 What boundaries does your market assume, that are of declining relevance in society in general? Like the boundary between home and work. Or between young and old.

5 What are the distinctions your reality design misses? Business travel is different on the way there (preparing) and on the way back (unwinding). Yet we're all lumped in together. Imagine a drinks party where people brought laptops to work on. Or that someone started on Tequila slammers in a meeting. This can't be right.

6 How are you manifesting what's new in what you do? The VW Bug launched an Internet ordering service in the US. To emphasize this, they only offered one colour – a bright yellow you couldn't get anywhere else than on the Net. How cool is that!

7 Why not switch from 'saying' to 'doing'? Virgin Atlantic's advertising suggests that media celebrities love 'Upper Class'. Wouldn't it be better if they gave free flights for anybody A-List? Imagine the word of mouth every time a passenger sat behind Bruce Willis.

8 What is the warmest, most nostalgic reality that would map onto your market as an added experience? What's your equivalent of the baked bread smells pumped into supermarkets, or the desktop graphical user interface?

9 What latent metaphors in your market could be turned into actual experiences? Many hotels describe themselves as having all the comforts of home. What about a hotel that really is 'a home from home' (because they customize your room with your favourite pictures, music, toiletries and that new movie you've been dying to see)?

10 How could you reach out into people's lives in new forms? What about media entertainment products that could build similar ideas in people's minds? If your 'desired mental model' was a TV show, what would it be? Starbucks, for instance, should be producing a new light entertainment show to eclipse *Friends*.

13

DIALOGUE MEDIA

Dialogue media are all those places where customers and companies can have a two-way interaction. Face-to-face service and phone lines are obvious examples. New media examples include e-mail, bulletin boards and interactive systems.

In the brand-image era, what was emphasized was consistency which led to inflexible, scripted encounters. Like when you buy a burger and the person serving says 'have a nice day'. This is minimal interaction. Whereas the point of good conversation and all other forms of dialogue, for level three marketing, is to build new mental models together.

What happens in good conversation is that two minds, by an intricate dance of exchanges, come to share a mental model. A good conversation leads both parties to a new third space. There is no dominant flow or focus. It is all those little cues, angles and insights that come from a random walk together that gradually reveal the great structure.

Dialogue in this sense is only an option when the company is as willing to be changed by the outcome as the customer. The prime example is any company whose product is partly made by customers. This is also potentially a good way of doing live market research and getting continuous feedback on an uncertain course. It is a good basis for handling a crisis situation, or the fallout from a dramatic change of direction, and it's also an essential ingredient of any service or knowledge (= knowledge exchange) business.

BIG BROTHER IS LISTENING TO YOU

One of the best demonstrations of the power of dialogue media came from the hit TV show *Big Brother*. The show originated in the Netherlands and has been aired in fifteen countries, across Europe and as far away as Australia and the US.

The crucial element of the show – the single feature which differentiates it from other reality shows – is the fact that viewers can vote on who gets kicked out of the house. This creates a level of public involvement unparalleled outside general elections. In the UK, *Big Brother* was aired during a general election and achieved higher ratings than the nightly news (4.4 million viewers versus 4.3 million for the *News at Ten*).

The show takes TV voyeurism to new levels too. In the original Dutch series, contestants were caught on camera having sex, and this must partly account for the high ratings – over 50 per cent of the Dutch TV audience tuned in for the live final.

The levels of voting have been equally impressive. 16 million votes were cast during the second UK series and at least 1 million viewers watched the house by video-streaming on the Web, as well as on television.

Big Brother is a show co-created by the audience. Witness the tactical voting over many weeks in the UK to keep one contestant (Paul) in the house, when all the housemates wanted him to leave. This ability to 'play God' is what makes it so special.

HOW CONVERSATION BUILDS TRUST

As well as being involving, dialogue also has a powerful side effect – it builds trust.

Conversations often start with a 'handshake'. Originally, this gesture of offering an open palm was probably a way of showing that you carried no weapons. There is no trust without a basic level of information about each other. To all intents and purposes, exchange is what a relationship is. After a handshake, hug or nod, we say 'hello'. And after that, depending on how deep the relationship is, we swap varying amounts of information. 'How are you?' is enough for a neighbour. But if that were all you said to your mum . . .

The principle of exchange as the basis of trust and developing a deeper relationship is a well-established one in social psychology. There's an old saying that if you want someone to do you a big favour ask them to do you a small favour first. Researchers set out to test this theory.[83] What they did was to test the effect of asking people to comply with a small request (to take part in a small survey) with compliance to a big request (allowing people to come to the home and 'enumerate every object you have there'). It worked; people who had agreed to the small request were far more likely to agree to the big one (52.8 per cent) than people who were just contacted with the big request directly (22.2 per cent).

But that's not to say you should pester your already busy customers with idle chat. Or, God forbid, phone them to ask a small favour as the prelude to trying to sell them something big. Your customers are smart, and never more so than in conversation.

Done the right way, good conversation can just be a joy in itself.

I was once asked for some ideas to feed into a project for London Transport on becoming customer centred. My main proposal was that they teach staff to be comics. Literally; send them off to holiday camps and teach them to tell jokes and keep people amused. There were already examples of this – for instance a famous announcer at London Waterloo who was very funny in a *Good Morning Vietnam* sort of way. Commuters are stressed and things are always going to break down from time to time. Why not help them relax and see the funny side? This is a terribly British way of defusing stressful and awkward situations. And I think it would have suited them.

Southwest Airlines, a low-cost US operator has built up a cult following by reframing cabin service into entertainment (added character is their equivalent of Go's added style). I love their famous landing announcement, 'and remember, no-one values your dollars as much as Southwest'. If it works for them why not London Transport?

What people value in conversation beyond the immediate enjoyment of the process is information. That's what we usually mean when we say someone 'is really fascinating'. We mean that, beyond the empathy, we sense we have a lot to learn from this person.

Companies have a lot of knowledge locked away that customers would find fascinating. And conversely companies have everything to gain from learning from customers in a closer, more attentive and fine-scale way. And this feedback loop, taken far enough can create whole new fields of opportunity and value . . .

I worked on the plan for a business-to-business Internet start-up called Zoolo.com. Zoolo's business idea was to take all the non-core activities of small businesses and make them efficient and cost-effective. Small businesses pay over the odds for all kinds of things, like stationery and bank charges, phone calls and insurance. Half of all small businesses go bust in the first two years. The main reason is cash-flow – they simply run out of money. Well-funded and managed businesses have a far higher survival rate.

Businesses have to submit their information and be vetted somehow every time they apply for credit, insurance or some other financial instrument. Zoolo would hold all their information and assign a credit/risk profile. We could do this by virtue of running small business financial back offices – billing, factoring and so on.

This would save the financial organizations a lot of time and effort. Our systems would work with their standards, and they would have the opportunity to bid not just for 'Bloggs the architects' but hundreds or thousands of similar businesses. In return they would offer much better terms – the kind of terms they would generally offer bigger companies with these systems and this volume of business.

The amount of information submitted would defend Zoolo from competitors. Just as people don't move bank accounts that often because there is too much information – standing orders, direct debits, etc. – invested in the current relationship.

It would only achieve the savings once it was an established business, with tens of thousands of customers. How could we get past the Catch 22 at the start of every relationship – 'I don't know you, so why should I trust you?' – and achieve these sorts of numbers?

My idea was to start the relationship with pure information. By offering a benchmark survey. One of the problems of running a small business is lack of management information. As a small central London marketing consultancy, it would be great to have a report outlining how my business costs compare with others, telling me for example that I have good value insurance and premises, but I am paying double the average for my IT and accountancy. That would give me something to work from.

We could offer exactly that, if you think about it, just by collecting information. 'Send us details of what you spend on the following . . . and we'll send you back a benchmark report comparing you with similar businesses.' How? By aggregating the data. The more people we got to reply, the more robust and/or fine-scale we could go.

CO-CREATION

Linux developed a whole operating system through dialogue between individuals.

Slashdot reports on what's happening in IT. It's published on the Net and written by the readers, who are IT insiders. In this way they have often managed to scoop the conventional journalistic media.

A milder version of co-creation is getting customers – as IKEA says – to do some of the work for some of the reward. Some of the work could include anything your company does – from design to distribution, and the easiest thing to swap is information.

When you look at your consumers this way, all kinds of opportunities both for you to help them through better information, and for them to help you, become apparent.

DIALOGUE BRANDING THE LIFE ACCOUNT FROM MOTHER

The first thing you'd notice when you walked into a Karma Cafe is the buzz of happy chatter. Conversation is key to the Mother model. The service would have more in common with management coaching and psychoanalysis than 'pension sales'.

That would be a hollow branding exercise, if the internal reality didn't match. So it implies an unusual recruitment and training programme. Staff would be taught the skills to listen, intervene and empower. They would also gain huge job satisfaction and personal development opportunities from the process. It's no good setting up your stall as 'the enlightened bank' (Mother's corporate slogan?) if you don't have enlightened people.

Mother, being an enlightened learning organization, understands that the best people to learn from are often people who are only a few steps ahead of you in the learning process, who have 'been there'.

The service targeting would be built on life stages and situations, with employees being linked with small groups of customers who had also just had a baby or worked as a free agent or were also a year from retirement.

An online network of fellow customers could help others research future life plans, by drawing on people's visions, decisions and experiences. There could be a case study database, even a contacting service (subject to consent). So whether you were thinking of setting up your own small business or looking ahead to retirement, you could find video diaries from people like you who had made a similar move.

This is a great possibility for network learning, incidentally. Why is it that every time we get into something new we have to repeat all the same little mistakes as others, simply because we are in unfamiliar territory? Some kind of vivid 'life as it is lived' journal database could help people avoid reinventing the wheel. It would also reinforce the learning of contributors by getting them to reflect on what they've learned.

PUTTING DIALOGUE BRANDING INTO ACTION – SOME STARTING POINTS

1 What processes do you use to make conversation part of your strategy development? Most companies would use focus groups, which put you the other side of a two-way mirror. A company in Amsterdam hosts conversations between clients like adidas and creative opinion leaders, which often leads to co-created ideas for 'happenings'.

2 Do you value the time spent in conversation with your market and tuning into customers' lives? Do you encourage volunteering, which gets people out there in the real world and builds empathy? A study by the Talent Foundation found that volunteering by employees correlates highly with Innovation.[84]

3 Why not audit all the exchanges of information between customers and your company? Where are the learning hotpoints? How do you transfer knowledge to partners and customers? How do they share information? How do you get their feedback?

4 Do the people in your company who talk with customers have charismatic conversation skills? Could you teach them? Do they have journalistic reporting skills? Could you give them an outlet to feedback their reflections?

5 You might think resistance to conversation comes from the customer. But customers are usually happy to talk when they have time. The resistance, in my experience, is often a kind of shyness in companies. IKEA store managers set a great example. One told me how he invited an unhappy customer in for a coffee, to talk about how IKEA could improve. (Smart move, as the customer turned out to be a local radio DJ.)

6 How could customers get more involved in your business? They might not mind doing more of the work if this saves them time and money in the long run. Have

you ever looked at your business in an IKEA way – seeing customers as part-time employees?

7 How could you create a neutral space where you and your non-customers can start a dialogue? One idea we discussed at an IKEA workshop in Spain was attracting older people to the stores on quieter days, by hosting day-time social events, like Bingo.

8 Does every customer have a variety of accessible ways to give feedback and get more involved, on the Web, by phone, fax or e-mail, a video booth, in real life? Some newspapers in America hold 'town meetings' to get the community's inputs.

9 How could the information customers give you be aggregated and fed back to them to add value to their lives? Could you help them 'benchmark'? Or to get inspiration from what other customers have done with their homes or lives?

10 Do you have an intelligence network to collect reports from the edges of society where change is happening? Studies in population biology show that new 'strains' often develop in partly isolated communities (where they are concentrated). Which niche groups are most likely to develop something new in your market?

14

MEMETIC MEDIA

Memetic media provide ways for people to copy each other. What these 'media' have in common is that they give people an opportunity to see what others are doing or thinking and copy it. A meeting place is a potential memetic medium, as is a bulletin board, an opinion poll, on a news report and, above all, the billions of conversations that take place between individuals. Few of these media can be bought, but they can be sought out and 'memes' (the bits that people will copy) can be designed to be contagious in these contexts.

There's nothing new about ideas spreading this way. Word of mouth and copying each others' actions are probably the oldest human media. But with interpersonal communication tools like e-mail, plus the fundamental uncertainty about our traditions and how to live, the importance of memetic trends has probably grown.

We need to distinguish between mere fashions, which belong in the brand-image era (and which these days tend to be quite transient) and deeper shifts in underlying mental models, which can drive the success of level three marketing. The fact that a new hairstyle or way of dressing can catch on is not all that significant. But a deeper trend like that of 'New Man' and male grooming is highly significant and worth developing.

There is, in my view, a danger in the black art of creating a brand image 'buzz' through viral marketing. This usually means getting 'opinion formers' to adopt the product, in the hope that others will copy them. Games makers have targeted 'alpha pups' (cool school children). Fashion brands have asked style leaders to adopt their product (although this has backfired on occasion, for example, G-Shock's attempts to get DJs to wear their new watch were refused point blank). Drinks marketers have gone as far as hiring people as 'ambassadors' to order their brand loudly at trendy bars.

These kinds of tactics are cheating. They are trying to fool people into thinking something is hip when it's not. People are already brand-image-manipulation-resistant. It's only a matter of time until the sneaky side of viral marketing is found out and the inevitable backlash ensues. The more enlightened level three approach is to create something counter-intuitive but readily believable and copyable. Not to force-feed people but to make a new concept appetising and highly digestible.

THE Y2K BUG

The Y2K bug is a great example of how new concepts can spread through memetic means. It was not overtly packaged or marketed by any individual or group. It is a spontaneous example of what it takes to make a succesful 'meme' catch on like wildfire.

The primary factor in meme success is the content (what mental model is being transmitted, how does it fit existing concepts and how does it put a new spin on reality?). Secondly, memes have factors which boost their transmission. This dual structure makes the 'viral ideas' analogy which is often applied to memes especially apt; a virus consists of some RNA code (partly mimicking what's already there in a cell and partly twisted to produce something new) and also a coating, which gets the virus through the cell wall in the first place.

The proposition contained in the Y2K bug mental model was DANGER. Normal clocks would count on at 00:00:00 but computer clocks would 'reset'. So there were two competing views of what would happen to time at this point. Given the fact that computers controlled the nuclear arsenals, power stations and so on, there was a horrible possibility that their version might win out. Which could mean the destruction of civilization, or at least a fairly big man-made disaster.

In itself that was a practical concern. Man-made designs often have unintended side effects, or unnoticed Achilles' heels, and generally they get found and fixed. But there was already a deeply rooted fear about the millennium as apocalypse. And so – by metaphor – the Y2K bug got its emotional force; it could mean 'the end of time'. This was emotionally powerful. Especially in places like the US where 70 per cent of the population (apparently) believe in God and the Devil.

If it had been the 1998 bug, it would not have had the same apocalyptic overtone. We were already programmed by Christian traditions to think of 2000 as a potential 'end of the world' date, and not just by traditions – modern American evangelists were preaching the 'end of times' throughout the 1990s.

Meme researcher Aaron Lynch interpreted the Y2K meme as reflecting a modern anxiety:

- the End Time has been promoted for thousands of Years as a 'hell on earth'
- experiences of modern life have led us to expect that things are at some kind of breaking point – that city wide riots can result from just an electricity black-out
- you don't have to be paranoid to believe that armaments have come perilously close to launching before; that we live with a hair trigger nuclear cease-fire.[85]

Lynch pointed out that it's unfounded to believe – as the meme suggests – that 'when the lights go out, the looting and shooting will start'. At times when huge disasters happen, people generally become their best selves – co-operative and altruistic – like in the Blitz.

And we know now that Y2K was all a big fuss about nothing.

But at the time it was a very big deal. Many companies and countries spent heavily on becoming 'Y2K compliant'. And not just because there was a superstitious 'image' reason for fearing this meme.

The Y2K bug reflects the general formula for a successful meme. It managed to sell people a counter-intuitive proposition (that the world was about to end) by wrapping it in emotional (apocalyptic myths and a 'hair-trigger' detente) and rational (computers often malfunction because of bugs) intuitions. It also had a number of 'replication' factors which made it highly likely to spread and overcome resistance:

Neologism (new name) – is a way to separate a new notion from all the fuzzily half-related notions that have gone before. It's an obvious point, but we think with words. And so when something is named, it becomes 'thinkable'. Trend memes work largely through just this device; as soon as someone says we are 'cocooning', 'telecommuting', or whatever, it seems a real possibility. As soon as it was called the 'Y2K bug', it went from being a contentious theory, to a definite phenomenon.

Formats – urban myths last longer than gossip, one theory says, because they have a good story structure. And this doesn't just apply to fictions. The health meme 'eat five pieces of fruit and vegetables a day' is specific in its prescription of how much/how often. If it had just said 'eat a lot of fruit' the scientific overtones would be lost. The Y2K Bug's core format was the 00:00:00 time code, which is highly intuitive.

Memorability – memes spread quickest and have most influence by word of mouth. People believe their friends, colleagues and relatives more than the media. Memes that are simple to remember and repeat, do much better in this. The Bolshevik propaganda meme that captured half a continent's support was 'Land, Peace and Bread'. What could be easier to remember than 'Y2K'?

Visibility – 'There's no smoke without fire.' If *everyone's talking about it* (as they were with the Y2K bug) then it must be true. Visual memes have an advantage here too. Which is the rationale for badges like the AIDS ribbon. And visual memes are vital for the media to show it happening. (This is the opposite with rumour or 'reports' which are much less 'realistic'.) Seeing is believing.

Imitability – how can I imitate this meme? There are literal imitation craze examples – like 'the gypsy look'. But the deeper question is how can I act on this? If there is a simple, low resistance path to action then people are far more likely to do it. The Y2K bug presented a choice – ignore it, or put it right.

Urgency – any kind of time limit or countdown increases the pressure to 'pass it on soon' or 'act now before it's too late'. That was a key factor in the Y2K bug meme. It was also used by PS2 (the new PlayStation) in the guise of scarcity – get your order in fast, if you want it by Christmas!

Sensation – anything that wants to be hyped needs to figure that the media want fast, vivid, abrasive stories. They need to sell papers. Viagra, or 'Sexstasy' as the British tabloids dubbed it was the most hyped drug in recent history. Why? It causes miracle erections! The formatting was perfect – little pill, hard to get hold of except on the black market (like ecstasy) – a name that sounds like it's short for 'Virility Niagara'! Front-page stuff. Even more gripping was the Y2K bug's story of 'the end of the world'.

Sociability – the memes that involve people getting together give their transmission a big boost. Pokemon re-engineered playground interactions. Every Hotmail had a post-script, inviting new account holders. BlueMountain – e-greeting cards – shot into the top ten websites through the very human tendency to 'send a greeting back'. The Y2K bug posed a question, which could only be answered by meetings, task forces and so on.

Third Party Support – memes don't just benefit memes. There are often interested parties that would benefit if a meme spread. These tend to get behind the meme. This drove the Internet bubble – investors were motivated to talk up the boom with other investors. One reason the Y2K bug spread so fast is that whole industries of software and consulting companies stood to gain from 'putting it right'. Also any government ignored it at their peril. The political risk outweighed any cost of being seen to support putting it right.

Resistance – just as bugs become antibiotic resistant, some meme strains have built in 'defence against your defences'. Political correctness – and burning causes like 'animal rights' – carry a resistance device, 'anyone who argues is a bigot'. They may be right, but this also neatly ensures that meme holders never get talked out of it. And it scares media into toeing that party line too. If you stood against the Y2K bug you were in danger of sounding like a technophobe, something many executives already hid from.

Authority – one form of modern authority is celebrity. The anti-fur campaign led by Greenpeace in the 1970s scored a major publicity coup when they enlisted Bridget Bardot to pose with poor defenceless baby seal cubs. This also gathered third party support – here was an image that would sell newspapers. The Y2K bug was given credence by the world governments and major corporations (like banks) that not only took it seriously but publicly urged others to do so.

Many of these factors are present in any successful meme. There are a few other traditional 'replication boosters' which meme researchers have found increase a meme's chances of long-term success; like sub-memes for having as many children as possible and parents playing a strong role in indoctrinating offspring. These, says Lynch, partly explain why the Mormon and Amish faiths have grown so fast within the US population. But these kinds of factors are relevant to fundamentalist groups rather than marketing.

VIRUSES OF THE MIND

The word 'meme' first surfaced in 1976 in a book called *The Selfish Gene* by Richard Dawkins. He wanted to illustrate his idea of 'evolution as replication'. So he came up with an example; the 'mimeme' (shortened to 'meme' to sound like 'gene') which is a 'unit of cultural transmission', or 'unit of imitation'.

Dawkins' main examples of memes were religious and scientific ideas, suggesting that he saw this as a process relevant to deeper structures. But he also mentioned 'tunes, ideas, catch-phrases, clothes, fashions and ways of making pots or of building arches'. It is these superficial examples of spreading 'units of imitation' which became popularized.

Taken literally, imitation is associated with rather limited, often short-term phenomena. Like when a catch-phrase ('Whaaassuup?'), or trouser shape ('flares') does the rounds. But taken as 'imitation in the broadest sense' – as the replication of mental models and resulting behaviours across the population – then it gets interesting.

The theory of memes – 'ideas that spread like viruses' – is one of its own best examples. The 'meme' idea has caught on – perhaps because it's noticeable that new ideas often do spread in a viral, person-to-person way in today's society.

How did we get ideas like: eating 'meals' divided into breakfast, lunch and dinner? Wearing different clothes for different occasions? Surfing the Internet? . . . Most of our behaviour is 'in the broadest sense copied', and so is what we think.

The kind of meme that is most interesting for level three marketing is one which creates a new insight or perspective; joining up the dots in a new way. When this happens we experience 'crystallization' – recognition of a new pattern in our old universe of experiences. All kinds of things, which were fragmentary, inconsistent, out of step with reality . . . cohere. Everything slots into place. History is re-written in the light of this new perspective. It all becomes clear.

That is exactly the task faced by many new inventions. At first sight they don't fit. Because they are new and so in some ways run counter to our intuitions. There is a big danger that they will be rejected. Because 'new' is scary. New inventions are often subject to Luddite counter-memes. Like that of 'Frankenstein foods' which led to genetically modified foods being banned from UK supermarkets, by popular demand. (In spite of the fact that many scientists and quite a few ecologists agree that GM foods are essential if we are to feed the still growing population in the twenty-first century.)

In the near future it is likely that fuel cell batteries will be introduced; they are lighter, longer lasting, more (cost) efficient and better for the environment. But there is a hurdle; they will need to have their liquid contents replaced, like a cigarette lighter. That creates a potential barrier to acceptance, as recharging your phone with a refill canister may seem 'not quite right'. The challenge is to create a meme which makes this desirable and acceptable. And which doesn't seem like it could leak in your pocket or explode.

I'd be tempted to launch separate, attractive, clear plastic fuel cells (I imagine they'd look like paperweights), which you could use as a 'mobile mains'. If you could run a power book, phone and other mobile equipment for 100 hours on one of these you'd probably try it, right? And if they came in a very visible and attractive design, they could soon catch on memetically. Once accepted fuel cells could then be 'hidden' in phones, etc.

The 'meme' meme is itself a good example of crystallizing new understanding. It is uncertain whether it actually adds any new details or cases to the social sciences. But what 'meme' theory does add is an essential, clarifying insight.

THE MEMES-EYE VIEW

Rather than seeing the ideas and artefacts of culture as all bound up in, and secondary to, the messy practice of human social life, meme theory separates them out. It says 'what if memes came first and people second?' Or 'what if the ideas that are best able to spread and endure determine human societies, rather than the other way round?'

It is this basic mental construct, culture having a life of its own, and memes competing for people's attention, acceptance and retention, which the 'meme' meme offers in place of the folk-lore, subjective belief that 'I make up my own mind'. That's what has led even the critics of memetics (as anthropology with new flashy packaging) to admit that:

> Memes are a wonderful teaching device for the student who wants to learn about human beings in general. They serve as a clear and imagination-stimulating concept for the beginner who needs to understand what makes human culture so very different. Furthermore, talking of 'memes' by-passes the trap of making culture seem transcendental, mysterious and immaterial.[86]

Memes are units of cultural replication. It is useful to understand that all of culture (and not just the bits we imitate) is made up of a limited number of such units.

Culture is like language. In each language we have a limited set of possible phonemes (sounds) – like k, or in Japanese, like ka, ki, ke, ko and ku. These units define not only what we say, but what we hear. Even within European languages we struggle with each other's phonemes. I was teased by clients, in Belgium, recently, for telling a waiter that '*J'ai femme*' (I have a wife). When I was really trying to say '*J'ai faim*' (I'm hungry).

Realizing that culture was a set of morphemes (units of meaning or structure) was a key breakthrough in anthropology in the early twentieth century. Culture is digital – made up of a distinct and limited set of units. It privileges some things and leaves others unnoticed – as unnoticed as the difference between *femme* and *faim*, to the English ear.

This is the most fundamental level on which human culture is shaped. A society either has, or has not, marked out a distinction – for example, A versus not-A. And a concept, if not recognized and named, doesn't enter people's thoughts, at least on any conscious level.

When the culture shifts at this building block stage, a profound unease and disintegration sets in. One of the pioneers in the culture-as-morpheme field was Ruth Benedict who quoted a chief of the Digger Indians called Ramon.[87] He was a Christian, but he had grown up in a tradition of 'shamans who transformed themselves into bears before his eyes'. Ramon told Benedict:

> In the beginning, God gave to every people a cup of clay. They all dipped it in the water. But their cups were different. Our cup is broken now. It has passed away.

The difference with this view of 'culture' (compare the use of the word in the media and market research reports) is that it is not this year's colour or a new fashionable attitude. It's something you acquire very early – like phonemes – and it's much harder to change or reacquire later. But it does change. Ask Ramon.

Compare the generations alive now. The pre-war generation have a completely different set of mental models about relationships, work and other matters to our own. Not just different 'attitudes' (conscious, changeable opinion), but different morphemes. Like duty. And the generation after us have another set again.

ESTABLISHING A NEW CULTURE

If you are going to drive your market, you need to drive your market culture.

There is an out-dated but very widespread view in marketing that 'it's not our job'. 'Let the Tea Council address the tea-drinking culture in general, we are just going to promote our brand over other teas: because it is fresher; cheaper; comes in round bags and is more "friendly" (ie it has well-loved advertising)', or whatever.

The brands that do drive the market culture have shown themselves to be far more powerful than those of the narrow brand-share persuasion. Look at Starbucks, which changed the way that people drink coffee. It didn't leave this to the 'Coffee Council'.

Being a strong brand now means changing the culture. That's what a brand is at level three – something which establishes a new tradition, which changes the way people live.

MEME BRANDING THE LIFE ACCOUNT FROM MOTHER

Financial assumptions are deeply ingrained. For Mother to spread its new mental model it's likely that it would need to get people to think in new terms. So part of the marketing would need to spread new words, concepts and behaviours.

Word of mouth is one of the quickest and most pervasive ways to change people's concepts. Catch-phrases, sayings and maxims bring ideas to people with the implicit endorsement of another speaker. They have 'social currency' attached.

The Little Book of Calm meme introduced a positive antonym for stress. Which has boosted cultural brands like yoga, feng shui and natural health . . . These are positive brands rather than their predecessors which were 'anti-' something.

Many of the financial memes we grew up with are coarse and timid at the same time:

- 'Look after the pennies and the pounds will look after themselves'
- 'Save up for a rainy day'
- 'A bird in the hand is worth two in the bush'
- 'Never a borrower or a lender be'
- 'On the never-never' (hire purchase).

The new concepts, which Mother needs to introduce, would be far more proactive about personal finance. It's likely that some form of self-help publication – a bit like *The Little Book of Calm* – would be helpful. It would aim to launch a different set of sayings:

- 'Build your life, not your savings'
- 'Plan first, budget last'
- 'Education always pays'
- 'Face your future with facts not fears'.

Mother might also launch a new board game to spread the memes in social settings. This would allow players to link life plans and money/success. The game would aim to do for financial karma what Monopoly did for real estate.

Giving every customer a beautifully produced basic board game, as part of their account opening pack, would kick start the game launch. It would also create a tangible expression of their philosophy.

Any creative marketing is only as good as the idea. Given the cost of any other marketing recruitment campaign, Mother could afford to go to town on this medium, to hire the best games designers in the world, and cut a deal on the revenues from public sales.

PUTTING MEMES INTO ACTION – SOME STARTING POINTS

1 Is there a negative convention holding your market back? Something that a new meme could defuse? In the 1980s an effective UK marketing campaign for safe sex tackled the 'condoms are embarrassing' issue in a very funny catchy way (by using cinema commercials aimed at young, dating couples).

2 What is the most exciting viral idea that has ever swept through your market or a similar one? How could you mutate this into a form that could spread now? Sales of yoghurt boomed in the 1970s when it was discovered that yoghurt-eating monks lived into their 100s. Could there be some new 'healthy eating' angles on longevity?

3 What are all the 'conventional wisdoms' in your market? Which might be the springboard for innovation. In the music equipment market it was a commonplace belief throughout the 80s and 90s that working with the new digital workstations was 'like trying to paint the hall through a letter box'. This was because the editing functions were accessed through menus in tiny editing screens. Now there has been a boom in instruments with easier interfaces – accessible through hundreds of knobs to twiddle (analogue modelling synths) or because they are computer screen-based (software synths).

4 What bits of (deeply rooted) mythology apply to your market? Take vehicle rescue services. In many fairy tales, a helper character gives a magical gift. What if the AA gave magical gifts; like a little flashing vehicle-tracking device in every member's car? So they could always find you (or your car, if it got nicked).

5 What vocabulary and jargon is used in your market? Could simple words for new concepts and behaviours be a driving force? The launch of Viagra was preceded by public relations which seeded the phrase 'erectile

dysfunction' which opened the way to discussion of this taboo issue.

6   If you could pass on some wise advice to customers in ten seconds what would it be? Can you create a few rules of thumb to help customers; such as the classic 'a hi-fi's only as good as its stylus'?

7   What controversy or inner conflict lurks in your market? How could you 'out' it? And launch a thousand dinner party and pub arguments in the process? For icecool.co.uk (diamond jewellery online), my friend James and I developed a guerrilla ad campaign which said: 'Diamonds are a Woman's Birthright'.

8   Many a true word is spoken in jest. What in-joke epidemics in your company could be released outside? 'FCUK' (French Connection UK) was already an in-joke on internal memos, before their ad agency picked it up.

9   What meme ideas can you think of, that would benefit your customers when they passed them on? (They have to be true, but you might be able to develop your concept in that direction.) Like Mercedes having the best resale value of any car.

10 How could you drive the culture of your market in a new, fruitful direction? I met an inspiring entrepreneur recently called Ann Addlington (of PetCareCo). Her vision is that pets are valuable because they teach human beings to care. Her pet centres are organized around this insight; they are about training and transforming the owners, not the pets. That would make a great campaigning theme (and potential partner) for one of the pet food brands. It's also very meme-able because it turns the typical culture of pets on its head – it's about cuddly people, not cuddly animals.

15

COMMUNITY MEDIA

Communities are an active version of the dated notion of a passive 'target audience'. They are 'active' in the development of symbolic shared meaning and even in the creation of the service and experience itself. Examples include user groups, clubs, associations and other networks. The Internet is the community medium par excellence because, even for pre-existing communities (like local clubs), it gives people more opportunities to find each other, to keep in touch and to share views and resources. Communities also form around venues and events.

The community media are a challenge to the idea that you advertise to individuals and they make up their minds alone. Communities inform many of our decisions, becoming both a source of opinions and information and a guide to 'what everyone else is doing'.

THE MINISTRY OF SOUND

The Ministry of Sound has turned a disused warehouse in a rundown part of London into a famous night club and the headquarters of a £120 million entertainment and media company, whose compilation albums and magazines sell. What the Ministry have done is they have branded a community.

Up until the early-1990s dance music was part of a wilder community of illegal raves. Then the Public Order Act (introduced by Margaret Thatcher after the Castlemorton rave, held by many to be the Woodstock of the 1990s) made unlicensed parties so punitively illegal that dance music was driven back into the clubs.

The Ministry was one of the first of the clubs in the UK to innovate away from the illegal party experience (= dangerously uncomfortable, with blocked fire exits, broken loos and the cold water taps not connected – to encourage mineral water sales). They modelled the club on chic New York venues. And tapped into a new phase and audience in the dance scene. They caught the mood of the mid-1990s; a new crowd that wanted to dress up, show off and drink champagne. This scene was more female-friendly, glamorous, comfortable and well-put-together.

With their commitment to quality at every level – the sound system, the DJs, the ambience – the Ministry slowly established an identity apart from other clubs. One which some stalwarts derided as 'corporate clubbing', but others found to be their natural home. A Ministry clubber is a devotee; more like a football fan (a loyal follower, who dresses and acts like they *belong* in that queue) than someone who has tumbled out of the pub and 11 pm and is just looking for somewhere to dance.

The focus on other factors in the experience (than popping-pills-and-dancing-in-a-disused-railway-tunnel) has allowed the Ministry to take on a tough anti-drugs policy, which further separates it from the clubbing mainstream.

Now the Ministry has a successful network of clubs and events (in Ibiza and further afield), record production, radio stations and magazines . . . and they have moved from being a venue to a way of life. It's a very exportable model and Ministry of Sound have just taken in funding from 3i, and are planning to invade the US with the same sophisticated community media mix.

COMMUNITIES IN A NETWORKED WORLD

Social groups – castes, clans, crazes – are at the heart of social order and change. They enact traditions. They have huge symbolic value. A person's identity is, even today, largely made up of community memberships, real and virtual; their job or trade, their religion and region . . .

But whereas the old social institutions were about 'Us' (as in 'Them and Us') the new institutions are more inclusive 'We' networks. They do not have an exclusive hold on allegiance and identity. 'I' can join many different 'We' groups; related to all the different areas of my life.

'We' groups are less fractious; but they often have a driving point of view. The importance of communities for concept marketing is most of all that they represent a kind of group mind and decision making.

According to Forum One, a consumer community specialist, there were over 300,000 community sites on the Net by the end of 1999, compared with 96,000 in 1997.

These communities take three main forms:

- **BULLETIN BOARDS:** where people post messages, which become threaded into discussions
- **LIVE CHAT ROOMS:** often hosted by a celebrity or expert, like the follow-up discussions that commonly take place after TV programmes these days
- **INSTANT MESSAGING SITES:** commonly used by groups of friends as chat-rooms, like the MSN messaging facility (also the basis of many file sharing sites).

There are also exclusive communities who share an Internet address and network of contacts as well as offline events. Like Disinfo.net the radical new media community, or The Well, an exclusive community which in the new media scene is a bit like an old gentleman's club and home to many a famous hacker, writer and cyber-guru.

Communities can be about exchanging knowledge and emotional support. Or can be a collection of individuals with a similar purpose or activity. Geocities with its 3 million members is divided into neighbourhoods on this basis. Members post their own sites detailing their interests or some thoughts or stuff they've made. The overall effect is a bit like a village fete for knowledge, with the topics of interest ranging from golf, to sociology.

Another great example is the patient support groups, which are brilliant sources of information and support for those across the world facing a particular health problem. A great benefit of belonging to a like-minded group of people who face a similar situation is that you get the reassurance that you're 'not alone'. A good analogy might be marathon running – you're carried along by the others.

In the 1920s and 30s there was a thriving network of listener groups in the UK. These would listen to an educational BBC radio broadcast and then sit and debate what they heard. The BBC produced a booklet with useful tips for those arranging discussion groups, and of course, in addition to the formal groups, families and friends would huddle around these programmes and chatter in their own informal way.

The programmes had a primetime slot, 7.30 pm and 8 pm Monday to Friday and a number of thought-provoking series were produced like 'A Changing World', which roved through topics like industry, science, politics and leisure in the early 1930s.

All of which reflected the BBC's mission to inform and educate as well as entertain. This mission has stood it in good stead in recent years – along with its values of creative integrity and objectivity.

But compare this 'lecture and discussion' format with a true Internet learning community pioneer . . .

HearMe.com was originally part of a modest LA online gaming site. The chat-rooms were designed for players to hang out in after a Quake (networked computer game with a first person perspective, where people shoot at each other) session, rather like a locker room after sport. All HearMe.com did was to pep up the format a bit, allowing chat room participants to actually chat – using sound rather than text.

On one level, this was an economic breakthrough. Given that local calls (to ISP) in the US are free, this gave people free phone conferencing facilities. But it wasn't the pricing that created a supernova. It was the applications. Created by thriving communities within this site. Like 'Divine Breath', a gospel singing class run out of New York.

It was these exciting new learning and interaction opportunities that took HearMe in mid 2000, from nowhere to be one of the top twenty-five sites in the US. It was an overnight runaway success. *Fortune* magazine proclaimed that 'Voice is the new killer app'.

The more popular sites generally do have some killer app bundled with the community spirit and experience. The greatest example of which is Napster, which attracted sixty million users in its first year, making it the fastest growing technology ever.

EXTENDED LEARNING COMPANY NETWORKS

User Groups are places where you can go to find out things; like why your old programmes won't work with your new operating system. The user groups are the first to know and to find quick fixes. They are valuable self-help communities to the millions like me who fumble with every new piece of hardware and software.

There is great potential for these communities to form an extended network with the product developers, for feedback and co-creation. This is already happening in the music studio niche, where companies are mainly staffed by enthusiasts, anyway.

Companies these days can track the community discussions and use this to sensitively monitor brand and product issues and the general climate of opinion and confidence. It is also becoming common to 'e-Street' – to hire legions of spokespeople to visit all the bulletin boards and put the company's point of view.

But I think these methods are in danger of falsifying the process. It's a great shame that more companies don't simply hang out with and listen to their customers.

ACTIVISM AND SOCIAL MOVEMENTS

'Consumer activism' is a phrase that strikes fear into the hearts of the biggest corporation or government: GM Foods; fuel protests; Nike Child Labour; McDonald's in France; anti-capitalism protests and many others.

Some of the most vibrant online communities are antagonistic sites; such as the ones which add 'sucks' after the company or brand name. Like 'Broadvisionsucks.com'.

How can you deal with the possibility that your company could be next?

Some good advice I read in a report on crisis management recently was – build up relationships beforehand. It's very hard to start the dialogue once the crisis is on. The other thing the report didn't mention is that it also pays to be ethical in the first place.

A company with a 'mission statement' isn't a patch on a company with a cause. I don't mean just companies with 'audacious goals' (shareholder profit by grander-sounding means). I mean genuine causes that some people will devote their lives to. That's a way to create sustainable, loyal communities of employees and customers.

CULTURAL CROWDS

For brands of a more cultural nature, the opportunity is to build a crowd behind your brand. Doing this is an exercise in cultural engineering; building a meaningful community vibe, that will have functional and cultural resonance.

Channel 4 did this with cricket in the UK. Old cricket was stuck with a flannels and public school image. Having bought the broadcast rights to UK cricket, to attract a new audience, they built a new cricket fan base, based on the passionate West Indian tradition. (That summer the main test series was against the West Indies).

This allowed them to create enticing ethnic festivals around the cricket, which they did in public parks. Channel 4 didn't just host a discussion, they created a Jamaican-style party around their screening of cricket matches. It worked wonders.

Mental models contain much more than 'information'.

Take Pokèmon. We live in a society, which in future will be based upon electronic exchanges and trading among individuals and companies. So along comes Pokèmon, a school playground stock exchange, as prophet and educator. Many a future network-negotiator will have first honed their skills on Pokèmon. Similarly, among a slightly older group, the Hollywood Stock Exchange predated the 1990s equities gold rush, by two or three years. Education with passion, indeed, and prescience.

This gets close to what Sociologist Alberto Melucci meant when he described communities and movements as 'social prophets'.[88] It is in the vibrant cultural fringes that we find the beginnings of the new mainstream culture. And these do have a kind of prescience about what lies ahead. If you want to track future trends you can do no better than read all the niche magazines and e-zines you can find.

COMMUNITY BRANDING THE LIFE ACCOUNT FROM MOTHER

Mother would revive a concept that has only recently shown signs of winding down – the mutual society. These co-operative banking organizations worked for their customers who were also shareholders. As would Mother. It's a natural system for a nurturing bank. The mutuality would extend beyond financial flows, because Mother is an enabler, not just a bank. A thriving self-help community would be created.

Mother would extend its activities from passive service to enabling customers to improve their lives through lifelong education and other means. Competence insurance (already exists in Scandinavia) would cover periods of 'going back to school'. Mother would also use aggregated bargaining power to get their private customers the same kinds of deals that corporate training offers. It would build partnership with key communities which engage in vocational education, like the professional societies. And ultimately it would probably invest in actual colleges.

The focus on *values* (not just value) would lead Mother to take strong positions on ethical issues. As the bank and its funds grew, it would gain influence over companies it invested in. The customers who took an active interest would be democratically involved in key decisions, with real time voting systems enabling them to have their say.

PUTTING COMMUNITY MEDIA INTO ACTION – SOME STARTING POINTS

1 What active social movements connect in any way with your market? Are they developing new ideas and life-styles that could transform your industry if they were widespread? Why not develop a whole new business line for each, just in case they are truly prophetic? You'd also benefit from the relationships these projects create.

2 Have you analysed social movements for their symbolic content? That may sound complicated, but it just means always figuring out *why* this movie, TV show, toy, dance or whatever has become a craze, and in every case, what could your company learn from what your customers think about and care passionately about?

3 When your customers are dealing with you, which of their many 'communities' are they part of at the time? Which others could be included, with added richness? A banking customer treated like a family accountant, when they deal with their bank. Banks could be addressing the full range of their customers' identities – as volunteers, or sports fans for example.

4 What are the most valuable ideas that customers ex-change now? It could be 'how to' tips. It could be inspir-ing ideas (decor or recipes). It could be emotional support. All of which are forms of customer learning. How could *you* replicate the most valuable ideas across your whole customer base, and how will you reward the sources of this content?

5 If you formed a learning network – like the BBC radio groups in the 1930s – what could you teach that would that help people live their lives? Remember that the key learning needs are vocational (employability) and self-development (quality of life).

6 Where is the nearest frustrating blockage or missed opportunity to your market? If you are a car company,

wouldn't it be great if there were fewer traffic jams? If you are a retailer, wouldn't it be great if kids loved going shopping?

7 Are you a committed Learning Organization? If so do you apply all the same principles to your marketing (or do you hide behind a dumb mass marketing 'image' façade)? Why treat customers any different from other stakeholders?

8 How would you fare in a marketing hotornot test? (Hotornot is a cult community site where visitors rank photos sent in as hotornot – i.e. attractive or not). What is the nearest hot trend that your customers *are* excited about?

9 What mass social event could form a community around your market? What is your 'festival' or 'demonstration' issue? Shouldn't that take centre stage?

10 What is the biggest thing your company could contribute to the future of humanity? It could be world peace (e.g. ABB Cable's mission to help the East to modernize). It could be better conversations (like BT's 'It's good to talk'). Why not focus more effort and energy on that great cause and make it your crusade?

16

STORY MEDIA

> Many think that stories are shaped by people. In fact it's usually
> the other way around.
>
> TERRY PRATCHETT

Story media are those forms which have 'life as it is lived' (or
could be lived) as their focus. These can range from fictional
dramas to news stories to computer games. They are places
where we can imagine how we would react in novel situations,
where we can come to understand what motivates us, where we
can research different ways of living.

Stories are especially relevant to any marketing situation
where introducing a new pattern of behaviour or action is appropriate. Stories in these contexts can provide powerful inspiration
and role models, as well as making whole choices in life vivid.

Stories were often used in image marketing (usually in TV
advertising) to weave mystique around brands. These were
escapist fantasies. This is not what I am suggesting. The stories
I have in mind will strike the audience as somehow true to their
situation and the choices they make. Which is not to say they
have to be 'realistic' in their setting. *Aesop's Fables* teach us a lot
about human nature without being news stories.

FROM A SEMINAR WITH A PENSION COMPANY

Retirement.

It's a terrible word (like 'retreating') and a concept that hardly still applies. It used to mean a peaceful last few years of life. Like the pit ponies being put out to pasture; a time when the working couple could rest their old bones and play with the grand-children. Now people are retiring younger – at fifty-five or even fifty is not uncommon – and they can therefore be looking for-ward to the second half of their adult life, in fairly full health. This is the age group that buys the most long-haul holidays, evening classes, leisure activities. It is a key market for new cars and investments, golf clubs and sun cream.

What pension companies do at the moment is target people in their twenties and thirties, take their money and then hand over a lump sum at retirement (hopefully). In branding terms this puts you just in front of the taxman, in the queue for customer interest and affection. If you are a pension company it would be reason-able to have a mission statement which said: 'helping people live well in the second half of life'. So why not actually do it?

There are three main initiation tasks I'd consider:

Create a positive image of the 'pensioner' – In the 1950s a 'teen' stereotype was born to give meaning to the new social realities then. It's time for wisdom or some other concept of the over fifties to be just as forcibly promoted. Dynamic, community-active, studious, wise and experienced . . .

Help people look forward to this time – People used to really look forward to retirement. At least that's the signal we get from the culture of the 1950s, 60s, 70s. Now how many do? What will they do with their lives? How will they form an identity?

Help people make the transition – There's not an obvious 'sales' rationale for this one, although it does fit our hypothetical com-pany mission and would create a big difference. What about a (virtual) college for people to start new directions and firm up their plans?

Given that any pension fund will spend millions on advertising, just to have awareness and warm values – why not gain these as the side effect of doing some good, in one or more of the ways I've suggested?

In all of these strategies, the natural learning mode is stories.

STORIES AS MAPS OF MEANING

In *Maps of Meaning*, psychologist Jordan Petersen explains how all cultures have told themselves stories to guide individual action.[89] The importance of stories derives, Petersen says, from the basic model, which we use as a motivational framework, in all behaviour. This model has three elements:

- who am I now and what is my current (undesirable) situation?
- where would I like to be as an (idealized) outcome?
- how could I get there?

A 'Where Am I Now?' Story

I've just seen an anti-smoking advert. It features a man with lung cancer who tells his awful, close-to-death story. And he ends this with 'And at 34 years of age you're thinking, this isn't supposed to happen to me.' I'm a 36-year-old smoker. And my denial is based on statistics which say if I'd given up before 30 I'd have a negligible extra risk (so about 0.5 per cent chance of getting lung cancer). If I smoke all my life, I'd have a 16 per cent risk. And if I give up before 50, I'll have a 2 per cent risk. So I'll give up around 40. The story attacks my 'it would never happen to me' tower of denial. It says: 'people do get cancer young, too. It's urgent to give up now, not around forty'.

It goes in much deeper than 'fear appeal' health marketing. You really feel for the guy. As in – selfishly – you don't want to be him. Coupled with the mid thirties onset of mortality fears. It's a powerful counter-argument because he's real and you absorb his story. Or I did. Belief-changing stories aren't necessarily statistically valid. They are psychologically true. One penetrating human story can challenge your belief system.

A 'How to Get There' Story

Cognitive researchers made a mathematics instruction video called 'The Adventures of Jasper Woodbury'.[90] Each episode of

Jasper's story ends with a challenge to the students to solve a problem. All the information they needed to solve the problem was embedded in the story. The information is gradually extracted from the video through discussion – the mathematical principles needed are agreed – and the problem is solved.

The researchers found that this story tool was more effective than traditional teaching of mathematical concepts. It allowed students at many different levels of prior knowledge tackle the problems together. It proved a great memory device. But most of all, it put doing mathematics into a living context; it positioned maths as a 'how to get there' tool.

Stories are most satisfying if they teach us something. Especially now that most of us are on a lifelong learning journey. So there are many opportunities for this form of story.

An 'Ideal Outcome' Story

There is no motivation without hope.

The promise of gain is what allows us to defer current gratification, to motivate ourselves towards some future goal; such as graduation, or a promotion.

In *Hoop Dreams* – a documentary spanning seven years – we watch three boys trying to emulate their hero Michael Jordan by making it into professional basketball. It caught the 'role model story' process beautifully; one teenager is forever saying 'I'm Jordan' while copying his hero's moves.

Public stories can have powerful side effects.

The film *Trainspotting* is not a story of hope, in the same misty-eyed sense as *Hoop Dreams*. Although there was an element of that in the portrayal of the junkies as latter-day gypsies – romantic, adventurous, articulate, good looking, funny and above all free from conformity. It's a contemporary *Carmen* – an advert for the wild side, an escape from the 'mind-numbing, spirit-crushing' banality of life in an empty consumer society.

The film's most important story effect was the journey into a scene. It took people there in their imagination. We all feel a bit like we are living in a film. And we 'paste' in bits of film to make up our lifestyle plans. The wild, decadent scene of *Trainspotting* struck a chord with viewers. So that many wanted to – and did – go to Scotland to sample the ambience, which was portrayed as a living pop video. A researcher working on a branding Scotland project told me that tourism to Scotland boomed in the three years following *Trainspotting*. It put the place on people's mental map.

The portrayal of a subject in a film – be it a place, an occupation or a cause – is like the packaging and display of something in a shop. Film-makers select the exact combination of elements calculated to produce a willing identification of viewer with this universe. In this way films can advertise lifestyles and points of view. And they also 'zoom in' our knowledge and sensory memories, making the unfamiliar accessible.

Educating Rita had a powerful effect. Applications to the Open University, where the film was set, doubled the year after its release. We grew up in a world where education was 'not for me' for many people. That's why *Educating Rita* was such a success for the Open University. It took people there in their imagination. It coloured in a life ahead, with possible romance, new confidence etc. It said 'this could be me'. Viewers of the film must have felt like university was now accessible. Whereas previously it was a great unknown – 'nobody I know has ever been there, and I've no idea what it'd be like'.

MULTIPLE LIFETIMES AND INITIATION

Stories are units of meaningfulness. The universe is a chaotic mess of things and events. A story joins up these dots in space and time. We have story-making minds or, more precisely, as Terry Pratchett said we have 'story-made minds'.

The importance of stories has probably never been greater. In the post-tradition-and-custom society we are not only aware of our personal autobiography, but are making it up as we go along. Stories give us ready templates.

Whenever people in traditional societies went through a change in identity and role, they were helped through this process by initiation. The best known example is coming of age, either reaching marriageable age, or adult-status. But ceremony surrounded all transitions.

The initiation process has both a functional and cultural side. The functional component involved instruction and sometimes, physical preparation – such as circumcision. But this was blended with the more unconscious, mythic and cultural component. To produce something we wouldn't recognize as education in the (Victorian) school sense. Initiation's main target is to help people form a new identity and role in life.

Nowadays we have many life-changing transitions – changes of job, divorce, children, starting your own business, redundancy, moving home, illnesses, lottery wins . . . plus an overall culture of self-direction and self-determination. You can see why *reinventing yourself* is a major theme of modern life.

These moments of total life change are big moments for marketing fortunes, which rely on long-term affiliation and purchase cycles. What would have been a once-in-a-lifetime decision can get recast in the re-scripting. This covers more than cars, homes and bank accounts – the most obvious examples. What people eat for breakfast, what they wear, what they do with their leisure time etc. are up for grabs. Few markets pass through one of these great 'resets' unchanged. On the contrary, people look for all kinds of little everyday signs that 'this is the new me'. It is at these times that people are really open to learning new things and actively thinking about life.

The result is that companies need to recruit and re-recruit again through all these zig-zags in life. Just as there are no 'jobs for life' any more there are no 'customers for life' either.

In media terms, *when* and *how* are much more important then *where*.

The weak, token approach is to target the easily identifiable life-change audiences, eg newlyweds and business start-ups, like banks do now. The stronger way is to actively help them through the change, thereby jumping the queue of competitors. To be inspiring or at least helpful, rather than just in the queue of marketers who are after customers' business.

Many hobbies are pursued with a vigour and independent sense of achievement and adventure, which is all too often lacking in the workplace. I worked on a photography book for my client Capco. They commissioned young photographers to capture their people's interests outside work; sky-diving, Indian art relics, motorcycle racing. . . . grand passions indeed.

This passionate vocational 'hobby thing' is characteristic of the intellect age. It's a turning from passive leisure, to passionate learning. One marketing application might be for companies and organizations involved with start-up businesses (banks, government agencies, accountancy software, computer and office suppliers, stationers . . .) to reach people through their hobbies.

In the UK, small firms employ 32 per cent of the workforce, with the self-employed accounting for another 13 per cent. The overwhelming majority of small firms are very small. 45 per cent of all working adults are in this sector; an increase from 25 per cent in the late 1960s.[91] So come to think of it, this is a major audience for any marketer.

Guess what the number one reason cited for starting your own business is? It's 'turning your hobby or leisure interests into a business' (HSBC Research); this accounts for about 50 per cent of all start-ups. So if you really wanted to get in at the ground floor of this cottage industry revolution, you wouldn't wait until the business plan stage. You'd become a massive sponsor of people's private hobbies and vocations.

REINVENTING YOUR SELF

As Forest Gump's mother said, 'Life is like a box of chocolates; you never know what you're going to get.' In the old days, you got to eighteen and had your life mapped out. As the son of the black-smith in your village, you were the next blacksmith in waiting, married and already defined as a character, in the minds of your neighbours and your family.

It's likely now that, at eighteen, you are heading to university or a skilled-vocation course and have some major goals. Perhaps you have your vocation *thing* in mind already. But your character and identity, your deep inner sense of who you are, are more flexible and prone to reinvention, and your further education is about to open your mind to new values and opportunities.

As you travel on your journey through life, you will go through many different phases. Punctuated by big discontinuities; the end of a relationship or the start of a new one; a company take-over or reorganization; a change in career; a new direction set by a new course of study; moving home, town, country; even a new hobby, or interest.

A key resource for reinvention is the role model. They'd be my first port of call on any story branding project. For instance, what if the pensions company mentioned earlier focused on Bill Clinton 'just retired', and followed him over the next few years?

STORIES AND THE LIFE ACCOUNT FROM MOTHER

Stories are central to Mother, because planning your life is an exercise in story-scripting.

So Mother would build the ability of customers to script their own life plans and to get inspiration from reading others. In the process, Mother would develop the 'Life Account' brand with a second, richer meaning: the life story. Short stories written by customers are Mother's added cultural medium and dimension.

Mother would create a mass e-publishing site, where customers could file and revise imaginative accounts of their future lives. This resembles the Peter Senge 'personal mastery' exercise (visualize your life in five years' time),[92] but would be elevated by the creative writing aspect into a twenty-first-century art-form. To help customers get the most out of this process, Mother would provide creative writing courses, guides and encouragement.

As you entered the Life Account site you'd pass a graphic of a gate with the inscription: 'Be careful what you wish for, personal visions tend to come true.' Inside the site, a thematic search engine would allow you to browse other people's visions for their future.

I might check out what the other 36-year-old free agent consultants were planning for ten years' time. In the process, I'd remember that I always meant to become a psychoanalyst at that age. And I'd click through to the 'research your future' zone, to gather materials I could use in my own next 'Life Account' story. Once there, I couldn't help being swayed by a competition; the top 100 Life accounts, as judged by the reader traffic, will get published globally in book form. So, knowing a little about memes, I revise my career-future plan slightly to sex therapist. Now this should be real fun to research. . . .

PUTTING STORY BRANDING INTO ACTION – SOME STARTING POINTS

1 What propositional beliefs keep customers from making the journey you'd like them to? Could you defuse these – as in the giving-up smoking example? Similarly for beliefs about end goals and knowledge of the steps that might lead there. Do you leave consumer motivation to chance, or are you a market mentor?

2 Are your customer learning aids in a form which is close-to-life? Like the Jasper Woodbury maths adventure video. Wouldn't it be better to see things applied in this lively way (eg video or cartoons)? Is learning in your market fun, or just a boring but necessary drudge?

3 How could you 'take customers there' in their imag-ination? If you have a new product that impacts their everyday way of doing things, shouldn't you show leader-ship? There are many ways – eg entertainment media – to showcase a vision. Can you expect customers to do something they have trouble visualizing?

4 How does the fact that adults go through regular reinven-tions – of their identity, mental models and goals – impact your market? Can you help them through these difficult transitions? IKEA does home-starter packs. New online services help moving home or job. Even banks do a half-decent job of advice to people setting up a business. What's your angle?

5 Could you take an existing piece of education in your

market and turn it into a compelling, passionate piece of entertainment? Or perhaps there are elements that could come to life; like an avatar, to guide people, and answer their FAQs (Frequently Asked Questions)?

6 What deeper desires and needs course through your market unrecognized? How could you make these explicit? For instance some goods and services are often bought as 'self-gifts' including make-up, CDs and fancy stationery. They are presents 'from me to me'; little affirmations. What if a store, in this market, tuned service into cult-like affirmation? 'May I just say, that you have a wonderful smile today?'

7 What if you helped people in their constant search for their vocation in life? For instance, some research in the US suggested that many high-achievers in their thirties were forming escapist ideas of an alternative career in their forties, that would be more fulfilling. What if an airline devoted a business class video channel to career escapism? Showing video documentaries of people who've made the break.

8 Could you help people to find their goals and values in life? Without starting a cult religion, you could still promote reflection and debate. If you got seven million young people to think about what they want to do with their lives, would that be more or less valuable in the long term than trying to sell the same group pre-paid phone vouchers, or jeans, or groceries etc. through 'image'?

9 Where do your customers get inspiring ideas of how other people live? Shouldn't it be from you? IKEA carried out a 'Home Audit' – a photographic study of UK homes, which was genuine research, but became a very popular public exhibition.

10 Do you conduct business gripped with the realization that your company touches the stories of so many lives? How could you spread this realization through your company?

17

REPUTATION MEDIA

Reputation media address the standing of the company, rather than its products and services. Corporate advertising and PR and publications assume this role now. But these image-making tools are often ill-suited to the task at hand. Big actions by companies are often far more impressive than any 'boasting'.

DEEP BLUE

IBM, or Big Blue as it was known, was for some decades seen as institutional and monolithic. That's why, rumour has it, 'HAL' in 2001 was so named; each initial being one letter ahead of IBM.

Apple played off IBM's 'Big Brother' reputation with a counter-meme, in their classic '1984' commercial which launched the Mac.

Behind the scenes, IBM was evolving fast. The Internet gave them a major spur to development. By the mid-1990s there was enough momentum for a bold first public move.

How could IBM position their computing products in a new intimate relationship with the user, yet also portray the company as having a new dynamism? Ideally they'd also tackle their other strategic worry; the IBM clones. They needed to justify paying extra for the 'original'. So they needed something which said IBM is human, powerful and impressive.

The answer was to pit their computing prowess against the world champion Kasparov, in a game of chess. It was an epic moment of myth making on all sorts of levels – are machines now smarter than us? Can American IT beat Russian aggression? It put IBM back on centre-stage as the company that was inventing the future.

REPUTATION IN A NETWORKED WORLD

Branding, in the form of trademarks, was introduced in the 1860s to guarantee the provenance and quality of a product. Nowadays, we hardly need trademarks. We can click on a website and check out the 'company X' behind what we are buying. We can research whether a company fits our values. And we have a fairly high ambient awareness of company news, their track record, and so on.

When I recently shopped for a digital camera, I did so in the knowledge that: Sony is a leader in electronics; their products are often ahead of the curve; they supply camera and filming equipment for broadcasting and their incoming president was felt by commentators to have revived the company ethos. I didn't feel that way about the Toshiba alternative, which – for all I know – may have been a better camera. So I bought the Sony.

Companies and countries are like tribes. They are the big continuity, history and future in our lives. We little people fit into their stories, as customers, employees, investors and citizens. They even make monumental temples (HQs or public buildings) to make this relationship of scale clear. That's why the epic (big story) is their natural branding form.

The US moon landing owes a great debt to Hollywood. NASA, that expensive bunch of scientists who were trailing the Russian space agency, were losing public support in the early 1960s. Then *Star Trek* came along. The programme re-kindled the American passion for space exploration; which is presented in the TV series as the 'American' myth retold. With all-American hero Jim Kirk; acting as frontiersman and town marshal. On this new wave of enthusiasm, Kennedy took space to the nation as a big election agenda, swept to power and did what he said he would; he 'put a man on the moon'.

A company's heritage determines what everyone, including their own people, expect. Good corporate branding often leverages this history to face new situations. The return of Steve Jobs the company's founder to Apple was a great rallying moment for the corporate brand. He made the story even more epic by doing the job in return for a salary of just $1.

Company branding (just like company value) is in the future tense; it's about expectations of a good return on investment, a secure job, a reliable partner or supplier. If I tell you 'I plan to climb mount Everest one day', I create a vision of my future in your mind. If I say I'm 'just planning to muddle through' I don't. Building future expectations requires a tangible proposition, because this gives you codes, the images and beliefs, for a new mental model.

Current events tend to be interpreted in the context of the heritage and goals of the firm. That's what stories do. They make sense of otherwise inchoate current events.

Company branding is not about the news. It's about what people read into it. Ericsson is thought of (outside Sweden) as a maker of mobile phones. So, when Nokia hammered them in the handset market, Ericsson's stock and reputation suffered badly. Ericsson's core business is communication networks. If their brand had said 'Ericsson is like Cisco' they might have been better thought of in 1999/2000.

Any story has a lead character. That character is the CEO, founder or other leading figure. This is a critical factor in modern business. As Warren Buffet says of the investor view, 'people vote for the artist not the painting'.[93]

Virgin means different things to a business journalist, a passenger on Virgin Atlantic, or a print supplier. But the leader myth binds these views together; the story of Richard Branson the adventurer-entrepreneur. His balloon flights were the *Star Trek* factor that make his court cases and competitive squabbles look heroic rather than vindictive.

THE RETURN OF THE PATRON

The need to build platforms that bind company branding into one symphonic theme is likely, in my view, to create a shift from sponsorship (back) to patronage.

A sponsor is someone who puts up money in return for cheap relevant ad space. Nobody believes that Andersen Consulting had more than this in their mind when they sponsored those big golf tournaments (except that they knew that their CEO audience liked golf).

Charles Saatchi is a patron of the arts. His Saatchi gallery and collection has been instrumental in the development of Britart. The aggressive 'sensations' featuring artists like Damien Hirst happened also to be the perfect fit with their advertising agency's aesthetics and swagger.

The financiers of Florence funded the Renaissance. They believed in shaping society as well as self-promotion. Usually the patron dictated the subject, right down to a sketch, the materials to be used and even composition, to the artist (who was seen as an artisan). But they also gave the Michaelangelos and Raphaels enough latitude to execute their brief with world-changing visions of humanity and artistry.[94]

There's a template here for a new relationship between business and the creative industries. With businesses being much smarter about what creative products will best advance their cause. And creative people producing works of great authenticity and grandeur, to these briefs. Working on a bigger canvas than 'brand image'.

The measure to hold up against patronage schemes is: is it relevant and yet inspiring? Deep Blue was. So was the New British Art.

Big ideas, in big media formats, inspire people.

THE OLYMPIC RINGS OF BUSINESS

To quote Gary Hamel, 'Industry revolutionaries take the entire business concept, rather than a product and service, as the starting point for innovation'.[95] A new business concept is one level higher than the 'business model'. The concept describes the plan. The business model details the practicalities; how the company will make money, defend their position, scale to enormous heights . . .

The business concept boils down to a simple question: 'How are we reinventing our industry?' Most business strategy I've seen is too timid and hidebound by convention to set the world alight. There are too many companies in the world making 'slightly better lampshades' and not enough which are 'changing the way we light rooms'. There are enough budding Thomas Edisons in the world to make this conservatism dangerous.

None of this superficially has anything to do with branding. Surely a company can come up with a new way of doing things and then use branding – concept branding, if they are truly forward-looking – to put it in people's minds? But there is an argument for expressing your company vision and strategy in a form which deeply inspires and informs people; for also branding what used to be 'just the business plan'.

Customers – are increasingly interested in the company behind their purchases. A great parent company adds excitement and high expectations. Also customers are increasingly educated and switched on. They need to understand *why* they should believe that this company's products and services are better. Knowledge of the company's authentic strengths and track record can provide this evidence. And they are increasingly questioning the ethics of business. They won't buy from just anyone.

Employees nowadays are involved both in coming up with business innovations and with implementing them with autonomy.

It used to be okay to come up with a five-year plan and brief a few managers on their division's targets. Now it's hard to plan in detail more than one year ahead. Those closest to the production or the customer are best placed to come up with ideas that make a difference; innovation is distributed. If they don't have a unifying concept of where the company is heading, the result is chaos. That's why purpose, values, vision and mission are such common words in the boardroom today.

Partners – we're moving from business monoliths to fragmented networks of partners, suppliers and intermediaries. Exciting people in other partner companies about your plans is not easy. Inside your company there are rich media available; the intranet site, company meetings, face-to-face briefings . . . But when addressing people in partner companies, the communications have to be compressed, and companies tend to be sceptical about other companies' grand plans. So a great concept needs a double-great expression, to cut through.

When K-World, my digital learning client, was first pitching to the US TV studios as potential programming partners, they honed their concept down to one line: 'We're going to do for knowledge what MTV did for music.'

Investors – shareholder knowledge, confidence and support for your ambitious plans are vital. The way one investment banker put it to me was: 'capital is like oxygen'. If shareholders believe that your plan is better than your competitors', they not only breathe life into it, they shut oxygen off from the others entering.

Nobody scrutinizes a business plan more carefully than someone about to stake their (or their clients') future wealth on it. But having human minds, they make decisions on the big picture, not the detail. Big, simple, compelling concepts that they can touch, believe in, comprehend and appreciate win out. In other words, investors' mental models are key.

The Media – companies, their activities, their leaders have become prominent news stories in the last five years. The individual investor boom has created a need for regular news information. There is a greater public interest in the activities of companies; both from sceptical customers, and also from workers trying to gauge the economic 'weather'. And business media have undergone a transformation, with high profile, successful new TV channels and magazines homing in on the new audience, and the new business spirit.

Business has gone from being frankly quite dull to very exciting. Anyone who's ever been interviewed will know that you have to be terse and yet compelling. And that journalists come with pre-conceptions which you have to work around. Managing business publicity now is similar to political electioneering. Only fiercer.

A new business concept needs to engage these five key stakeholders; the 'Olympic Rings' of modern business, and the marketing campaigns that target each group, while not identical, do need to be consistent.

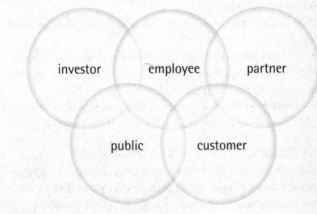

Fig. 40 | *The 'Olympic rings' of business*

LEADERSHIP FROM MOTHER

Mother's values set it apart from other banks.

The company ensures that a good proportion of its profits are ploughed into strategic philanthropy which underlines the company's positioning, develops new markets and makes society a sustainable place for it to do business in. Mother Trust initiatives include grants and content provision for business education in sub-Saharan Africa (the most popular course in this region, along with maths, English and IT).

To maximize the effects, Mother employs an incentive scheme with customers. Those who meet eco-standards set by the Mother community receive discounts on services.

BRINGING LEADERSHIP BRANDING TO LIFE – SOME STARTING POINTS

1 Are you *the* authority in the markets in which you operate and those in which you will wish to operate in future? What strategic acquisitions, partnerships and actions could plug the gaps?

2 What inside stories energize your company? Why are they only known inside?

3 Try scripting your strategy as a newspaper article. What's the four-word headline? What's the clinching example? Is it credible? Would it make the front page?

4 Try writing the story of your market past-present-future, from the perspective of different stakeholders: employees, investors, customers, partners, the public, even your competitors. What does this helicopter tour reveal as the unifying thread? I did this exercise on the fly for PlayStation and came up with the answer – instinct.

5 Are your stakeholders optimistic or pessimistic about you, overall? And why?

6 Taking a compendium of classic stories – for instance an encyclopedia of mythology – and an afternoon, try fitting your vision to different epic archetypes. Perhaps you could be David, in 'David and Goliath'?

7 What's the most inspiring thing about your business? It probably isn't putting a man on the moon. But it might be a cause like curing cancer or feeding the world (biotech), battling corruption (accountancy), or bonding friends

and family (telco), or upholding the truth (the BBC). What would a good movie producer do with that theme and a budget? Why not ask one?

8 If you analyse your company into story components – the leader, the heritage etc. – where are the key strengths and weaknesses? What alternative stories can be made from the same company ingredients?

9 What 'happening' (think Deep Blue) would bring your vision to life?

10 What's the most exciting creative product you could be a patron of?

PUTTING THEORY INTO PRACTICE

The four segments of the new marketing paradigm can be used as a framework for planning marketing campaigns:

- *Why? – guides the business concept development.*
- *Who? – matches business ideas to real life needs, situations and people.*
- *What? – guides the development of branded concepts.*
- *How? – guides the interactive media strategy and helps build a molecule of branding initiatives.*

The evolution of the mobile phone market provides a worked example of this four stage planning process in action.

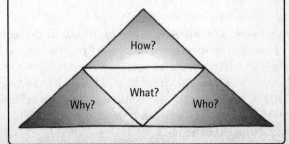

DEVELOPING A LEVEL THREE STRATEGY

How do you put the ideas in this book into practice?

I use the pyramid model to develop strategies for my clients. The process tends to be iterative; new business models, new audience insights, new concepts or new media platform ideas can each change the way you look at the other sections, and the total strategy needs to be coherent. So in practice you need to work on all of them at once.

However as a first pass, it makes sense to work through the sections in order:

- start with the business situation and goals (the Why?)
- then gather audience insights and trends (the Who?)
- then create branded concepts (the What?)
- then look for media and learning strategies to transmit these concepts (the How?).

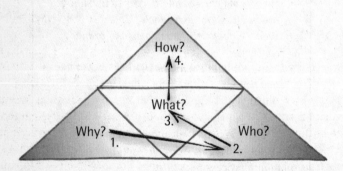

Fig. 41 *The pyramid model*

I'm going to use the mobile market as a worked example. I've been approached by several companies with potential projects in this area. The following chapters reflect my authentic early process of getting to grips with the market. I have yet to be briefed by any of these companies, so I am working with scant information. My initial ideas may be flawed. But they do serve to demonstrate the thought process in action.

18

(WHY?) BUSINESS ANALYSIS
AND HYPOTHESES

A proper flow of information generates a creative stream. People
with access to multiple sources of information (about customers, products, social development, markets, competitors
etc.) can make links and recognise opportunities at a rate far
exceeding those who have access to limited or narrow sources
of information.

TERRY FINERTY

I interviewed Terry Finerty for an article I wrote for the *Financial
Times* on creativity in business.[96] Most of the other people I interviewed emphasized fun, diversion, sources of inspiration and
creative environments. Terry (who was my main client at Arthur
Anderson on a project to evolve their business strategy) emphasized information – and lots of it. In my experience Terry is right,
accessing information and problem-finding are by far the most
important contributors to developing compelling yet relevant
new creative ideas.

At the start of any project the best approach is to become a
sponge. That's easy when you know very little about the market,
and is much harder when you have 'seen it all before'. Then
you have to force yourself to look at your market through new
eyes.

That's why it is often valuable to include qualified beginners
in your project team as well as experts. My project to re-brand
the country of Sweden came about because the government-

sponsored task force decided they needed a non-Swede to lead their thinking along new lines.

Whether you are a beginner (like me with mobiles phones) or an expert, there are two important factors: how much information you gain and also your attitude to that information. The right attitude is being accepting enough to take in new information, but not so accepting that you get taken in by it and become trapped by conventional wisdom. It's a mixture of 90 per cent humility ('there's so much more I could know about this subject') with 10 per cent arrogance ('I could do this much better').

Provided you keep your critical, questioning, sifting side alert, then the quality of the output is proportional to the quantity of the input. You simply cannot know too much.

It's also important to take in a diverse set of views on the same topic. If all you read is industry reports you will form the idea that the future has already happened (and that it went very smoothly in a predictable direction). You will also fall prey to the most generic strategies which 'everyone knows are right'. Which at best will put you several years behind competitors who have already chosen this course. You need to take in dissenting voices and search for anomalies and gaps, to get confused in order to achieve a higher level understanding than is present in what 'everyone thinks is happening'.

Most industry revolutions start with either a counter-intuitive strategy or an adjacent possibility, which was overlooked. Both are possible when things change. When deep change happens, the old mentality that served the industry well in a past era develops inaccuracies and omissions when applied to a new situation.

Blockbuster was a category killer in the video-rental market. Probably because the founder's previous business was in transportation and refuse collection. He thought in terms of efficiently shifting boxes (taking advantage of new logistics). The aggressive *bulk* of Blockbuster (size of stores, copies of film per store) brought a 'supermarket' mentality to what had previously been a 'delicatessen'. This was counter-intuitive for the video industry because they were caught in the image of their 'Hollywood' product.

Karaoke established a whole new entertainment industry in social venues. The technology consists of a backing track and an autocue – nothing really revolutionary there. The real breakthrough was spotting an adjacent possibility. Look around any disco when a popular song comes on and you see people mouthing the words. People who are out having a good time like to sing along. The karaoke machine was a product that filled an existing need. And in the process changed the social life of modern society (especially in Japan).

The Internet has made it possible to access diverse information very easily. Search engines such as Google give you a wealth of articles, reports and trends within seconds. So much so that it is easy to get buried by the sheer quantity of information. A search for Web pages on 'mobile phones' returned 921,000 entries. So it's important to home in on your questions; what do I actually want to find out? and then search using much more defined questions and criteria.

The typical questions would include:

- basic statistics – market size, trends, key players, customer penetration, key segments
- business models – what makes this industry tick? How do the different players make money? From what exactly? What is the value network (including retailers, partners, suppliers, even competitors)?
- what is the vision and mission stated by the key players in annual reports and interviews?
- what makes your business unique and competitive? What are your key strengths, weaknesses, opportunities and threats? What company culture factors drive you?
- what is your company's positioning and what does that sacrifice? What else are customers doing in their lives that might be relevant?
- context – what business are you in? What adjacent businesses could you be in? What are the key success stories in your industry? What inspiring cases in other industries could be a template for doing things differently?
- what's new? What are the main lines of development? What

are the key choices and options ahead? What do the experts and advisors suggest as scenarios?

■ what's the one key fact that could drive your thinking in a new direction?

Analysis is supposed to have a point. For developing a new marketing paradigm, the sharper that point the better. All of this diverse information should drive you to the realization that there is one new direction the company *must* take.

THE MOBILE MARKET

I have been on a trawl through information on the mobile market. I'm assuming that my 'client' is a mobile phone *manufacturer* as opposed to operators and service providers – for convenience I will take Ericsson as my hypothetical case example (they are not one of the companies which have approached me). The global mobile market is huge and has grown very fast:

Mobile service revenues (source ITU):

	$ billion
1990	11
1992	23
1994	47
1996	104
1998	154
2000	230

This total revenue in 2000 is the same size as the whole economy (GDP) of countries like Sweden ($227 billion), Switzerland ($241 billion) and Belgium ($227 billion).[97] Between 1900 and 2000 users have grown 60-fold (50 per cent per year) and revenues have grown 30-fold (40 per cent per year). There were 684 million mobile phone subscribers in year 2000, which is about 70 per cent of the number who have fixed phones. So it's not all that surprising that the market is approaching saturation. . . .

Mobile Phone Sales Hit a Brick Wall

405 million mobile phones were sold in 2000 and even optimistic industry estimates now predict that about the same number will be sold in 2001.

Why have mobile sales suddenly stopped growing?

According to Jorma Ollila, Nokia's chairman and CEO, 'We believe that this slowdown is a result of a general market deterioration driven by economic uncertainty, the ongoing technology transition and less aggressive marketing by the operators.' Commentators add that mobile phones – which had never been through a major recession before – are highly discretionary, because most handset sales in recent years have been replacements for older models, rather than purchases by new users. It is easy, this view says, for users to stick with their current model as hard times approach.

I am sceptical about these explanations.

They suggest that there has been a temporary setback in a market that is destined to grow at 50 per cent a year again. That may be true in regions with fast developing new user bases, like China. But this is unlikely to be Ericsson's core opportunity, unless it is through a joint venture with a local firm. And fast though China's development may be, it won't double the global phone market every two years.

The slowdown in IT markets (like computers) has been driven by companies placing fewer orders, not by consumer spending, which if anything is overheated in markets like housing, fashion and holidays. Japan, which has been in deep recession for the last ten years, has been one of the most buoyant markets for mobile phones.

It seems to me much more likely that the market has simply reached a plateau. It might be very interesting, therefore, to look at recent successes and failures.

It's New Services, Not Handsets Which Will Drive the Market

The market has run out of new users. So the natural next stage, to drive replacement of 'outdated' models is to develop new uses. That's exactly the reason why i-mode succeeded in Japan, while WAP failed in Europe.

With nearly 16 million subscribers in less than two full years of commercial service experience, i-mode is the leading success story of today's mobile market.

The surest way to have a good idea is to have a lot of ideas.

LINUS PAULING

NTT DoCoMo launched the i-mode service in 1999. i-mode is quite basic compared to WAP. The language is based on a subset of HTML (the Web protocol) rather than WAP's more advanced and mobile-specialized XML. How i-mode scores over WAP is firstly in the user experience and applications. It has a great graphical user interface (GUI) with full colour and large displays. And secondly it uses a packet network; without going into details this means the Internet connection is 'always on' rather than dial up.

DoCoMo's business model is based on revenue sharing with 250 content and application service providers. They have relied on these experts to supply the services, rather than trying to do it themselves. It's exactly the same way that PlayStation attacked the computer games market. It encourages a fast developing and diverse range of applications. It also leads to much more creative and effective solutions.

The result was that great applications led the market. When ringtone downloads became possible with new handsets, the partners created more than 1000 ringtones by the time the phones were launched.

The most popular i-mode services include: e-mail, Bandai (down-loadable cartoon characters), Nikkei News, mobile banking, ringtone and music downloads and navigation. One of the killer applications was MP3 music downloads, which was not even technically possible with the original WAP handsets. Another great service was city navigation; which provides real-time information on restaurants, cafés, bars, hotels and parking space.

The early WAP applications were fairly boring, and first impressions count. I remember some friends arriving excitedly for brunch one Sunday to show off their new WAP phones. But all they had to show were slow-to-connect news and weather reports – we were soon back in our Sunday newspapers.

According to Takeshi Natsuno, a DoCoMo business manager, the key to i-mode's success was starting with the business model (not the technology) and realizing that it was content that would sell the service.[98] His four criteria for this content were:

- it should be fresh ('once a day is too slow')
- it should be 'deep' (ie rich and satisfying)
- it should encourage repeat visits (e.g. games)
- the user should be able to see the benefit.

Another factor in i-mode's success was that the fixed Internet had been slow to take off in Japan (Internet penetration was only 13 per cent). i-mode took people online for the first time. The biggest ISP (Internet Service Provider) in the country is DoCoMo. Not only was DoCoMo leading the Internet access charge, but it is profitable, making about $200 in revenue, per subscriber, per year. The core user base for this service is 24–35 year olds. The heaviest users, in contrast with other areas of the Internet, are women.

One huge challenge to the conventional wisdom that has been driving mobile phone development is that, with i-mode you don't need much bandwidth. DoCoMo's packet network actually supports speeds of up to 28.8 kbps. But the tiny size of the phone screen means that less is needed – i-mode content runs at 9600 bps. The average homepage size is 1.2 kilobytes; e-mails are limited to 500 bytes and each phone can store up to 100 e-mails.

One significant side-effect of i-mode is that Japanese users change their handsets at least once a year, compared with much slower replacement rates in Europe.

Now DoCoMo are leading the way into third generation (3G) phones. Whereas European operators are doing their best to get WAP (2.5G) right with a new mobile-services initiative, which has similarities with i-mode as a common user-friendly standard format. They need to recoup some of their heavy investment in this level, before going onto the (even more costly) high bandwidth 3G phones in about two years' time.

The Next Revolution?

The failure of WAP (and of the hoped for boom in m-commerce, m-finance and so on) have put a big question mark in investors' minds about the potential for the next generation mobiles, which the operators paid crippling amounts to license. In the UK, operators paid £22.5 billion, in Germany the figure was 50.5 billion Euros . . . Good news for governments perhaps but terrible news for the industry and also the subscribers who will somehow eventually have to pay for this, if 3G services are to repay investors.

The generations in mobile phones have been based on new technological paradigms:

1G. 1980s. Analog signals. Voice only.
2G. 1990s. Digital signals. Voice, data, SMS.
2.5G. 2000. Enhanced data, WAP, packets. 'Better' internet connection.
3G. 2001+. High bandwidth (up to 2Mb/s). Streaming multimedia capability, broadband.

3G is already on test in Japan. It is planned for 2002/3 in Europe, which is now rolling out GPRS (always on) technology. The US is unlikely to even roll out GPRS until late in 2002.

The Crux of the Current Situation

Ericsson face a nest of challenges. The bottom just fell out of their handset market. The operators should be driving the services that sell the new (2.5 and 3) generation handsets, but they are even more strapped for cash. There is also a possibility that software and service providers will do to the hardware makers, what Microsoft did to IBM. So things are getting interesting.

Ericsson got hammered by Nokia in round two of a boxing contest (although half way through this round, both got pretty beaten up by the failure of WAP). Now they have a whole new round, and the rules will change dramatically. This might even suit the underdog.

Counter-Intuitive Solutions and Adjacent Possibilities

The big limit on mobile phone companies may be assuming they will make money from mobile *phones*.

Over 70 per cent of people who have fixed phones now also have mobile phones. These mobile phones are small, reliable and attractive. They do the job. When did you last replace the fixed phone in your home? Why should mobile phones be any different? This is now officially a very mature market.

On the other hand if you see it as making mobile *devices*, for many other uses than phoning people, then there is an unlimited future market.

The industry knows this and is busy making prototype handsets that can be phones *plus* lots of other things at the same time. They have dual-band operation, with the phone part using the old GSM networks. That is still phone-centric thinking.

My hypothesis for mobile equipment makers is that *the future is in non-phones*.

Some generalist competitors will offer 'everything in one unit'. Like DoCoMo and their partners who will have up to two years start in the Europeans. Let them. Just as PlayStation doesn't mind that there is a PC gaming market alongside their highly adapted console. The problem they will face is persuading people to trade up to a very expensive, bulky and heavy phone that also plays games and does other stuff. While the light, low bandwidth, cheap i-mode type predecessors have great games and services etc. already.

The personal digital assistants (PDAs) like Palm and Handspring (whatever their current business slowdown woes) have shown that a dedicated unit can outgun an adapted phone. PDA's are much better for office-type admin. Phones are good for phoning each has fought and held its own corner, because users see the clear benefits of having one of each. Putting both in one unit makes it too bulky, heavy and pricey.

Ericsson would go from serving a mature market with diminishing opportunities and returns to supplying a completely new market. And why stop at one device? This intuitively feels right. It's the way markets develop.

- **THE PLAYSTATION FACTOR:** the features would be optimized for the function. So that the experience would be great and not 'squashed into an all-purpose phone'.
- **THE I-MAC FACTOR:** they'd be desirable objects in their own right. Because being specialized, they could have powerful design aesthetics too.
- **THE 4WD FACTOR:** the car market started like mobile phones with a simple A-B device. But matured into 4-wheel-drive vehicles, sports cars, and people carriers . . .
- **THE MAKE-UP BAG FACTOR:** there is no limit to people's desire for little portable luxuries. Why not have two or even five mobile devices in your bag? With the extra volumes driving down costs of the basic technologies, to make this affordable.

The business is driven by killer applications (because these get people to buy new handsets). My hypothesis is that the way to deliver these is through specialist non-phone devices. The big question then of course is *which applications for whom?*

19

(WHO?) AUDIENCE
INSIGHTS AND TRENDS

> If I'd asked people what they wanted, I would have made a faster
> horse.
>
> HENRY FORD

The market research industry has evolved to help level two (brand-image) marketing optimize products and communications in mature markets. It is very good at extrapolating existing needs. It is equally bad at helping companies envision future markets, customer segments and needs which are based on discontinuous change.

Many have pointed this out since Henry Ford. Most take it as an excuse to use no research and rely on their instincts instead. Barry Diller tells the story of when he took over at QVC. In the first year his quick-win new initiatives brought success. He then had a disastrous second year which, according to Diller, was because he listened to the research experts. He fired these experts and went on to have a great third year.

That's okay if you have great instincts. But those great instincts have to come from somewhere. My view is that real-world social insights are still vital to marketing. Without them you may behave with low 'EQ' (like the dot-coms).

But those insights need to go beyond researching your current market and audience. They need to anticipate and create a future market and audience. Which takes us from scientific dissections of society into science fiction. The imagination is the most powerful research tool ever invented.

The big difficulty is escaping the grip of the present reality. Because our brains were invented to do things like market research most of the time and things like science fiction only with great effort. It's all too easy to fall back on lazy thinking.

Think about a market you've worked in recently. And your mind floods with clichés, stereotypes, and the ways 'things have always been'.

If you've worked in the baby products market your mind would probably now be full of 'mother and baby' images. If you wanted to drive this market somewhere new you'd need to look at emerging realities, not traditional ones; like father and baby. Or babies in work crèches. Or baby-sharing among busy part-time professionals (a real trend in the US apparently). To develop new audience concepts, you need to lead your mind into new possibilities. Ones that anticipate the future, rather than repeating the past.

This is where the insights of cognitive science are useful in ordering your own thoughts and directing your mind to productive ends. Earlier I briefly touched on a very important finding of research into categories of knowledge, which is that we think on three levels:

High Level, Abstract – e.g. 'mammal'
Basic Level, Normal – e.g. 'dog'
Fine Scale, Discriminating – e.g. 'cocker spaniel'

In everyday thinking and communication we use the basic level for convenience. You don't say (or think) 'there's a mammal on the porch' nor (in most circumstances) 'there's a cocker spaniel on the porch'.

The problem for our challenge of inventing new social realities is that basic-level thinking leads the mind along familiar lines (that's why it is convenient). Instead you need to zig-zag between abstract high-level thinking and very fine scale, true-to-life-as-it-is-lived thinking. To alternate between being a 'philosopher' and a 'novelist'.

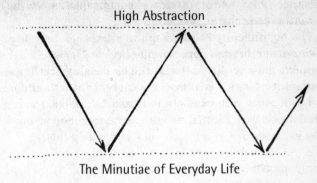

Fig. 42 *Thinking patterns need to change to invent new social realities*

In this way it is possible to explore beyond the obvious. To spot things which are not usually visible because they are too big (slow, broad trends) or too small (quirks of human nature that escape everyday attention). With these realms in mind, market research suddenly becomes tremendously helpful again. Because you approach it like a philosopher trying to discern some very abstract notion behind what is said, or like a novelist researching a new book (and you filter out all the trite stuff in the middle).

On the abstract level the main questions to ask are:

Which major un-met human needs might be relevant?
It's tempting to see human beings as sated with modern consumer markets. It's at a more abstract level that huge unmet needs make themselves visible. For instance, stable and full relationships (lover, family, friend and colleague . . .) are a core human need. And judged by longevity, loyalty and loneliness modern relationships are not working.

Which major abstract trends in human societies might have a bearing?
For example, anthropologist Mary Douglas described modern societies as being characterized by a growth of 'gentleness'. When trends are as abstract as this, they are more thought-provoking than the 'basic level' trends that do get noticed in everday life (and reported in the news) like 'New Age', 'vegetarianism' or

'new man'. A key test of abstract concepts is that they *do not bring to mind a ready mental image.*

What possibilities and opportunities can we apply?
Here I'm talking about the kinds of insights that appear by combining abstract qualities. For instance, in the Internet, a cheap network of previously localized information and media created new possibilities. These can be understood as offering both richness and reach (whereas previously this was a trade off).

The danger of the high altitude abstract plane on its own is creating unrealistic ideas. That's why we also need to keep dipping down into the earth of real-life insights. The questions you need to ask here are much more broad-ranging, loose and unstructured. The essential attitude is curiosity about what makes people tick and imaginative projections about what could work if society changed:

- if our product did not exist what would people do instead?
- how does our product fit into their lives?
- how do they first meet us?
- what are their habits around us?
- what do they love and hate?
- why do some people get much deeper into this stuff than others?
- what vivid experiences have stuck in their minds?
- what desires and frustrations segment our market for us?
- what else are they doing in their lives that might be relevant?
- how have similar parts of life worked in different societies and ages?
- at some point in history this category was exciting. What was exciting about it?

We are our own best research subjects. We can imagine new ways of living, on this authentic everyday level of our own thoughts, feelings and experiences that no amount of objective questions could ever get to.

This is a time to daydream, to go out and watch people, to imagine a world which was subtly different from what you see around you, but still true to human nature and mores. Another major resource is fiction. You'll learn more about modern young women by reading *Bridget Jones's Diary* than research groups will ever tell you. Remember that television, the atom bomb and space satellites were all invented by 'science fiction'.

MOBILE DEVICES – NEW INSIGHTS AND NEEDS

Let's look at this the normal way first. Many obvious applications have already been suggested for 3G. Perhaps we don't need to look any further?

Mobile Television. If people spend so many hours watching TV at home, why not when they are in transit? TV handsets would need much bigger screens than 3G mobile phones – more like the screens in handheld PCs and DVD players.

Mobile Computer Games. Networked games are already predicted to be the key application that drives 3G handset sales. A specialist mobile console game could run existing computer games software, using a state of the art graphics card and CPU and with a proper games controller. The Internet connection means live network gaming.

Mobile Gambling. Gambling is the fastest growing leisure market in the UK and has been in the top three for the last five years. The device would have television features so you could watch sports events live, and also specialized interactive gambling buttons and menus (click on the horse to readout its current form and the odds).

Mobile Life Management. A rich media device could combine the best of administration (eg PDAs and mobile banking) with lifestyle content. A typical application might be viewing a holiday hotel and resort, before clearing the funds into your bank account and booking direct. The device would also be a credit-card-like payment device linked securely to your bank, and an advice channel.

Videophone. This would increase the intimacy of existing (voice) conversations so it might be most applicable to intimate relationships. One-to-one uses would also get it past the first hurdle, which is how to sell the device when the number of users in the network is low. Imagine a heart shaped device that is used for virtual blind dates and also by couples who spend lots of time apart. Spiced up perhaps with video clips, icons and role-playing games in shared spaces . . .

Enterprise Applications (for business use). The first one being a laptop 3G card to create a permanent high bandwidth connection for us mobile professionals. Why plug a phone into your PC when you can connect direct? Later a specialist console could be developed to solve the problem of remote meetings among sales forces and other itinerant professionals, with a rich interface combining videoconferencing with multimedia clips, slides and shared spaces . . .

Music. Why even download MP3s? Why not have a super-high-fidelity device that has jukebox direct access to all catalogued music in the world? You could tag favourites or even set it to any radio station in the world if you were feeling lazy. The interface would in due course become voice-operated. 'I'd like to listen to the most recent Paul Oakenfeld set . . .'

It seems to me that all of these ideas suffer from 'clinging to the side of the pool'. They take existing multimedia markets and hope that a mobile version with screen and high bandwidth will create a whole new market.

But if you look at them a bit closer to life as it is lived, you begin to wonder how they are truly valuable as advances on what is available now. After all, the devices will cost hundreds of pounds and the connection fees will be high (because the new network technology and licenses must be paid for).

Will gamblers, who already bet by phone and Internet and betting shop, switch to mobile with streaming video? Most of the new gambling happens from work, especially from workers in the financial markets, which is where half the phone calls to Gamblers Anonymous came from last year.

A typical high-tech gambler is sitting around in a city dealing room, bored, in a lull in the day's trading. They are placing spread bets on a horse race or football match next weekend using their trading skills to spot combinations of odds and probabilities which might beat the bookie. They are using their computer screen and maybe a phone call or two. They do not have any unmet needs that a bulky, expensive handset could solve. If they did want to go mobile, they don't need high bandwidth so much as security.

Then there are computer games. These are solitary, concentrated, screen-staring contests, with high tactility (the games controller or joystick) and incredibly advanced graphics, which demand high quality big screens. The PlayStation 3, out around the same time as 3G, will have real-time animation three times more advanced than what you saw on screen in *Jurassic Park*. Whereas a portable small screen version would take things right back to pre-PlayStation levels. The disposable, low resolution, portable, short play games are already well catered for by Gameboy. The networked games already work well at fairly low modem speed, because the fast processing is kept local on the games engine in the console.

I'm not saying that high-bandwidth mobile gaming devices won't take off. But it's going to be a tough, tight space to develop and justify. The world is not short of computer gaming opportunities. And the natural location is either in your bedroom (console games) or at work when the boss isn't watching (PC games).

There is a general problem with the screen-based mobile entertainment models. They require you to stare at the screen. So you can't be walking around or driving. What's worse, the high bandwidth is only technically possible when the receiver is nearly stationary. In a train travelling at 100 miles per hour the bandwidth would be reduced to existing i-mode levels.

Even at the highest rates (of 2Mb/s) 3G would be far from offering decent definition TV. While laptops offer convenient DVD drives as standard, with incredible screen quality. And who knows, the 'price per view' could actually be cheaper on DVD than 3G?

Enterprise applications were supposed to be the mainstay of WAP. But studies show that most usage has been for voice rather than additional features and that companies are now shifting back from WAP to simpler, basic phones. Plus the handheld digital assistants will hold their own. And video conferencing is a very stilted way to hold a meeting.

Music, shopping and banking are already great i-mode applications and they will be pushed very hard in the 2.5G mobile services stage (an attempt to revive WAP's flagging fortunes). It's very hard to see how the benefit of high bandwidth to these services (streaming media and video) would outweigh the huge cost, especially in a market which may have got out of the habit of replacing old handsets just to 'keep up'.

The most promising of these services is probably videophone for personal use, which is at least a 'sci-fi' application we've been waiting for. I'd buy it, provided it wasn't too expensive and all my friends were buying it too. But I'd probably buy it in a standard 3G handset (built-in cameras are already planned in some prototypes), so that I could alternate between using videophone and voice-only.

While I have probably been over-pessimistic in my assessments, my main point is that there is a case for looking beyond the obvious. Especially given our (hypothetical) strategy of launching specialist non-phone devices which could compete with all the generalist handsets offering all these services together with the old standards like e-mail, SMS and phone calls too. We need to come up with something special and new . . .

Let's start at the abstract level. What does 3G actually offer over existing technologies? The screens and other features (like being always on) will be available from 2.5G phones. The only real difference is one significant new feature – high bandwidth.

Now switch to real-life details. High-bandwidth Internet connection is already available for fixed computers. I've just bought a DSL connection. Not for streaming video, networked games or anything like that. But because I am sick of paying huge connection charges and waiting hours every time I want to download a big file. I have a fairly fast line already (ISDN) and a recent download (of some developer software) took eight hours.

This isn't just a business-user insight. File sharing sites are very popular with the 'underground' of music swapping

(Napster clones like Morpheus and Bearshare) and also to trade in 'cracked' software files (using Hotline and other hacker community sites).

So downloading massive files may be a lead worth following. It's not immediately obvious what content or software people would need to download to their mobile devices. But that's only because I haven't specified a big unmet need yet. . . .

Let's take our lead from the 'learning ethic' trend I described in detail earlier:

- There is an explosion of formal education going on – with more people going into higher education, work-based training and other forms of life-long learning.
- There is a broader trend in existing media towards smart culture, which feeds your mind with knowledge-rich content (that's also passionate and vivid).
- Learning and self-development are taking over (from status and instant gratification) as the core driving motivations of individuals and society.
- The prime cause of these shifts is uncertainty; in fluid times of rapid change where traditions and past knowledge fail us, and we each need to work things out for ourselves.

Put these abstract lifelong-learning trends together with the ability to deliver big information files in rich and varied forms and you get – for instance – something that you'll recognize immediately from science fiction as something like *The Hitch-Hiker's Guide to the Galaxy*.

This could be a live source of instant knowledge, that could help us navigate through life: in an art gallery, a book about ecclesiastical theology, a foreign city airport, or even today's newspaper . . . whenever we had frustrating gaps in our knowledge, we could call it up in vivid, varied forms.

That is a very promising real-life un-met need. It's more knowledge than you could ever fit on a thousand hard drives. Only a high bandwidth mobile device could hope to satisfy this need in the living contexts where it arises. Of course it's only a hypothetical case. The main point was to show how abstract trends and close-to-real-life insight can combine to take marketing beyond the obvious.

One final point is that it's best at this stage not to close down your options. The device that meets the need for high bandwidth learning might be like *The Hitchhiker's Guide.* It might work in a thousand other ways too – using positioning satellites, AI (to learn how you learn and what you already know), it might be for business, school or pleasure . . . It's best to leave all that open for the concept stage.

20

(WHAT?) THE CORE CONCEPT

Many are stubborn about the means, but few are stubborn about
the ends.

FRIEDRICH NIETZSCHE

Introducing a new human concept (as opposed to giving a product an image) is an exercise in pure discipline. For the last fifty
years we have developed sophisticated techniques for branding
tangible products and services. Now it is the turn of intangible
concepts, which drive whole new markets. And that's far harder
to do.

These can (and must) take tangible forms. Either as novel
products and experiences, like the DVD disc. Or as intangible
cultural concepts, like netiquette (the etiquette of the Internet).
In either case, new concepts succeed in gaining acceptance
when they have clear, distinct and consistent components which
add up to a new mental model:

Building a new concept is tentative work. It is all too easy to
be led by past mental models, using predictable and established
elements. This is only natural as these models are held in
our brains as well-worn pathways (frequently fired circuits of
neurons).

I find it is essential to put down definite markers in the coding
part of the concept – strong, evocative sense impressions and
clear, logical propositions. Once these are in place, it is much
harder to slip back into cliché and stereotype.

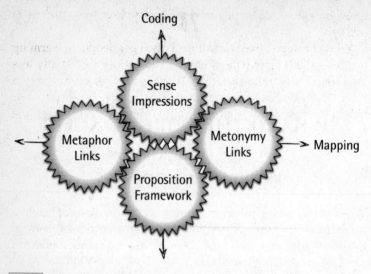

Coding

Sense
Impressions

Metaphor
Links

Metonymy
Links

Mapping

Proposition
Framework

Fig. 43 | *A new mental model*

These markers hold the new concept to its new intentions, but it is the mapping elements which make a concept sticky, lively and engaging. Metonymy selects the part to be foregrounded, simplifying the concept considerably. And metaphor relates it to known emotional and cultural territories, giving it resonance with other human experiences.

The nearest existing process I know to this is design. Designers make 'the skin of culture'. Gary Swindell, creative director of an Oslo design agency, told me that he once started a project for an airline by studying the history of flight (= propositions). And his team made an award-winning breakthrough in ski-wear design when they decided to take moto-cross clothing as their starting point instead (= sense impressions).

Designers have the right skills to build new concepts, but are somewhat hampered by the fact that their product is 'designs'. In rare projects, such as the design of the i-Mac, a designer is working on the redefinition of a category. But more often they are commissioned to update a company or brand's image. As Swindell once complained to me, '90 per cent of the briefs we get say "modern, friendly and innovative".' With these propositions in place, achieving any kind of conceptual change is unlikely.

When I run creative workshops I often get people to warm up by 'designing a new type of chair'. The results are usually less than impressive. I then ask them to try again with a new concept brief: 'design a chair for whales' (or similar). By forcing our minds to work on unusual propositions and mental images, the result is guaranteed to be creative.

MOBILE LEARNING DEVICES

When you plant a sapling, you often strap it to a piece of bamboo for support. As it grows into a tree it outgrows this support. In fact you'd usually remove the piece of bamboo before it starts to stunt the tree's growth or shape.

The early ideas in a project (which tend to be metaphors) are like this piece of bamboo. They tend to draw on established, emotionalized and easy to accept ideas. The *Hitchhiker's Guide* is a perfect example of this. On the one hand it points to a familiar and well-loved piece of culture which does roughly the job that our new device might do. On the other hand it is very limiting compared with the full potential of the concept.

The original book by Douglas Adams was written in the 1970s and was first produced as a BBC radio broadcast in 1978. It is a child of its time in terms of the technology, certainly as portrayed in the later TV series. The display was in green text and lines (like computer monitors at the time). And it's basically a fixed database. You can now buy a CD-Rom encyclopedia which performs roughly the same functions (although it's admittedly short on wittily inventive content, like aliens who torture people by reading them bad poetry). What I have in mind is something far more ambitious.

A better sensory reference point can be found in the pioneering video work of Peter Greenaway, artist and film-maker. His BBC film of *Dante's Inferno* layered the screen with scrolling text, film images and the head of John Gielgud who is the narrator. This work positively crackles with electronic information. It's the best example I've ever seen of a possible future for multi-media, beyond the limiting conventions of Web pages.

Imagine you were in an art gallery and could call up images of other works by that artist, snippets from documentaries, text from the catalogue, commentaries by art critics, video diaries by current artists who were inspired by this work . . . all in a rich video collage. With modern artists there could even be footage of the work in progress.

Imagine you were on your way to a business meeting. Perhaps, if you were me, you'd be on your way to a workshop with a new client in the mobile phones market. The same collage format could be applied to the history of the company, videos of speeches by the CEO, news items, advertising, business case histories and product brochures.

Imagine you were reading a news item about the Middle East conflict and you realized that you were short on background knowledge to put this into context. Your collage might include documentaries, footage from the Helsinki peace summit, interviews with people on all sides of the conflict, maps and pages from history books written by each side.

What this kind of material would do is richly annotate as well as inform. Before I saw the BBC *Dante*, I had only a dim notion of the references in the book. Through the TV show I learned what wolves meant in medieval symbolism, why the journey into Hell circled in one (superstitious) direction, about the compromise in medieval theology over the place of Greek philosophers (not baptised and saved, but otherwise quoted and admired), how Dante's work was driven by his unrequited love for Beatrice (who he loved so much on first sight that he held his chest because he thought his heart had stopped beating) . . .

Rich media annotation would perform two functions. It puts information in a more engaging, diverse and entertaining form, and it stimulates our whole brain, not just the rational rote learning part – it puts us 'in touch' with the subject . . .

The key propositions I have in mind also go beyond the *Hitchhiker's Guide* (*HHGG*).

Like the *HHGG*, the device would be:

- portable
- encyclopaedic
- used while mobile
- to fill knowledge gaps that arise in context, instantly
- characterful, personal and cultural.

But unlike the *HHGG*, our device would also be:

- interactive (touch screen commands for 'more like this' etc.) rather than one-way
- customized, to fit the preferences and learning style of the user
- drawn from a huge repository of existing human knowledge and media content
- a rich multimedia learning experience
- a commercial service, which charged (by the megabyte) for content.

The most obvious metaphor for a richer learning service would be some kind of human character – an oracle avatar who 'reveals all'. That's after all why documentaries in television have their presenters. We relate to the material through another human being.

But having a human guide could make the service too 'linear'. It emphasizes passive receiving, not active discovery. It would limit the interface, and also the experience/system which would work better as a de-structured collage of material, which assembles itself from downloaded elements in your browser.

Instead I think we should go for the device as 'a second brain'. Let's call it BRAIN2.

It is a collective memory 'plug-in'. Brain science is a hot cultural property, and this invention is probably the first in a long line of cognitive amplifiers to come, the later ones being 'wet-ware' (ie changes to our brains). The metaphor says what the BRAIN2 does; it makes us smarter because it expands our store of knowledge.

In line with this organic theme, I think the metonymy should be tactile control. This makes the device feel like an extension of our bodies (rather than using voice operation and/or button pressing which would emphasize its separation). This is a chance to put touchscreen interactivity in the place of number pad and keyboard – a familiar interface for Palm users, and a natural step for the video game and computer mouse generation.

21

(HOW?) DESIGNING
A MEDIA PLATFORM

'It wasn't very civil of you to sit down without being invited,'
said the March Hare.

LEWIS CARROLL, *Alice's Adventures in Wonderland*

People are sick and tired of brands invading their personal and
cultural space. As one 13-year-old girl in a Dutch research report
from a music festival said, 'I wish brands would just leave us
alone'. Brands keep butting into our lives uninvited – between
TV programmes, in junk e-mail, along every city sight-line, in
movies and computer games (product placement), and now
even from friends who are participating in 'viral marketing'
(customer-to-customer) promotions.

This is not quite as simple as a rejection of brands. As I argued
earlier, brands are intrinsic to the way we make sense of the
world. And can play a valuable role if they step up a level in
helping us live meaningful lives.

Relevant media, which are accessed on demand, are welcomed. When I was buying a new computer recently I immersed
myself in websites, chatrooms, advice from Apple-owning
friends, visits to Apple retailers. I was hungry for knowledge and
stimulation to help me make a decision. That knowledge included quite deep research into things like the Java capabilities
of old versus new operating systems. For about a week I lived,
breathed and slept Apple and much besides. And I loved it.

The problem of the old mass media marketing is its carpet

bombing of all users, non-users and never going to be users, with useless information in the hope of hitting a few strategic targets in the process. On the other hand, permission marketing (wait to be invited) is usually too passive to establish bold general concepts. We need to meet people halfway.

The general solution to this problem is to build your own media platforms. If you want to establish a new concept in cookery, make cookery TV programmes. If you want to develop a dress code, launch books and magazines. If you want to establish a new social ambience or relationship, get into venues and create experiences. Or use many of the other strategies covered earlier, like working through communities, memes, patronage. And use new interactive media such as Internet forums and interactive TV.

Even when working within existing media, inventing your own genres (a media within a media) is a good way to think. It forces you to justify your presence.

THE MOBILE KNOWLEDGE PLATFORM

Our BRAIN2 device could be a key medium for twenty-first century learning.

The device (its inventor hopes) will be to the IQ age what television was to the Image age. If so, the question is not what other media platforms can do to market it, so much as what it can do for whole other domains of culture and commerce.

What the i-mode case study highlighted earlier is a universal law of media adoption: a medium is only ever as good as the content. Like i-mode the key link in building this medium would be partners who would supply the content and services.

To start we'd need deals with major quality content owners, like the BBC, the Gutenburg project (classic texts), major newspaper and book publishers and Encarta. They wouldn't need to develop anything new, but they would need to agree an unlimited license for the back catalogue. Naturally we'd ensure that the device and file format would not allow users to abuse the system for pirating. And the content owners would get extra revenue.

To give it more grit we'd also partner with schools and universities, to upload their intellectual properties in the form of video lectures, papers and so on. Again they would be getting extra revenues (and prestige) for little cost. And we could do a contra deal to provide hardware at very low prices, allowing them to run distance learning courses on the system (a booming sector in education).

Ideally we would supplement this base with rich, context-based content. This would be free because it would be there to enrich the experience of something else that is being paid for. Perhaps we could get Stockholm's tourist industry to upload *HHGG* type content, to be accessed by a global positioning system (GPS) as you moved around the city? Less ambitious, but no less valuable, would be venue-specific experiences – for galleries, operas, museums, universities, public buildings, even TV channels (like *Big Brother's* website) and shops (I'd ask IKEA first).

Our BRAIN2 device would aim to become a universal, rich knowledge-transfer medium. Put in on your kitchen table and cook with the Naked Chef, courtesy of Sainsbury's. Use it to navigate your company's knowledge base in an engaging form. Use it to revise for an exam by browsing around a historical period or physics discovery. Or even to watch a lecture you missed. With two services over and above the device and connection fee; *premium* for public content and *free* for marketing partners.

When media like this exist, everything I've described in this book will be ten times easier. In the meantime we'll have to keep building our own media platforms.

THE LAST WORD

DOING THE RIGHT THING?

Marketing in the old image-aspiration mould has given itself, and business, a bad name.

It has promoted stereotypes.

It has contributed to a climate of envy and superficial materialism.

It has clogged up our lives with crass and ugly noise.

It has charged customers for expensive advertising, design and other hidden extras.

This book describes the opportunity to create real value (changing people's lives) and to be part of the education and enlightenment revolution that's sweeping through society.

Given the huge knowledge gaps and shortage of great content, marketing could become welcomed, not zapped.

These new higher forms of marketing suit increasingly complex and intangible company concepts and the wholesale reinvention of markets.

And they are tailor-made for the new media landscape.

Only our 'legacy' mindsets are holding us back.

Even if this is just one marketing future among many, it's the most wholesome, sustainable and decent one I can think of.

So let's say goodbye to the image age.

And face up to a brand new tomorrow.

NOTES/BIBILIOGRAPHY

1 Guy Debord, *The Society of the Spectacle*, tr. Donald Nicholson-Smith (London, 1967)
2 Flynn, 'Massive IQ gains in 14 Nations: what IQ tests really measure.' *Pyschological Bulletin*, vol. 101
3 Horn, 'Organisation of abilities and the development of intelligence.' *Psychological Review*, vol. 75 (1968)
4 Claude Hopkins, *Scientific Advertising* (Moore Publishing, 1923)
5 Margaret Horsfield, *Biting the Dust* (Fourth Estate, 1998)
6 John de Graff, David Wann & Thomas H. Naylor, *Affluenza* (McGraw Hill, 2001)
7 Ernest Dichter, *Handbook of Consumer Motivations*, (Mc-Graw Hill, 1964)
8 The OECD Jobs Survey (1994, OECD Paris)
9 http://www.anycast.com
10 Robert Aunger (ed.), *Darwinizing Culture* (OUP, 2001)
11 M. Czikszentmihalyi, *The Evolving Self* (HarperPerennial, 1994)
12 Larry Downes & Chunka Mui, *Unleashing the Killer App* (HBS, 1998)
13 Manuel Castells, *The Rise of the Network Society* (Blackwell, 2000)
14 Manuel Castells, 'Informationalism and the Network Society,' in Pekka Himanen, *The Hacker Ethic* (Secker & Warburg, 2001)
15 Boulton, Samek & Libert, *Value Dynamics*
16 Gary Hamel, *Leading the Revolution* (HBS, 2000)
17 Ibid.
18 DTI MARIA report
19 Bob Garratt, *The Learning Organization*, rev. ed. (HarperCollins-Business, 2000), & see also Peter Senge, *The Fifth Discipline* (Doubleday, 1990).
20 CSFB E-Learning Report (1999)
21 US Bureau of Labour statistics

22   *www.vpskillssummit,org*
23   Campaign for Learning, MORI
24   See 20
25   US Census Bureau/Merrill Lynch
26   Ghoshall & Bartlett, *The Individualised Corporation* (William Heinemann, 1998)
27   Mal Leicester & John Field (eds.), *Lifelong Learning* (Routledge-Falmer, 2000)
28   Campaign for Learning research; MORI & NALS
29   Pekka Himanen, *The Hacker Ethic* (Secker & Warburg, 2001)
30   M. Czikszentmihayli, *Flow, The Psychology of Optimal Experience* (HarperPerennial, 1991)
31   'Gen X & Work', Demos
32   www.gradresources.com
33   DFEE
34   US Department of Education
35   'The Independents', Demos, 2000
36   Audience Selection, 1998
37   Beautiko, 2001
38   *Blow* magazine
39   Willis, 'Teenage boys study', *Challenging Codes*
40   *2020 Vision* (Industrial Society, UK)
41   Northwestern Mutual Life, USA
42   *Newsweek*, Australia
43   *Star Tribune*
44   *Business Week*, USA
45   Y&R Brand Futures research
46   John Berger, *Ways of Seeing* (BBC, 1993)
47   Francis Fukyama, *The Great Disruption* (Profile Books, 2000)
48   *Financial Times*, 25 April 2001
49   De Wit capital, quoted in *Red Herring*
50   *Red Herring* brand supplement
51   Peter Doyle, *Marketing Management & Strategy* (PrenticeHall, 1997)
52   George Lakoff, *Women, Fire & Dangerous Things* (University of Chicago Press, 1987)
53   Rosario Conte, in Robert Aunger (ed.), *Darwinizing Culture* (OUP, 2001)
54   Eysenck & Keane, *Cognitive Psychology* (Psychology Press, 2000)
55   George Lakoff, *Women, Fire & Dangerous Things* (University of Chicago Press, 1987)
56   Ekman in George Lakoff, *Women, Fire and Dangerous Things* (University of Chicago Press, 1987)
57   Paivio in Michael Eysenck & Mark T. Keane, *Cognitive Psychology* (Psychology Press, 2000)

[58] George Lakoff & Mark Johnson, *Metaphors We Live By* (University of Chicago Press, 1980)

[59] Roman Jakobsen, *On Language* (Harvard University Press, 1995)

[60] Theodore Zeldin, *Conversation* (Hidden Spring, 2000)

[61] George Lakoff, *Women, Fire & Dangerous Things* (University of Chicago Press, 1987)

[62] Ibid.

[63] Neal Stephenson, *In the Beginning was the Command Line* (Avon Books, 1999)

[64] Carl Jung, *Man and his Symbols* (Doubleday, 1964) reprinted (Picador, 1983)

[65] From a Merril Lynch draft paper, 2001

[66] Plotkin in Robert Aunger (ed.), *Darwinizing Culture* (OUP, 2001)

[67] Flynn, 'Massive IQ gains in 14 Nations: what IQ tests really measure.' *Psychological Bulletin*, vol. 101

[68] Adam Westoby, unpublished manuscript (availabe at http://ase.tufts.edu)

[69] Laland and Odling Smee, in Robert Aunger (ed.), *Darwinizing Culture* (OUP, 2001)

[70] Manuel Castells, *The Network Society* (Blackwell, 2000)

[71] Euro RSCG

[72] Gerhard Steiner, *On Learning* (Cambridge University Press, 2000)

[73] *Companion to Cognitive Science* (Blackwell, 1998)

[74] Connectis supplement, *Financial Times*, May 2001

[75] Source AOL/Roper Starch

[76] Eg Stephen Covey

[77] C.J. Jung, *The Archetypes and the Collective Unconcious* (Routledge and Keegan Paul, 1959)

[78] Nobuyyuki Idei, Sony President, quoted in Fiona Gilmore (ed.), *Warriors on the High Wire* (HarperCollinsBusiness, 2001)

[79] Herriot Watt University

[80] See 68

[81] Ed Douglas, 'Darwin's natural heir', the *Guardian*, 17 February 2001

[82] See note 73

[83] See note 73

[84] From Freedman and Fraser, 1966 in Aronson, *The Social Animal* (Freeman & Co, 1973)

[85] Talent Foundation study

[86] Aaron Lynch, *Thought Contagion* (Basic Books, 1996)

[87] Maurice Bloch in Robert Aunger (ed.), *Darwinizing Culture* (OUP, 2001)

[88] Ruth Benedict, *Patterns of Culture* (Houghton Mifflin, 1934)

[89] Alberto Melucci, *Challenging Codes* (Cambridge University Press, 1996)

[90] Jordan B. Petersen, *Maps of Meaning* (Routledge, 1999)

[91] See 73

[92] David Storey, *Understanding the Small Business Sector* (International Thomson Business Press, 1998)

[93] Peter Senge, *The Fifth Discipline Fieldbook* (Nicholas Brealey Publishing, 1994)

[94] *Fortune*, 'America's most respected companies' (1998)

[95] Lisa Jardine, *Worldly Goods* (Norton, 1996)

[96] Gary Hamel, *Leading the Revolution* (HBS, 2000)

[97] John Grant, 'Goodbye pork pie hat', *Financial Times*

[98] OECD National Accounts, July 2001

[99] Americas Network, March 2000

INDEX

Learning from people you want to
be like.
Follow successful people on their
working day. Vignettes.
Live?
Follow specific people through the
year.